Reading Medieval Studies Volume 32

Incipient Globalization? Long-Distance Contacts in the Sixth Century

Edited by

Anthea Harris

BAR International Series 1644
2007

Published in 2016 by
BAR Publishing, Oxford

BAR International Series 1644

Incipient Globalization? Long-Distance Contacts in the Sixth Century

ISBN 978 1 4073 0078 8

A Special Issue of *Reading Medieval Studies* Volume 32 for 2006
Reading Medieval Studies is a peer-reviewed journal, published annually since 1975.
Papers on subjects between AD 500 and 1500 are welcomed and should be sent to:
The Editor, *Reading Medieval Studies*, Graduate Centre for Medieval Studies,
The University of Reading, Whiteknights, Reading, RG6 2AA

BAR Publishing is the trading name of British Archaeological Reports (Oxford) Ltd.
British Archaeological Reports was first incorporated in 1974 to publish the BAR
Series, International and British. In 1992 Hadrian Books Ltd became part of the BAR
group. This volume was originally published by Archaeopress in conjunction with
British Archaeological Reports (Oxford) Ltd / Hadrian Books Ltd, the Series principal
publisher, in 2007. This present volume is published by BAR Publishing, 2016.

Printed in England

BAR
PUBLISHING

BAR titles are available from:

BAR Publishing
122 Banbury Rd, Oxford, OX2 7BP, UK
EMAIL   info@barpublishing.com
PHONE   +44 (0)1865 310431
FAX   +44 (0)1865 316916
www.barpublishing.com

Contents

Introduction

Anthea Harris

University of Birmingham

This volume comprises the publication of a one-day conference held at the University of London (School of Oriental and African Studies) on 19th November 2005. The conference carried the same title as this volume, *Incipient Globalization? Long-distance contacts in the sixth century*, and was designed to bring together a selection of papers dealing with both material culture and theoretical issues and to represent as many geographical regions of the sixth-century world as possible. The idea of holding a conference on this subject grew out of an increasing realisation that analysts within International Relations Theory and International Political Economy had become deeply interested in the long-term history of the process of globalization, and that the transition from the Roman to the Medieval periods is often characterised as a significant change within the scholarly field of International Relations.[1] Studies on the formation of new, contemporary 'globalized' international orders have made reference to the evolution of the Roman and medieval international systems; yet archaeologists of Late Antiquity have largely remained apart from this debate.[2] This volume is offered as a contribution to the discussion on the origins and process of globalization; it is hoped that it will prompt further work on this subject within Archaeology and the cross-fertilisation of ideas across Archaeology and International Relations.

The title of this volume is borrowed from Jan Aarte Scholte, who uses 'incipient globalization' to describe what he sees as the second historic stage of globalization: the period between the 1850s and 1950s, when means and modes of communication such as the telegraph, radio, television, aeroplanes and cars were developed.[3] The period of incipient globalization follows a period of 'global imagination' from 1600 onwards, in which world religions burgeoned and scientific revolutions had global reach in their implications. These stages are preliminary to the stage of 'full-scale globalization' which the world is in the throes of today, with global institutions, banking, markets and production. For Scholte, a growth of supraterritorial spaces underlies these stages, which has transformed (and is transforming) social geography, although the process remains an uneven one. This for him is at the heart of globalization, and thus he rejects some previous understandings of the term – as either the spread of Western control, of 'global' culture, increased trade links and cross-border activities – as unsatisfactory.

Although Scholte's work is concerned with the modern period, these analytical categories have much import for late antiquity, too. Archaeologists have long been interested in long-distance exchange and the collapse and formation of international systems.[4] In terms of its place in any putative globalization process, the sixth century AD can be seen as beyond the stage of 'global imagination' insofar as it had already seen the spread of Christianity and Buddhism as 'world religions' beyond regional borders, and technologies such as weapons manufacture, silk production and architectural expertise had also taken on a supranational dimension. Instead, it might be argued that the sixth century AD witnessed a period of 'incipient globalization', where modes of communication (such as pilgrimage) and means of communication (such as ships capable of deep-sea / ocean-going voyages) became more plentiful, not less, as the political and administrative structures of the Roman state diminished in reach. This increase in complexity was, in many cases, born out of (and took place alongside) the spread of world religions and newly refined technologies. The analytical categories outlined here are, it must be remembered, an impetus to a deeper understanding of the origins of globalization, rather than a stricture.

The first paper in this volume, by Ken Dark – one of the few scholars who has written both on the archaeology of this period and on International Relations theory – introduces and explores many of these themes and demonstrates that Archaeology is ideally placed to engage with the questions surrounding globalization. Dark's paper is the only theoretical paper in this volume; the rest aim to offer case-studies of long-distance contacts in the sixth century, showing what types of transnational and international relations are available for study, what characterised these linkages and what material objects

[1] This field was opened up by scholars working with a World Systems Theory approach to International Relations, such as J. Abu-Lughod, *Before European hegemony: the world system A. D. 1250-1350* (Oxford, Oxford University Press, 1989) and A. G. Frank and B. K. Gills (eds.), *The world system: five hundred years or five thousand?* (London, Routledge, 1993). Since then, key work outside World Systems Theory has included K. R. Dark, *The Waves of Time: Long-term change and International Relations* (London, Continuum, 1998); B. Buzan and R. Little, *International Systems in World History: Remaking the Study of International Relations* (Oxford, Oxford University Press, 2000); S. Sassen, *Territory, Authority, Rights: From Medieval to Global Assemblages* (Princeton, Princeton University Press, 2006).
[2] Recent notable exceptions are M. McCormick, *Origins of the European Economy: Communications* and Commerce *AD 300 – 900* (Cambridge, Cambridge University Press, 2002); C. Wickham, *Framing the Early Middle Ages: Europe and the Mediterranean, 400-800* (Oxford, Oxford University Press, 2006). These scholars write as historians, yet engage with archaeological data and interpretation.
[3] J. A. Scholte *Globalization: a critical introduction* (2nd ed.) (Basingstoke, Macmillan, 2005), pp. 65-74.

[4] Most recently, C. Bell, *The Evolution of Long Distance Trading Relationships across the LBA/Iron Age Transition on the Northern Levantine Coast* (Oxford, British Archaeological Reports International Series 1574, 2006), with bibliography of earlier work.

travelled along them. Thus, Dark's paper is followed by two papers on two different types of artefacts – gold bracteates and pottery ampullae, respectively. The former, as Charlotte Behr demonstrates, have proved excellent diagnostic tools for the sixth century, in terms of dating and in terms of long-distance contacts. The latter have been much more problematical, for reasons that Susanne Bangert examines, yet potentially provide a key insight into religious politics of the sixth century. The fourth paper, by Kate da Costa, serves as a deliberate 'counter-balance' by focussing on local and regional exchange in the sixth-century Arabian peninsula, and provides a reminder that long-distance contacts must be considered in the context of shorter-range exchange. Two more papers on artefacts then follow: Mei Ling Chen examines Byzantine and Sasanian glass imports in China, while Jörg Drauschke contributes an important paper on 'eastern' imports into the Merovingian Empire, arguing that scholars now need to be more critical of the criteria by which archaeological finds are deemed to be evidence of long-distance contacts. This is followed by Niall Finneran's paper on the role of Ethiopia in the sixth-century *oikoumêne*, in which Ethiopia is demonstrated to occupy a crucial place in religious, political and economic dynamics, with links to both Byzantium and India. The volume concludes with a comparison between the archaeology of sixth-century Britain and China, using the numismatic evidence to analyse various points of commonality and of difference.

All the papers given at the conference are published here, with the exception of Geoffrey King's paper on the Sasanian Empire. It is with great sadness that I record that Mei Ling Chen fell seriously ill during 2006 and so her paper is published here largely as it was presented at the conference.

I am deeply grateful to Professor Françoise Le Saux, the editor of *Reading Medieval Studies*, and other members of the Graduate Centre for Medieval Studies at The University of Reading for suggesting that I publish these papers as a special volume of *Reading Medieval Studies* and for supporting me throughout. I hope that its subscribers will enjoy this issue and its focus on a crucial century on the crux of late antiquity and the early medieval period.

The conference was held during my tenure of a Paul Mellon Foundation Post-doctoral Fellowship at the School of Oriental and African Studies. I am grateful to the School for its sponsorship of the conference and for its generosity in permitting me, an archaeologist principally of Europe and the Byzantine Empire, to spend time studying the East. In particular, I would like to thank Professors Colin Bundy, Stephen Chan and Craig Clunas at SOAS for their support, and Professors Xu Jia-Ling and Zhang Xu-Shan for discussing the Chinese evidence with me at length. For help with translation and access to Chinese-language sources, I am grateful to Xu Jia-Ling, her PhD students at Northeast Normal University, Changchun, as well as Wang Tao at SOAS. Rebecca Naylor and Zoë Harris helped enormously with organisation on the day of the conference and also deserve grateful thanks.

Globalizing Late Antiquity:
Models, metaphors and the realities of long-distance trade and diplomacy

K. R. Dark

University of Reading

Introduction

This contribution addresses the 'big picture' of conceptualising the long-distance contacts between the lands around the eastern Mediterranean and other geographical regions in the first to seventh centuries AD. These contacts will be discussed in relation to the Roman Empire prior to the fifth century, and then to the period of Late Antiquity – understood here as from the early fifth to the late seventh century. Discussion of these contacts provides an opportunity to evaluate the analytical relevance to both the Roman period and to Late Antiquity of the much-debated theoretical concept of 'globalization'.

The imperial Roman economy

In recent years, long-held interpretations of the Roman imperial economy have come under intense criticism from both ancient historians and, especially, archaeologists. These, which envisaged a 'Classical' economy based on agricultural production and the spoils of war, have been challenged both through the implications of new archaeological evidence and by new directions in scholarly debate. In particular, the minimal roles assigned by Finley and others to long-distance trade and large-scale production have been comprehensively rejected in the face of overwhelming material evidence. This revolution in thinking about the Roman economy, associated most closely with the work of Kevin Greene and David Peacock, has placed archaeological evidence – especially that relating to production and exchange – 'centre-stage' in such discussions.[1]

Work by many scholars on data from across the Roman world has shown convincingly that long-distance bulk trade played a significant role in Roman economic life, and manufacturing took place on a large scale. Basic commodities such as oil, grain, pottery and building materials were produced in large quantities and transported over long distances. This has rendered the argument that long-distance trade in the Roman Empire involved only luxury goods no longer tenable.[2]

Simultaneously, the assumed centrality of slavery and of the military in the Early Roman economy have come to be questioned. While the Early Roman rural economy was – at least in specific provinces (especially in Italy) – heavily dependent on slaves, the economic role of the free – if oppressed – provincial 'peasantry' and of urban populations has been increasingly emphasised. Towns can be seen as centres of production and the provision of services, rather than parasitical 'consumer cities'. Even the role of 'Roman' culture within the Empire has become hotly debated, so that the social matrices within which economic activity took place, and its societal consequences, have become contested among alternative interpretations.[3]

Again, the key evidence here is archaeological, although textual sources also attest low-status economic actors operating in what is effectively a laissez-faire capitalist economic system based on profit and loss. This economy appears to have been transformed after the mid-third century into one in which state control played a larger role, even perhaps to the effect of becoming a 'command economy' in which the state operated as the principal economic actor. However, private enterprise,

[1] M. I. Finley, *The Ancient Economy* (revised 3rd ed.) (Berkeley, University of California Press, 1999); J.H. D'Arms, *Commerce and social standing in Ancient Rome* (Cambridge Mass., Harvard University Press, 1981); P. Garnsey and C. R. Whittaker (eds.), *Trade and Famine in Classical Antiquity* (Cambridge, Cambridge Philological Society, 1983); P. Garnsey, K. Hopkins and C.R. Whittaker (eds.), *Trade in the Ancient Economy* (London, Chatto and Windus, 1983).
[2] K. Greene, *The Archaeology of the Roman Empire* (London, Batsford, 1987), pp. 14-15; D.P.S. Peacock and D.F. Williams, *Amphorae and the Roman Economy* (London, Longman, 1986); R. Duncan-Jones,

Structure and Scale in the Roman Economy (Cambridge, Cambridge University Press, 1990); R. Duncan-Jones, *Money and Government in the Roman Empire* (Cambridge, Cambridge University Press); C.E. King and D.G. Wigg (eds.), *Coin Finds and Coin-Use in the Roman World* (Berlin, Mann, 1996); M. Polfer (ed.), *L'artisanat romain : évolutions, continuités et ruptures (Italie et provinces occidentales). Actes du coll. intern. des 26-28 oct. 2001 à Erpeldange* (Monographies Instrumentum 20), (Montagnac, Editions Monique Mergail 2001). See also: D.J. Mattingly, 'Oil for export? A comparison of Libyan, Spanish and Tunisian olive oil production in the Roman empire', *Journal of Roman Archaeology* 1 (1988): 33-56; C. Howgego, 'Coin circulation and the integration of the Roman economy', *Journal of Roman Archaeology* 7 (1994): 5-21.
[3] 'Capitalist' is meant in this paper to designate any economic practice of buying and selling for profit, rather than (for example) networks of the consumption or transfer of material goods and of services embedded in social, cultural or religious relationships. Thus, an economy based only on socially-prescribed dues and renders would not be classified here as 'capitalist' while one in which the sale of goods for personal, family or institutional profit was the convention would be categorised in that way. For evidence of a capitalist market economy in the Roman Empire: B. Levick, 'The Roman economy: trade in Asia Minor and the niche market', *Greece & Rome* 51 (2004): 180-198; P Temin, 'A Market Economy in the Early Roman Empire', *Journal of Roman Studies* 91 (2001): 169-181; D. Rathbone, *Economic Rationalism and Rural Society in Third-Century AD Egypt: The Heroninos Archive and the Appianus Estate* (Cambridge, Cambridge University Press, 1991); W. Scheidel, S. Von Reden (eds.), *The Ancient Economy* (Edinburgh, Edinburgh University Press 2002); D.J. Mattingly and J. Salmon (eds.), *Economies beyond agriculture in the Classical world* (London, Routledge, 2001); B. W. Frier, 'The Rental Market in Early Imperial Rome', *Journal of Roman Studies* 67 (1977): 27-37.

entrepreneurship and associations of free, non-state, traders all remain extensively attested. Local and regional producers, unlikely to be under direct state control, flourished in the provinces and a greater provincial and diocesan self-reliance are visible, as evidenced for example in the regionalisation of both pottery and iron production in Late Roman Britain.[4]

Other recent work, both in archaeology and ancient history, is revising even this newer model of the Roman imperial economy, suggesting that the Roman Empire had what economists and economic historians term a 'proto-industrial' economy. A 'proto-industrial' economy is one in which mass-production of standardised goods based on traditional manufacturing practices serves regional or even inter-regional markets. Such economies were common in pre-modern contexts and characterised the immediately pre-Industrial economies of Europe. There is even evidence that the so-called 'long waves' of economic 'boom' and 'bust' characteristic of capitalist market economies may also be visible in the Roman period.[5]

These patterns of long-distance exchange and domestic growth appear more akin to those of seventeenth- and early to mid-eighteenth-century England rather than to those of medieval feudalism. However, it must be stressed that a 'proto-industrial' economy is one in which full industrialization has not occurred and in which agriculture remains the basis of economic production.[6]

Nevertheless, revising economic models of the Roman world in this way has the potential to open new debates in the study of the economy regarding, for example, the exploitation and commoditization of labour and time, the part played by innovation and technology and the relevance of neo-classical economic models to pre-modern economic history.

This economic system had profound implications for the provinces of the Roman Empire. Despite the current debate over the validity of the term 'romanization', it is hard to dispute that populations in the Roman Empire frequently had unprecedented access to manufactured goods, often including goods standardised between provinces, and that material standards of living (at least for many urban communities) were transformed. In the western provinces of the Empire, urbanism and bureaucratic government were introduced as a consequence of incorporation into the Roman state.[7]

This is a long way from the model of the 'Classical economy' envisaged by earlier scholars such as Finley, or even the 'peasant economy' model of the Roman world favoured by archaeologists in the 1970s and 1980s. Our knowledge of the extensity – the geographical range – of the Roman economy has also been transformed by recent archaeological work. In particular, it is clear from excavations and other work in Egypt – especially at Berenike on the Egyptian Red Sea Coast – and in South Asia, that Roman trade across the Indian Ocean was far more intensive and wide-ranging than previously thought, and that its products reached across the Empire, being especially common in the Eastern provinces. While Roman material in South Asia has been systematically studied since Wheeler's seminal work in the area, and the existence of trading centres such as Broach and

---

[4] Concerning technology see also: P. Leveau, 'The Barbegal water mill in its environment: Archaeology and the economic and social history of antiquity', *Journal of Roman Archaeology* 9 (1996): 137-53; A. Wilson, Machines, power and the ancient economy', *Journal of Roman Studies* 92 (2002): 1-32; Ö. Wikander, *Exploitation of Water-Power or Technological Stagnation in the Roman Empire* (Lund, Gleerup, 1984); K. Greene, 'Technology and innovation in context: the Roman background to mediaeval and later developments', *Journal of Roman Archaeology* 7 (1994): 22-33.

[5] K.R. Dark, 'Proto-industrialization and the end of the Roman economy', in *External Contacts and the Economy of Late Roman and Post-Roman Britain*, ed. K.R. Dark (Woodbridge, Boydell, 1996), pp. 1-22. For economic 'long-waves' in the Roman economy: C. Going, 'Economic "long waves" in the Roman period?', *Oxford Journal of Archaeology* 11 (1992): 93-111. The propensity for 'long-waves' of expansion and decline in modern capitalist market economies was first identified by the economist N.D. Kondratieff in the 1920s, and is widely (although not universally) credited in modern economic theory. Note also Hitchner's work on sustained growth and productivity in the Roman economy: R.B. Hitchner, 'The Advantages of Wealth and Luxury: The Case for Economic Growth in the Roman Empire', in *The Ancient Economy. Evidence and Models*, eds. J.G. Manning and I. Morris (Stanford, Stanford University Press, 2005), pp. 207-222; R.B. Hitchner, 'Olive production and the Roman economy: the case for intensive growth in the Roman empire', in *La production du vin et de l'huile en Méditerranée*, eds. M.-C. Amouretti and J.P.Brun Bulletin de Correspondance Hellénique supplement 26) (1993): 499-506; R. Saller, 'Framing the Debate Over Growth in the Ancient Economy', in *The Ancient Economy. Evidence and Models*, eds. J.G. Manning and I. Morris (Stanford, Stanford University Press 2005), pp. 223-238. For a radical but interesting suggestion concerning Roman-period credit and finance without using coinage: M. Shaheen, 'Credit Cards in Ancient Times', *Anistoriton* 23 (2002): unnumbered pages.

[6] K.R. Dark, 'Proto-industrialization and the economy of the Roman Empire', in *L'Artisanat Romain: évolutions, continuités et ruptures. Actes due 2e Coloque d'Erpeldange 26-28 Octobre 2001*, ed. M. Polfer

(*Instrumentum* monograph 20) (Montagnac, Instrumentum, 2001), pp. 19-29. See also: D. Whittaker 2003 'Roman Proto-industry in Southern France: Some Indian Comparisons' *The Medieval History Journal* 6.2, 293-301.

[7] For the results of cultural and economic interactions across Roman frontiers: L. de Blois and J.W. Rich (eds.), *The Transformation of Economic Life under the Roman Empire* (Impact of Empire 2) (Amsterdam, Gieben, 2002); N. Roymans, 'Romanization and the transformation of a martial elite-ideology in a frontier province', in *Frontères d'empire. Actes de la table ronde internationale de Nemours 1992*, eds. P. Brun et al (Nemours, Mémoires du Musée de Préhistoire d' Ile-de-France, 5, 1993), pp. 33-50; A. Gardner, 'Military identities in late Roman Britain', *Oxford Journal of Archaeology* 18 (1999): 403-17. For an alternative concept of Classical cultural integration: I. Morris, 'Mediterraneanization' in *Mediterranean Paradigms and Classical Antiquity*, ed. I. Malkin (London and New York, Routledge, 2005), pp. 33-55. For the Mediterranean as an analytical unit: P. Horden and N. Purcell, *The Corrupting Sea. A Study of Mediterrnanean History* (Oxford, Blackwell, 2000). For the recent debate on the term 'romanization': E. Fentress, 'Romanizing the Berbers', *Past and Present* 190 (2006): 3-34; D. Mattingly. 'Being Roman: expressing identity in a provincial setting', *Journal of Roman Archaeology* 17 (2004): 5-25; P.W.M. Freeman, '"Romanisation" and Roman material culture' *Journal of Roman Archaeology* 6 (1993): 438-445; J. Webster, 'Creolizing the Roman Provinces', *American Journal of Archaeology* 105·(2001): 209-225.

Arikamedu has not been in doubt, the intensity of this contact has only become apparent in recent decades.[8]

Whether or not these goods arrived in Roman, Arabian or Indian ships – or in a combination of these – the commodities of this trade included spices, exotic wood, ivory, valuable stones, pearls and silk. Not only luxury goods were involved, as work in Roman Egypt has shown, but bulk everyday items such as pottery. This trade, apparently outside of state control, again offers strong evidential grounds for doubting minimalist interpretations of the Roman economy. Moreover, it was much more long lived than previous supposed: involving – in its Roman-period phase – dateable material from the second century BC to at least the fifth century AD.

At the other end of this commercial link, Roman material in South Asia includes pottery, glass and over 6,000 coins, some of the latter in large hoards as at Akkampalle, which contained 1,531 *denarii*. Local potters copied Roman ceramic forms and cultural connections can also be seen, with early first millennium AD Indian art, and perhaps religion, being influenced by Roman models. To give an example, excavations in Kerala at Pattanam (which may be the ancient port of Muziris) have revealed hundreds of sherds of Roman pottery and a large hoard of Roman coins was found c.6 miles from the site. Finds of gems and precious stones may hint that these were among the material being exported.[9]

The quantity of Roman material in South Asia is matched by its wide distribution. Roman coins have been found on at least 130 sites, with a concentration in the Krishna valley in Andhra and the Coimbatore region in Tamilnadu. Local counter-marking shows that these were in use as coinage within the subcontinent and Roman material of the same range and date as the authenticated Indian finds is not just found in India, but also in Sri Lanka and southeast Asia also.[10]

This link with the Roman Empire involved not only the export of things but also beliefs, values and concepts – so that South Asian cultural history will need to be revised in the light of this pattern of links. For example, in 180, Pantaenus, a Sicilian Christian sailing from Roman Alexandria could even, it seems, find a local Christian community in India. Thus archaeology and texts leave us in no doubt that there was regular contact between the Roman Empire and India, with both economic and cultural consequences.[11]

How much further East Roman traders ventured remains a problem. Roman contacts with China are a relatively new area of archaeological investigation, although these may have been much more extensive than often supposed. However, it is unlikely that such regular contacts were maintained as with South Asia, due to the rigours of the overland route and the difficulties of maritime contact.[12]

Closer to the Roman Empire, in Persia, one need only look at the Persian town of Jundeshapur to realise just how much evidence of Roman contacts one can see outside the Empire in the East. The town, built on the plan of a Roman fort, became the centre for Roman culture in Persia and was even the place to which the pagan philosophers of the Academy Athens later fled when Justinian I closed down their school in the sixth century. A few other cities in Persia also followed Roman plans. For example, Bishapur had a temple constructed in the manner of Roman Syria, an honorific column commemorating its foundation and townhouses decorated with what appear to be Antiochine mosaics. Although the settlement of Roman captives may have

[8] On the nature and permeability of Roman imperial frontiers: C.R. Whittaker, *Rome and its Frontiers. The Dynamics of Empire* (London and New York, Routledge, 2004); R. Talbert (ed.), *Barrington Atlas of the Greek and Roman World* (Princeton, Princeton University Press, 2000); H. Elton, *Frontiers of the Roman Empire* (London, Batsford, 1996). There is a vast academic literature on Roman contacts with India; for surveys see: S. Suresh, *Symbols of Trade: Roman and Pseudo-Roman Objects Found in India* (New Delhi, Manohar, 2004); G.K. Young, *Rome's eastern trade: international commerce and imperial policy, 31 BC-AD 305* (London, Routledge, 2001); P. Lunde and A. Porter (eds.), *Trade and Travel in the Red Sea Region Proceedings of Red Sea Project I held in the British Museum October 2002* (Oxford, British Archaeological Reports International Series S1269 / Society for Arabian Studies Monographs 2, 2004); J. Moorhead, *The Roman Empire Divided 400-700* (Harlow, Longman, 2001) p. 294, n.19; R. Tomber, 'Indo-Roman trade: the ceramic evidence from Egypt', *Antiquity* 74 (2000): 624-631; J.I. Miller, *The spice trade of the Roman Empire* (Oxford, Clarendon, 1998); W. Ball, *Rome in the East* (London and New York, Routledge, 2000), pp. 123-133; R.M. Cinimo (ed.), *Ancient Rome and India* (New Delhi, Munshiram, 1997); V. Begley and R.D. de Puma (eds.), *Rome and India: The Ancient Sea Trade* (Madison, University of Wisconsin Press, 1991); L. Casson, 'Egypt, Africa, Arabia and India: patterns of seaborne trade in the first century AD', *Bulletin of the American Society of Papyrologists* 21 (1984): 39-47; V. Begley, 'Arikamedu Reconsidered', *American Journal of Archaeology* 87 (1983): 461-481. The starting point for this work is: R.E.M Wheeler, *Rome beyond the Imperial Frontiers* (Penguin, London, 1954). On long-distance overland trade, see also: F. Millar, 'Caravan cities: The Roman Near East and long-distance trade by land', in *Modus Operandi: Essays in Honour of Geoffrey Rickman*, eds. M. Austin, J. Harries and C. Smith (London, Institute of Classical Studies, University of London 1998), pp. 119-137.

[9] Ball, pp. 139-48, 400-404; N. Durani, 'Pepper Port. Muziris Found', *Current World Archaeology* 2.6.1 (2006), 18-19, quoting Tomber. Note also the fifth- and sixth-century material reported by: N.D. Sheth 2006 'Roman relics found near Elephanta', *India Daily News*, 15 September

2006 http://www.dnaindia.com/report.asp?NewsID=1053100 (accessed 29 May 2007).

[10] P.J. Turner, *Roman Coins from India* (London, Royal Numismatic Society, 1989); D.P.M. Weerakkoddy, *Taprobane: Ancient Sri Lanka as known to the Greeks and Romans. Indicopleustoi: Archaeologies of the Indian Ocean* (Turnhout, Brepols, 1997); D.P.M. Weerakkoddy, 'Roman Coins of Sri Lanka: Some Observations', *The Sri Lanka Journal of the Humanities* 21.1-2 (1995): 1-30; Ball, p. 469, n. 85.

[11] Ball, p. 130.

[12] Ball, pp. 133-9. One should note also that South Asia and China were closely connected throughout the period discussed by this paper: X. Liu, *Ancient India and Ancient China: Trade and Religious Exchanges AD 1-600* (Delhi and Oxford, Oxford University Press, 1994). I am currently collaborating with a Chinese team which is attempting to catalogue Roman and Byzantine material found in China. For a recent review of this period in Chinese history: J.C. Wyatt, *China: Dawn of a Golden Age 200-750 AD* (New York, Metropolitan Museum of Art, 2004).

had some part in promoting Roman culture in these places, the employment of craftworkers such as mosaicists from the Empire attests continuing cultural connections and trade. These were not isolated prisoner-of-war camps, but thriving urban centres that retained their connections with the Mediterranean world.[13]

There is also evidence of links southeast into Arabia and the Persian Gulf, and northeast into Armenia and Georgia. The integration of Arabia into the trade with Asia is especially interesting, given its role in medieval commerce in the Indian Ocean. These were the connections that took Christianity into these areas from the fourth century onward.[14]

The long-distance contacts of the Roman Empire far beyond its frontiers extended not only to the East but also to the North and South. Roman contacts stretched into Scandinavia, as Lotte Hedeager and others have shown. These links were also varied in intensity and character, involving both unofficial (even illegal) and official interactions with people beyond the Rhine. There they connected with other networks operating to the North of the Roman World and encompassing much of Scandinavia and the Baltic coasts.[15]

To the South, Roman beads have been found at the Rufiji Delta in Tanzania. In this zone, work by Felix Chami has shown that twenty iron-working sites have evidence of long-distance contacts, including Roman pottery, glass and beads at Kivinja, and the site at Unguja Ukuu also received goods from the Roman world. Gold/silver-in-glass beads from Rhodes dating to between the first century BC and fifth century AD have been recorded at Mkukutu near Kibiti. Roman material was, therefore, reaching sub-Saharan Africa whether directly or indirectly.[16]

That is, an extensive series of overlapping networks of long-distance contacts can be recognised throughout the first to fourth centuries. The Roman world played a major role in these and its citizens may have been the instigator of at least some of them. The nature of these contacts varied both in context and intensity, so that their affects also differed from the adoption of provincial Roman culture to the use of artefacts manufactured in the Empire devoid of any Roman connections. This was an extension of the large-scale production and inter-regional trade evidenced within the Roman world, and a flourishing market economy capable of generating large-scale profit from high-risk trade may have been what enabled traders to engage in perilous but lucrative extra-European trade. Thus, the Roman Empire seems to have had both a proto-industrial economy and an economic system in several other respects similar to that of the post-medieval states which facilitated later European global imperialism and ultimately contemporary globalization.

Long-distance contacts in Late Antiquity

Such commercial and cultural interactions did not disappear as the Western Roman Empire collapsed, although they were re-configured and perhaps reduced in volume by changed circumstances. These interactions involved the flow of information, material and beliefs both around the Mediterranean and across political and cultural borders to its West, North, East and South. For example, we see fifth-century 'barbarian' kingdoms in

---

[13] Ball, pp. 115-17.

[14] Arabia and the Persian Gulf: G.W. Bowersock, *Roman Arabia* (Cambridge and London, Harvard University Press, 1983); D.T. Potts, *The Arabian Gulf in antiquity* (Oxford, Clarendon Press, 1990); Casson, 'Egypt, Africa, Arabia, and India'; B. Isaac, 'Trade-routes to Arabia and the Roman provinces in the Desert,' in *L'Arabie préislamique et son environment historique et culturel*, ed. T. Fahd (Strasbourg, Université des sciences humaines de Strasbourg, 1989), pp. 241-256; Ball, pp. 60-64 and 101-5; D.F. Graf, *Rome and the Arabian frontier from the Nabateans to the Saracens* (Aldershot, Ashgate, 1997); M. P. Spiedel, 'The road to Dumata (Jawf in Saudi Arabia) and the frontier policy of praetensione colligare', *Historia* 36 (1987): 213-221. For Armenia: N.H. Baynes, 'Rome and Armenia in the Fourth Century', *English Historical Review* 25 (1910): 625-643; R.W. Thomson, 'Armenia in the Fifth and Sixth Century', in *The Cambridge Ancient History Vol. XIV Late Antiquity: Empires and Successors AD 425-600*, ed. A. Cameron, B Ward- Perkins, M. Whitby (Cambridge, Cambridge University Press, 2000), pp. 662-677; D. Braund, *Georgia in Antiquity* (Oxford, Clarendon Press, 1994). Christianization included Persia: T.D. Barnes, Constantine and the Christians of Persia', *Journal of Roman Studies* 75 (1985): 126-136. See also: D.J. Mattingly, 'Impacts beyond Empire: Rome and the Garamantes of the Sahara', in *The transformation of Economic Life Under the Roman Empire, Proceedings of the Second Workshop of the International Network 'Impact of Empire' Nottingham 2001* eds. L. de Blois and J. Rich (Amsterdam, Gieben, 2002), pp. 184-203

[15] L. Hedeager, *Iron-Age Societies: from Tribe to State in Northern Europe, 500 BC to AD 700* (Oxford, Blackwell, 1992); L. Hedeager, 'Empire, frontier and the barbarian hinterland: Rome and northern Europe from AD 1-400', in *Centre and Periphery in the Ancient World* eds. M. Larsen and K. Kristiansen (Cambridge, Cambridge University Press, 1987), pp. 125-140; U. L. Hansen, *Römischer Import im Norden* (Copenhagen, Det Kongelige nordiske Oldskriftselskab, 1987); M.G. Fulford, 'Roman material in barbarian society c.200-BC-AD 400' in *Settlement and Society. Aspects of West European prehistory in the first millennium BC*, ed. T.C. Chapman and J.V.S. Megaw (Leicester, Leicester University Press, 1985), pp. 91-108; K. Randsborg, 'Beyond the Roman Empire: archaeological discoveries in Gudme on Funen, Denmark', *Oxford Journal of Archaeology* 9 (1990): 355-366; P.O. Thomsen et al, *Lundesborg- en handelsplads fra jernalderen* (Svendborg and Omegns Museum, Ringe, 1993) ; P.O. Thomsen, 'Lundeborg – a port of trade in Southeast Funen', in *The archaeology of*

Gudme and Lundeborg, eds. P.O. Nielsen, K.Randsborg and H.Thrane (Copenhagen, Akademisk Forlat, Universitatsforlaget Kobenhavn, 1993), pp. 23-29; U. Rald, 'The Roman swords from Danish bog finds', *Journal Roman Military Equipment Studies* 5 (1994): 227-241; M. Jansen, 'The Archaeology of Danish Commercial Centers', in *The Voyage to the Other World* eds. C.B. Kendall and P.S. Wells (= *Medieval Studies at Minnesota* 5) (Minneapolis, University of Minnesota Press, 1992), pp. 171-181 (171-3); M. Axboe, 'Danish kings and dendrochronology: archaeological insights into the early history of the Danish state', in *After Empire. Towards an Ethnography of Europe's Barbarians* ed. G. Ausenda (Woodbridge, Boydell, 1995), pp. 217-238, esp. pp. 255-6; R. Hodges, 'Gudme and Lundeborg: "Rome" beyond the frontier', *Minerva* 12.1 (2001): 30-31.

[16] F. Chami, 'East Africa and the Middle East relationship from the last millennium BC to about 1500 AD', *Journal de Africanistes* 72 (2002): 1-2; Moorhead, *The Roman Empire Divided 400-700*, p. 257; F. Chami, 'Roman Beads from the Rufiji Delta, Tanzania: First Incontrovertible Archaeological Link with the *Periplus*', *Current Anthropology* 40/2 (1999): 237-241.

Europe engaging in regular interactions with the Eastern Roman, at this period one may say Early Byzantine, Empire and such links spread the distribution of fifth- and sixth-century red-slipped wares and amphorae from the Mediterranean to Ireland and Britain.[17]

As the work of Anne Bowman, Ewan Campbell, Anthea Harris and others, has shown, in Britain this distribution was in part probably the result of direct long-distance contacts with the eastern Mediterranean, at least partly for non-commercial reasons. This involved what may be directional – and perhaps diplomatic – contacts between western Britain and the city of Constantinople itself. Mike Fulford has credibly argued for a Constantinopolitan pottery assemblage at Tintagel, and the same arguments could be extended to other British settlements. Sherds of distinctive Byzantine ships' water jars and the ceramic stoppers from amphorae imply the arrival in Britain both actual Byzantine ships and amphorae intact from the eastern Mediterranean. Medieval church dedications in Cornwall and Wales suggest that Byzantine saints, again some with specifically Constantinopolitan connections such as St Ia (whose shrine was near the Golden Gate), were also venerated in Britain. Remarkably, the dedication to 'St Stinian' at a tiny chapel near St David's appears to retain a memory of the great Byzantine ruler Justinian, whose role in sixth-century East-West contacts is well known.[18]

Another long-distance route – perhaps relating to Egypt – brought so-called 'Coptic Bowls' and other Byzantine objects to eastern Britain and Gaul, while a scatter of Eastern (especially Egyptian) glass finds occur across the West. Pilgrimage also brought new long-distance connections, evidenced for example in the so-called Menas flasks (or *ampullae*), found widely within and beyond the Empire, including the West as Susanne Bangert's paper shows.[19]

These contacts can be conceptualised in terms of two separate routes: one broadly East-West and motivated by diplomacy as much as trade, the other North-South and more strictly mercantile. The first – connected perhaps with Syrian merchants and with the city of Constantinople itself – also resulted in a series of Byzantine mercantile communities across Europe, which served both diplomatic and economic roles. These, identified in political centres in Italy, Gaul, Spain and North Africa, may have existed in Britain also.[20]

South of the imperial frontiers in the Mediterranean the East Byzantine trade and diplomacy still encompassed Ethiopia, Nubia, the Sudan, and adjacent areas – the former regions sharing the continuous tradition of Byzantine church architecture and Byzantine Christianity. Ethiopia in particular appears to have been deeply affected by Byzantine culture, as discussed in Niall Finneran's paper. The extent of Byzantine contacts in Arabia, while still in need of further study, was clearly wide-ranging and had long-lasting consequences.[21][22]

Persia, although the principal superpower rival of the Byzantine state, was pervaded by Early Byzantine culture. Christianity had arrived as early as the reign of Shapur II and within a generation reached to the Merv oasis, where Christians are still recorded as late as the tenth century. One sixth-century city, populated with captives from Antioch, had something like 30,000 –

[17] In general: A. Cameron, *The Mediterranean World in Late Antiquity* (London, Cambridge University Press, 1994); A.D. Lee, *Information and Frontiers: Roman Foreign Relations in Late Antiquity* (Cambridge, Cambridge University Press, 1993); A. Gillett, *Envoys and political communication in the Late Antique West* (Cambridge, Cambridge University Press, 2003), pp. 411-533. For specific example of the expanding pattern of interactions around the eastern Mediterranean in the fourth to seventh centuries: J.W. Hayes, 'From Rome to Beirut and Beyond: Asia Minor and Eastern Mediterranean Trade Connections', *Rei Cretariae Romanae Fautorum Acta* 36 (2000): 285-98; P.M. Watson, 'Ceramic Evidence for Egyptian links with northern Jordan in the 6th-8th centuries AD', in *Trade, contact, and the movement of peoples. The Eastern Mediterranean. Studies in Honour of J.Basil Hennessy,* eds. S. Bourke and J.-P. Descœudres (Sydney, Meditarch, 1995), pp. 303-320; C. Abadie-Reynal, 'Céramique et commerce dans le bassin égéen du IVe au VIIe siècle', in *Hommes et Richesses dans l'empire byzantin I, IVe-VIIe siècle* (Paris, Lethielleux, 1989), pp.143-159. For the western Mediterranean: P. Reynolds, *Trade in the western Mediterranean AD 400-700: the ceramic evidence* (Oxford, British Archaeological Reports International Series 604, 1995); S. Keay, *Late Roman amphoras in the western Mediterranean. A typology and economic study. The Catalan evidence* (Oxford, British Archaeological Reports International Series 196, 1984).
[18] K.R. Dark, *Britain and the End of the Roman Empire* (Stroud, Tempus, 2000); J.M. Wooding, 'Cargoes in trade along the western seaboard', in *External Contacts and the Economy of Late Roman Britain and Post-Roman Britain,* ed. K.R. Dark (Woodbridge, Boydell, 1996), pp. 67-82. See also: M. Comber, 'Trade and Communication Networks in Early Historic Ireland', *The Journal of Irish Archaeology* X (2001): 73-92, pp. 82-3 and 87; C. Thomas, '*Gallici nautae de Galliarum provinciis* – A sixth/seventh century trade with Gaul, reconsidered', *Medieval Archaeology* 34 (1990): 1-26; A. Harris, *Byzantium, Britain and the West: the archaeology of cultural identity, AD 400-650* (Stroud, Tempus, 2003); E. Campbell, 'The archaeological evidence for external trade contacts: imports, trade, and economy in Celtic Britain A.D. 400-800', in *External Contacts and the Economy of Late Roman Britain and Post-Roman Britain,* ed. K.R. Dark (Woodbridge, Boydell, 1996), pp. 83-96.

[19] A. Harris, *Byzantium, Britain and the West,* Bangert, this volume.
[20] K.R. Dark, 'Early Byzantine mercantile communities in the West', in *Through a Glass Brightly* ed. C. Entwistle (Oxford, Oxbow, 2003), pp. 76-81; S. Lebecq, 'Les échanges dans la Gaule du Nord au Vie siècle', in *The sixth century: production, distribution, and demand,* ed. R. Hodges and W. Bowden (Leiden, Brill, 1998), pp. 185-202.
[21] Again, there is an extensive scholarly literature on these interactions. For summaries and critical evaluations see: D.N. Edwards, *The archaeology of the Meroitic state: new perspectives on its social and political organization* (Cambridge Monographs in African Archaeology 38) (Cambridge, Cambridge University Press, 1996); L. Török, *The Kingdom of Kush: Handbook of the Napatan-Meroitic Civilization* (Leiden, Brill, 1997); I. Wallerstein, *The Modern World-System* (3 vols.) (New York, Academic Press, 1974-1989); S. Munro-Hay, *Aksum: an African civilisation of Late Antiquity,* (Edinburgh, Edinburgh University Press, 1991). See also the paper by Finneran, this volume.
[22] L. Török, *Late Antique Nubia: history and archaeology of the southern neighbour of Egypt in the 4th-6th century A.D.* (Budapest, Antaeus, Communicationes ex Instituto Archaeologico Academiae Scientiarum Hungaricae 16, 1988); V. Bernard and J.F. Salles 'Discovery of a Christian Church at Al-Qusur, Failaka (Kuwait)' *Proceedings of the Seminar for Arabian Studies* 21 (1991): pp. 7-21; J. Bowman, 'The Christian monastery on the island of Kharg', *Australian Journal of Biblical Archaeology* 2/3 (1975/6) 49-64.

mostly Christian – inhabitants living in a Roman-style city with a hippodrome, baths and other comforts of home.[23]

These 'transnational' interactions across political frontiers between separate polities were accompanied by intensive cross-border economic and information flows within the Byzantine Empire itself. In all of these areas not just commercial and diplomatic, but also religious and cultural contacts took place. Christianity, and heretical beliefs derived from the Byzantine world, spread widely in Asia. There is textual or archaeological evidence for Christian communities in Late Antiquity in Arabia, China, India and across Central Asia. There were Christian states in Ethiopia and the Sudan with close ties to the Byzantine state and Church. These contacts were expanding throughout the sixth century – for example, Byzantine missionaries introduced Christianity to the city of Soba on the Blue Nile in 580.[24]

In Ireland, this period saw the introduction of aspects of Roman culture, which were not found in the Roman period, alongside large-scale Conversion to Christianity. By the seventh century this had affected both technology and many aspects of daily life including language, social organization, building design, everyday artefacts, art styles, burial practices and probably personal appearance. The introduction of Latin literacy, scripts and learning during this period proved of enduring significance to both Ireland and broader European cultural history.[25]

Links with South Asia appear also to have been sustained. The published Roman coin series runs to the seventh century, and recent work by Roberta Tomber is beginning to show that ceramic evidence also supports continuing contacts through the fifth and sixth centuries. For example, an examination of amphorae from coastal and inland sites in western India, from Gujarat to Kerala, identified continuing contact with the Mediterranean from the fourth to sixth centuries.[26]

[23] On the relationship between the Byzantine and Persian empires in Late Antiquity: J. Howard-Johnson, 'The two Great Powers in Late Antiquity: a comparison', in *The Byzantine and Early Islamic Near East III: States, Resources and armies*, ed. A. Cameron (Princeton, Darwin Press, 1995), pp. 157-226; G. Greatrex, 'Byzantium and the East in the Sixth Century', in *The Cambridge Companion to the Age of Justinian*, ed. M. Maas (Cambridge, Cambridge University Press, 2005), pp. 477-509 esp. 501-503; A. Cutler, 'Silver across the Euphrates. Forms of exchange between Sasanian Persia and the Later Roman Empire', *Mitteilungen der Spätantiken Archäologie und byzantinische Kunstgeschichte* 4 (2005): 9-37. For Persia's maritime contacts: D. Whitehouse, 'Sasanian maritime activity', in *The Indian Ocean in Antiquity*, ed. J. Reade (London, Kegan Paul, 1996), pp. 40-42. For fifth- and sixth-century silver finds in Central Asia: M. Mundell Mango, 'The archaeological context of finds of silver in and beyond the Eastern Empire' in *Acta XIII Congressus Internationalis Archaeologiae Christianae*, eds. N. Cambi and E. Marin (Vatican City and Split, 1998), pp. 207-52. Christians in Persia are considered by: Z. Rubin, 'The Sasanid monarchy', in *The Cambridge Ancient History XIV Late Antiquity. Empire and Successors, A.D. 425-600*, eds. A. Cameron, B. Ward-Perkins and M. Whitby (Cambridge, Cambridge University Press, 2000), pp. 638-661, esp. 638-677; G. Greatrex, 'Khusro II and the Christians of his empire', *Journal of the Canadian Society for Syriac Studies* 3 (2003): 78-88; S. Brock, 'Christians in the Sasanid empire: a case of divided loyalties', in *Religion and National Identity*, ed. S. Mews (Oxford, Blackwell, 1982), pp. 1-19; F. Millar, *The Roman Empire and its Neighbours* (2nd ed.) (London, Duckworth, 1981), pp. 249-69, esp. 264; N.G. Garsoïan, 'Byzantium and the Sassanians' in *Cambridge History of Iran (Vol. 3)*, ed. E. Yar-shater (Cambridge, Cambridge University Press 1983), pp. 568-592; P. Gignoux, 'Sceaux chrétiens d'époque sasanide', *Iranica Antiqua* 15 (1980): 299-314; F. Decret, 'Les Conséquences sur le christianisme en Perse de l'affrontement des empires romain et Sassanide de Shapur Ier à Yazgard Ier', *Recherches Augustiniennes* 14 (1979): 91-152; R.N. Frye, 'Irano-Byzantine commercial and diplomatic rivalry', *Bulletin of the Asia Institute* 1.4 (1976): 1-18; O. Reutner, 'Sasanian churches', in *Survey of Persian Art*, ed. A.U. Pope (Oxford, Oxford University Press 1939), pp. 560-566; Elton, *Frontiers of the Roman Empire*, p.101; Ball, *Rome in the East*, pp. 115, 122 and 134.

[24] S.J. Trimingham, *Christianity among the Arabs in Pre-Islamic times* (London, Longman, 1979); C. Balint (ed.), *Kontakte zwischen Iran, Byzanz und der Steppe im 6.-7. Jahrhundert* (Budapest-Naples-Rome, Publicationis Instituti Archaeologici Academiae Scientiarum 2000), pp. 185-92; D. Welsby and C.M. Daniels, *Soba I. Archaeological research at a medieval capital on the Blue Nile* (London, British Institute of East Africa, 1998); D.W. Phillipson, *Aksum: its antecedents and successors* (London, British Museum Press, 1998); D.A. Welsby, *The Medieval Kingdoms of Nubia. Pagans, Christians and Muslims along the Middle Nile* (London, British Museum Press, 2002), esp. chapters 3 and 9; J.A.

Langfeldt, 'Recently discovered early Christian monuments in north-eastern Arabia', *Arabian Archaeology and Epigraphy* 5.1 (1994): 32-60; C.J. Gardberg, *Late Nubian Sites: Churches and Settlements (The Scandinavian Joint Expedition to Sudanese Nubia, Vol. 7)* (Jonsered, Astrom, 2001); A.V. Sedov, New archaeological and epigraphical material from Qana (South Arabia)', *Arabian Archaeology and Epigraphy* 3/2 (1992): 110-37; A.V. Sedov, 'Qana ' (Yemen) and the Indian Ocean. The archaeological evidence', in *Tradition and Archaeology. Early Maritime Contacts in the Indian Ocean. Proceedings of the International Seminar Techno-Archaeological Perspectives of Seafaring in the Indian Ocean 4th cent. B.C. – 15th cent. A.D. New Delhi, Feb. 28-March.4, 1994*, eds. H.P. Ray and J-F.Salles (Lyon/New Delhi, Manohar 1996), pp. 11-35; Y. Okakda, 'Ain Sha'ia and the Early Gulf Churches: An Architectural Analogy', *al-Rafidan* 13 (1992): 87-93; Y. Okakda, 'Early Christian Architecture in the Iraqi South-Western Desert', *al-Rafidan* 12 (1991): 71-83; Bernard, Olivier Callot and Jean Francois Salles, 'L'eglise d'al-Qousour Failaka, Etat de Koweit', *Arabian Archaeology and Epigraphy* 2 (1991): 145-181.

[25] For Ireland in this period: T. Charles-Edwards, *Early Christian Ireland* (Cambridge, Cambridge University Press, 2000); D. O'Croinin, *Early medieval Ireland 400-1200* (London, Longman, 1995); H. Mytum, *The origins of Early Christian Ireland* (London, Routledge, 1992); N. Edwards, *The archaeology of early medieval Ireland* (London, Batsford, 1990).

[26] R. Tomber, 'Beyond western India: the evidence from imported finds' PANEL: Issues in Indian Ocean Commerce and the Archaeology of Western India, summarising lectures by L. Blue, S. Gupta, Rukshana Nanji & Vishwas D. Gogte, Pia Brancaccio, V. Selvakumar, Shajan, K.P.,P.K Gopi, R. Tomber, http://www.ucl.ac.uk/southasianarchaeology/Indo-Roman%20Commerce.pdf http://www.ucl.ac.uk/southasianarchaeology/Conference%20Handbook%20Vol%202.pdf (accessed 10 February 2007); Turner (op. cit. n. 10) lists Byzantine coins dating to the fifth to seventh centuries from India: pp. 46, 48, 60, 86 and 125. See also: A. Wink, *Al-Hind, the making of the Indo-Islamic World. Vol. I, early medieval India and the expansion of Islam* (Leiden, Brill, 1990). A report entitled: 'Search for India's ancient city' on BBC News, 11 June 2006, http://news.bbc.co.uk/2/hi/south_asia/4970452.stm (accessed 29 May 2007) recounts the discovery by K.P. Shajan and V. Selvakumara of Muziris in Kerala at Pattanam, including large quantities of Roman pottery at a site with glass beads, gems and precious stones. This is about six miles from the findspot (in 1983) of a large hoard of Roman coins. A reported comment by Roberta Tomber indicates that there is growing evidence that trade continued much longer, if not necessarily continuously, into the sixth and early seventh centuries. Reports of more recent excavation at the site (up to March 2007 at the time of writing) can be found on the Nasrani Syrian Christian Network at

Diplomacy may also have played a part in such South Asian links. In 631-2 a 'king of Indians' is said to have sent Heraclius congratulatory presents of pearls and precious stones after his victory over the Persians. Heraclius also displayed Indian elephants, which may have been from this or another exchange, in a triumph. In this context it may be relevant that the only real (as opposed to mythical) animal from outside the Empire depicted on the, possibly Heraclian, Great Palace peristyle mosaic currently displayed in the Mosaic Museum in Istanbul is an Indian elephant.[27]

Formal contacts with East Asia also remained. As late as 605-17, the emperor Yang Ti attempted to form a diplomatic relationship with Constantinople and official Chinese visitors recorded their awe at seeing Constantinople. In contrast to current perceptions of the relative technological development of East and West in the first millennium AD, one of their principal observations was how advanced the 'Roman' technology was. They noted, for example, the (otherwise unattested) use of a cooling system for the capital's buildings in which cold water flowed over the roof. They also note how formidable 'Roman' military capabilities were compared to those of China.[28]

Nor did links with the North lose their intensity. Intensive and long-lasting contacts between eastern Britain, Scandinavia and continental Europe are widely attested. In fact, as Näsman has pointed out 'one of the important changes which followed in the wake of the fall of the Western Roman Empire was the new cultural and political network which developed between regions on both sides of the fallen *limes*.' This included long-distance interactions involving Byzantine objects extending into Scandinavia, although the role of Byzantine merchants is unclear. Whether or not traders from the Mediterranean were present in this region, the consequences of these interactions had profound affects on Scandinavian and other northern European societies.[29]

So we can reasonably envisage long-distance trading and diplomatic networks, along with cultural and religious exchanges, based on the Byzantine Empire throughout Late Antiquity. These were maintained and expanded up to the early seventh century. At least at some times, such networks extended across the known world, from Britain (and perhaps Ireland) to China, from Scandinavia to Africa south of the imperial frontiers. Other networks of contact, for example that bringing amber into Anglo-Saxon England, were not focussed on the Empire, although Byzantine merchants and customers may have been involved. Taken together, such networks connect almost every part of the 'World of Late Antiquity' either directly or by, at most, a single indirect step in the communication system.[30]

The international networks of Late Antiquity seems to be continuous with that of the Roman period, at least in part, so it is reasonable to consider it as a continuation of the same system. That this system was perhaps expanded in Late Antiquity need not surprise us, as increasingly evidence from shipwreck and ceramic studies supports the view that the fifth and sixth centuries were a period of exceptional material wealth and economic vitality in the eastern Mediterranean.[31]

Conceptualising long-distance linkages

This raises the question of how should we conceptualise this very extensive long-distance network of contacts, ranging perhaps from the first to seventh centuries? Archaeological theory offers surprisingly few of its own models for long-distance interactions of this sort, with only two models widely used since the demise of diffusionist theory in the 1970s.

The first of these models is genuinely 'archaeological' in that it was proposed in the course of archaeological debate rather than imported from another field. This is Renfrew's 'Peer-Polity Interaction' theory, which – at least in its usual form – is related more directly to inter-

http://nasrani.net/2007/03/17/muziris-pattanam-%E2%80%93-follow-up-on-the-excavations-i/ and http://nasrani.net/2007/03/24/muziris-pattanam-significant-evidences-boat-follow-up-on-excavations-iii/.

[27] Moorhead, p. 258; C. Mango and R. Scott (with G. Greatrex) (translation, introduction and commentary), *The Chronicle of Theophanes. Byzantine and Near Eastern History AD 284-813* (Oxford, Clarendon Press, 1997), pp. 631-2; K.R. Dark, 'Roman architecture in the Great Palace of Byzantine Constantinople from the sixth to the ninth centuries', *Byzantion*, in press.

[28] Conveniently translated into English in F. Hirth (ed. and trans.), *China and the Roman Orient* (Chicago, Ares Press 1885) (reprinted 1975). (The water-cooling system is described on page 58). Note that these Chinese sources include descriptions of structures in the Eastern Roman/Byzantine capital that can be independently checked in Western sources, for example the Chalke Gate and the covered passage from the Great Palace to 'Great Church' of Hagia Sophia (93, 57-8). P. Schreiner, 'Eine chinesiche Beschreibung Konstantinopels aus dem 7. Jahrhundert' *Istanbuler Mitteilungen* 39 (1989): 493-305.

[29] H. Näsman, 'The Justinianic Era in South Scandinavia', in *The sixth century: production, distribution, and demand* eds. R. Hodges and W. Bowden (Leiden, Brill, 1998), pp. 255-278, pp. 265-7; J. Callmer, 'Oriental Beads and Europe, A.D. 600–800', in *Rome and the North* eds. A. A.Ellegård and G. Åkerström-Hougen (Jonsered, Sweden,

Astrom, 1996), pp. 53–71, esp. fig.2 on p. 65 and p. 631. For North Sea networks at this date: I. Wood, 'The Channel from the 4th to the 7th centuries AD', in *Maritime Celts, Frisians and Saxons*, ed. S. McGrail (CBA Research Report No. 71) (London, Council for British Archeology, 1990), pp. 93-97; M. Welch, 'Contacts across the Channel between the fifth and seventh centuries: a review of the archaeological evidence', *Studien zur Sachsenforschung* 7 (1991): 261-9; J. Hines, *The Scandinavian character of Anglian Englana in the pre-Viking period* (Oxford, British Archaeological Reports British Series 124, 1984).

[30] Harris, *Byzantium, Britain and the West*; J. Huggett, 'Imported grave goods and the early Anglo-Saxon economy', *Medieval Archaeology* 32 (1988): 63-96.

[31] L. Ellis and F.L. Kidner (eds.), *Travel, communication and geography in late antiquity: sacred and profane* (Aldershot, Ashgate, 2004); S.A. Kingsley (ed.), *Barbarian Seas: Late Roman to Islam* (London, Periplus Publishing, 2004); S.A. Kingsley and M. Decker (eds.), *Economy and exchange in the East Mediterranean during late antiquity* (Oxford, Oxbow 2001). Harris has recently argued that these relationships constituted a 'Byzantine Commonwealth' in Late Antiquity: Harris, *Byzantium, Britain and the West*; A. Harris, 'Commonwealth, Byzantine', *Encyclopedia of Greece and the Hellenic Tradition (vol. 1)* (London and Chicago, Fitzroy Dearborn, 2000), pp. 368-371 (370).

state interactions rather than those transcending state borders. According to the model, interacting polities come to resemble each other more closely over time through the process of interaction itself. This is very similar to the neo-classical economic theory of 'convergence', in which competitors become increasing alike through competitive emulation.[32]

The second derives from work at the interface of 'Structuralist' International Relations theory and Marxian historical sociology. This is 'World-Systems Theory', based on the existence of unequal centre: periphery relationships in the global economy. These can be resolved into a series of sets of concentric circles, in which an inner core exploits an outer periphery. The emergence and decline of such relationships (the 'world-systems' of the theory) depends on patterns of economic boom and bust, according to the principles set out by Kondratieff (so-called 'Kondratieff Cycles').[33]

World-Systems Theory ('WST') has been widely applied to both contemporary and earlier economic patterns, and some archaeologists have been especially enthusiastic about adopting this model. The principal shortcoming of all purely economic approaches, such as WST, is that they fail to capture the prominent role of cultural and political interactions in long-distance contacts. The 'core' in classic WST of the type used in archaeological theory is characterised on economic grounds alone, so that economic relationships also circumscribe the relationship of the 'core' to the 'periphery'.

However, other 'cores' and 'peripheries' may be recognised in social, cultural, religious, and military terms, all potentially with their own separate dynamics, as we see in the case of the relationship between fifth- and sixth-century interactions around the North Sea and those focussed on the Mediterranean. These might overlap and conflict with the economic relationships of core:periphery relations. So, 'core' and 'periphery' in the sense these terms are used in classical WST are categories produced by considering the international system in a narrowly historical materialist fashion that few contemporary social, political or economic theorists would countenance.[34]

One should not overlook the considerable academic literature on WST in other fields. A characteristic of this has been to abandon increasingly both the materialist concept of the 'world system', and its intrinsic link with modern capitalist economies. The latter development, exemplified by the rise of 'World System Analysis' (note the lack of a hyphen and plural!) is to suggest that there

has only ever been one world system, originating in Mesopotamia in the 4th millennium BC, and that this is to be conceptualised in terms of an expanding network of *mostly* economic relationships between states. This network retains the core:periphery relations of WST but is neither dependent upon capitalism nor is it visible only in purely economic terms. Even those favouring a more economically based version of WST have reconsidered the basis of such systems so radically that almost any unequal economic relationship can be described in terms of core: periphery relations. For example, Chase-Dunn and Hall envisage 'very small world-systems' in a single valley![35]

Unsurprisingly, in the context of such theoretical confusion over basic concepts (such as 'what is a world-system') and faced with the cognitive and socio-cultural critique mentioned above, the credibility of both WST and WSA has become somewhat strained. It might be questioned whether, beyond the 'commonsense' concepts of core and periphery themselves (concepts that are not an invention of World-Systems theorists, even in their academic form), this theoretical tradition has anything to offer archaeologists beyond that of a Classical Marxist analysis. Thus, some world-systems theorists (notably Kristian Kristiansen) have explored what may be more strictly classified as a regional approach.[36]

[35] For example: R.F. Newbold, 'Centre and Periphery in the eye of the late Roman Empire', *Florilegium* 3 (1981): 72-103; K.R. Dark, 'Culture and the Myth of Economic Determinism in Global History and World Politics', in *Cultural Factors in Economic Growth,* eds. M. Casson and A. Godley (New York, Springer, 2000) pp. 182-209; L. Zucker, 'Production of Trust: Instituational Sources of Economic Structure 1840-1920', *Research in Organization Behavior* 8 (1986): 53-111; P.J. Di Maggio, 'Interest and agency in institutional theory', in *Institutional patterns and organizations: culture and environment,* ed. G.L. Zucker (Balinger, Cambridge MA, 1988), pp. 3-21; M.C. Casson, Cultural Determinants of Economic Performance', *Journal of Comparative Economics* 17 (1993): 418-82; M. Granovetter, 'Economic Action and Social Structure: the Problem of Embeddedness', *American Journal of Sociology* 91.3 (1985): 481-510; R.A. Dodgshon, *Society in Time and Space. A Geographical Perspective on Change* (Cambridge, Cambridge University Press, 1998). Dodghson makes the important point (chapter 5) that the creation of material cultures and modification of environments, in effect, 'institutionalise' human cultures and practices. For the contrast between North Sea and Mediterranean 'centres' of economic interaction: M.O.H. Carver, *Arguments in Stone. Archaeological Research and the European Town in the First Millennium* (Oxbow Monographs 29) (Oxford, Oxbow Books, 1993); M.O.H. Carver, 'Pre-Viking traffic in the North Sea', in *Maritime Celts, Frisians and Saxons* ed. S. McGrail (Council for British Archaeology Research Report No. 71) (London, Council for British Archaeology, 1990), pp. 117-125; H.B. Clarke, 'The North Sea. A highway of invasions, immigration and trade in the fifth and ninth centuries', in *The North Sea: a highway of economic and cultural exchange* eds. A. Bang-Anderson, B. Greenhill and E.H. Grude (Oslo, Norwegian University Press, 1985), pp. 39-49.
[36] C. Chase-Dunn and T. Hall, *Rise and Demise. Comparing World-Systems* (Boulder, CO., Westview, 1997); C. Chase-Dunn and K.M. Mann, *The Wintu and Their Neighbors: A Very Small World-System in Northern California* (Tucson, AZ., University of Arizona Press, 1998); C. Chase-Dunn and E.S. Manning, 'City systems and world-systems: four millennia of city growth and decline', *Cross-Cultural Research* 36.4 (2002): 379-398; C. Chase-Dunn and A.K. Jorgenson, 'Regions and Interaction Networks: an institutional materialist perspective', *International Journal of Comparative Sociology* 44.1 (2003): 433-450.

[32] A.C. Renfrew and J.F. Cherry (eds.), *Peer polity interaction and socio-political change* (Cambridge, Cambridge University Press, 1986).
[33] Wallerstein (op. cit., n. 24)
[34] For a review of the utility of this sort of 'classic' world-systems analysis in relation to the Roman Empire: G. Woolf, 'World systems analysis and the Roman empire' *Journal of Roman Archaeology* 3 (1990): 44-58.

Strangely, Marxist archaeology has had surprisingly little to say about past international systems, beyond stock critiques of imperialism and exploitation dating back at least to the time of Lenin's work on modern imperialism. That is, there is no distinctive archaeological Marxist tradition in archaeology of characterising international networks.[37]

If archaeological theory has a surprising lack of theory relating to long-distance and international networks, then one option would be to turn to the theory of global politics, that is, to International Relations ('IR') theory. It is worth noting at the outset that IR is often misunderstood as an analytical field and is far more wide-ranging both in scope and time than usually supposed. IR theorists are concerned with all inter-regional and long-distance interactions, and their local consequences and sources, from their origins to the present. IR is, therefore, about more than governments and their foreign policies, but includes social, cultural, religious and economic beliefs, values, institutions and activities and their contexts in, and effects on, the natural world. If it seems as if IR claims every part of human life to be within its remit, then one should recall that so often does archaeology. The fields have many other similarities, not least their highly eclectic character and willingness to move rapidly into new fields of inquiry and challenge long-held historical interpretations.[38]

In addition, the origins of IR as a field of study have given it an enduring interest in pre-modern, especially Hellenistic, Roman and medieval, polities and their neighbours. In my experience it can come as a surprise to some archaeologists to find just how central a role the 'distant' past plays in the main themes of IR debate, just as IR theorists were until the 1990s generally unaware of archaeologists' interest in, and potential contribution to, their field.[39]

What is significant here is that IR is a field in which, of course, scholars have long needed to discuss such interactions both in relation to the present and in relation to pre-modern international interactions. As already noted, although archaeological theorists seem often not to realise this, WST itself derives from, and has played a major part in, IR theory. As a consequence it is, as already mentioned, long debated and widely criticised in IR. In fact, numerous alternative perspectives on analysing long-term transformations and large-scale networks of contact have been developed in IR that have not yet been sufficiently explored in archaeological research, such as David Wilkinson's concept of networks of urban centres or George Modelski's linkage between urbanism and long-cycles in the development of states.[40]

However, recently, archaeologists of the Roman world have been showing an interest in the area of IR theory that is particularly relevant here: the theory of globalization.

Thinking about globalization in relation to the Roman world

Although Bruce Hitchner has discussed the relevance of the concept of globalization to the Roman world in unpublished lectures, only two scholars have yet published substantial academic works on the subject. Tadeusz Aleksandrowicz has considered the question of whether or not the Roman world was globalized, and in *Globalizing Roman Culture* Richard Hingley has argued that 'globalization theory' has a direct relevance to analysing the Roman world. Aleksandrowicz's work has largely gone un-noticed in archaeological debate but Hingley's book has been a basis for further discussion, for example with a Theoretical Roman Archaeology Conference session in 2006 on the subject of 'Making ends meet or early globalisation? Economies of power, culture and identity in the Roman world'. Consequently, it may be useful here to discuss Hingley's theoretical framework as a starting point for evaluating how globalization theory might contribute to understanding the Roman-period and Late Antique interactions already outlined.[41]

Hingley's use of the concept of globalization is as a conceptual tool to investigate non-state transnational linkages rather as a way to understand the domestic affairs of the Roman state. Although his discussion ranges widely across the Roman Empire, the basis of his theoretical position is that 'Roman culture' formed as

Note also: S.K. Sanderson (ed.), *Civilizations and World Systems* (Walnut Creek, CA. and London, Altamira & Sage, 1995); R. Denemark, J. Friedman, B.K. Gills and G. Modelski (eds.), *World System History: the social science of long-term change* (London, Routledge, 2000); G. Modelski and W. R. Thompson, *Leading sectors and world powers: the co-evolution of global politics and economics* (Columbia, SC., University of South Carolina Press, 1995); A.G. Frank and B.K. Gills (eds.) *The World System: Five Hundred Years or Five Thousand?* (London, Routledge, 1993); A.G. Frank, 'The bronze age world system and its cycles', *Current Anthropology* 34 (1993): 383-413.

[37] M. Rowlands, M. Larsen, and K. Kristiansen (eds.) *Centre and Periphery in the Ancient World* (Cambridge, Cambridge University Press, 1987); K. Kristiansen, *Europe Before History* (Cambridge, Cambridge University Press, 1998).

[38] On the scope and character of IR in relation to archaeology and other fields: K.R. Dark, *The Waves of Time. Long-Term Change and International Relations* (London and New York, Continuum, 1998), chapter 1.

[39] On the potential value of a close relationship between archaeological research and theory and IR theory, see: Dark, *The Waves of Time*. As far as I am aware the only in depth and lengthy analysis of the external relations of the Roman Empire by an IR theorist remains: E.N. Luttwak, *The Grand Strategy of the Roman Empire from the First Century A.D. to the Third* (2nd ed.) (London, Weidenweld & Nicholson, 1999).

[40] D. Wilkinson, 'Civilizations as Networks: Trade, War, Diplomacy, and Command-Control', *Complexity* 8 (2002): 82-86; D. Wilkinson, 'Central Civilization', *Comparative Civilizations Review* 17 (1987): 31-59; C. Chase-Dunn and T.D. Hall (eds.): *Core/Periphery Relations in Precapitalist Worlds* (Boulder, CO, Westview, 1991), pp. 113-166.

[41] On globalization theory in IR (excluding works mentioned in the text of this article): M. Castells, *The Rise of the Network Society* (Oxford, Blackwell, 2000); D. Held et al, *Global Transfromations: politics, economics and culture* (Cambridge, Polity, 1999).

series of structures and contexts for both complex interactions between people and the state, and between local and more generally Roman identities and customs. In this respect, Hingley's discussion attempts to attach a theory of 'global culture' to the 'post-colonial' perspectives currently popular among some 'post-processual' archaeologists working on the Roman Empire.[42]

However, globalization theory is not designed to be a theory of intra-state or local interactions. As we shall see shortly, there is no single 'globalization theory', but the basis of almost all of the theoretical schools that could be classified as 'globalization theory' is quite the opposite. These almost all contend that long-distance ('global') interactions and cultures transcend existing political and cultural identities and frontiers, usually with transformative affects promoting commonalities between originally disparate groups. Yet Hingley argues for the persistence of local tradition in the face of transnational imperial forces. This is a theory of resistance, not of transformation, and of the precedence of the local over global dynamics – arguably the opposite of what is usually understood by the process of globalization![43]

If we use globalization theory in archaeology at all, it is perhaps wiser to use it in the way it has been intended, by applying it to understanding long-distance contacts and their effects. This does not address the question of what we mean by globalization, let alone how to draw on the vast theoretical literature concerning it, and before we can use the concept at all we need to ask a basic question: what is globalization and how might this possibly relate to the Roman world or Late Antiquity?

Globalization and the Roman and Byzantine worlds

It might be said that the Romans and Byzantines could not have been globalized because they had no concept of the earth as a globe. In fact, this assumption is a myth: the Romans frequently conceptualised and depicted the earth as a sphere, as illustrated at the centre of the Empire by the recently discovered fourth-century imperial regalia

found in Rome. Furthermore, Roman scholars also believed the sky also to be spherical, so that the globe of the earth was contained within another sphere. Pursuing this argument to its logical conclusion one could say that in this fashion the Romans were more 'globalized' than we are today![44]

Hingley's discussion gives the impression that globalization is a single fixed and clear-cut concept. However, when we look at IR theory, it is immediately apparent that there is much debate over what globalization is, and if it even exists in the modern world, let alone the ancient world. This is certainly not the place to enter into a full discussion of the extensive academic literature on this subject written by IR analysts in the last decade, but it is perhaps useful to start with a relatively straightforward characterisation of globalization and discuss that.[45]

Globalization can be said to be the 'becoming worldwide' of interactions between people, states and institutions. If one works from our everyday understanding of the term 'worldwide', no pre-modern political or economic system was ever globalized, because it did not have a network of linkages across the entire globe. Unless one wished to claim that the Romans, or for that matter Byzantines, ever reached America or Australia – and I for one would not – then no Roman, Late Antique or Byzantine political, cultural or economic context was ever globalised in this sense.

However, this depends upon what we mean by 'global'. If one conceptualises the world not in strictly geographical terms but as it is known at a given time to a particular people, then the world for the Romans, Persians, Indians and Chinese in this period could be understood in terms of the Eurasian continent and Africa. In this way, Roman and Byzantine political and economic systems *could* have been globalized, in that they had links to all parts of that 'world'. Other ways of conceptualising globalization also depend on beliefs not interaction. In what has been called the 'world polity' model it is the role of a shared culture that brings about globalization, while in the 'world culture' model, which is that used by Hingley, one needs just to view the globe

[42] Tadeusz Aleksandrowicz, 'The Roman Empire as a model of globalization', paper read at the conference 'Society as text – in the thought of Richard Harvey Brown' held on 31 May - 1 June 2003 at the University of Silesia, Katowice, Poland, http://brownsym.cm.umk.pl/abstract.php?abstract=1 (accessed 10 February 2007); R. Hingley, *Globalizing Roman Culture. Unity, diversity and empire* (London and New York, Routledge, 2005). R.B. Hitchner is currently preparing a book: R.B. Hitchner, *The First Globalization: The Roman Empire and its Legacy in the Twenty-First Century,* forthcoming. Postcolonialism is explored in relation to the Roman world in J. Webster and N. Cooper (eds.), *Roman Imperialism: post-colonial perspectives* (Leicester, University of Leicester, 1996).
[43] On the processes of globalization in the post-medieval international system: I. Clark, *Globalization and Fragmentation* (Oxford, Oxford University Press, 1997); M.W. Zacher, 'The Decaying Pillars of the Westphalian Temple: Implications for International Order and Governance', in *Governance Without Government: order and change in world politics,* eds. J.N.Rosenau and E.-O.Czempiel (Cambridge, Cambridge University Press, 1992), pp. 58-101.

[44] A representation of the earth as a globe formed part of the imperial regalia of Maxentius found by Clementina Panella on the Palatine in Rome in 2007: N. S. Gill, 'Archaeologists in Rome uncover the only existing example of Maxentius' regalia', *The International Herald Tribune,* 3 December 2007, http://ancienthistory.about.com/b/a/257931.htm (accessed 29 May 2007). A photo of the globe is shown in R. Owen 'Emperor's treasures found', *The Times,* 31 January 2007, http://www.timesonline.co.uk/tol/news/world/europe/article1303241.ece (accessed 29 May 2007). For the only complete celestial globe of Roman date: E. Künzel, 'The globe in the Römisch-Germanisches Zentralmuseum Mainz' *Globusfreund* 45/6 (1997/1998): 81-153.
[45] For sceptical views: D. Held and A. McGrew, *Globalization/Anti-Globalization,* (Cambridge, Polity, 2002); P. Hirst and G.Thompson, *Globalization in Question* (2nd ed.) (Cambridge, Polity, 1999).

as one place and consider that there are global issues to be addressed.[46]

Alternatively, one could adopt a concept of globalization in which only political or economic interactions between states are considered only worthy of analysis, what IR theorists call a 'Realist' view of international politics. According to Realist IR theory the 'world' is the sum of interactions between states. At specific points in the history of the first millennium AD (prior to primary state-formation in the Americas) it could be claimed that there were no states outside of the network of interactions of which the Roman Empire was a part, and so the entire world really was globalized because every state was linked to each other at least indirectly. Of course this would also depend upon how one understands the state, which is another subject of mutual interest to IR theorists and archaeologists.[47]

This demonstrates how alternatives ranging from Roman-period globalization to no globalization at all, can be generated just by changing how the term globalization is understood. This may suggest that, if we use this term at all, we should be very careful to say what exactly we mean by it and to set out the relationship between our sense of the term and those used by other scholars. To explore the concept further one might consider two of the more detailed recent attempts to say precisely what is meant by globalization and then explore the term's applicability to the twenty-first century. Both attempts find the term useful, but both use globalization to mean somewhat different things.

In a recent book, *The Globalization of World Politics*, Anthony McGrew characterises globalization in terms of the following seven criteria. These are: *economic transformation* (especially transnational trade flows and interdependence), *communications* (especially the impact of this on the formation of social groups), *global culture* (in that urban centres increasingly resemble each other), *homogeneity* (diminishing inter-cultural differences), *fundamental changes in the perception of time and space* (changes in how communications undermine traditional perceptions of time and geographical distance), *the emergence of a global polity* with the transference of loyalty to new, higher level, political units, a culture in which people 'think globally and act locally', and – finally – a *risk culture*, in which people realise that some problems are global and cannot be addressed at the state level.[48]

Seen in this way, the Roman Empire could be understood as showing globalization in several of its aspects. One can trace economic transformation and enhanced communications – by road and by ship – and perhaps the development of shared features of a Roman urban culture (however re-worked in local contexts). One might also argue that differences between elites decreased as a result of these interactions and that time and space were re-conceptualised. Finally, of course, the Roman state at least aspired to being a global polity, although not in the sense meant by McGrew.

So, in that sense one might argue that the Roman world was globalized, although there is no evidence of a risk culture in the Roman Empire. Not until the rise of Christianity, and the perception that there are worldwide moral and spiritual issues and identities, do we see a risk culture and the true sense of McGrew's global polity emerge – a global identity superseding that of any individual people or state with individuals thinking in global terms. This also transformed perceptions of time and space. That is, if the McGrew model fits the Roman world at all, it is not the empire of Augustus or Trajan that it fits but rather the Christian Roman empire of Late Antiquity.[49]

In his appropriately titled work *Globalization: a critical introduction,* Jan Aart Scholte uses the reconfiguration of social geography and inter-continental and supra-territorial connections between people that to characterise globalization. He emphasises the changes to these engendered by globalizing forces – political authority that is not dependent on the state, non-national identity and what he calls 'non-rationalist' (he means, in a non-pejorative sense, non-scientific) knowledge. Scholte stresses that the process has had positive and negative effects, even disregarding those directly derived from its economic consequences – effects such as the heightened insecurities as conflicts become more easily internationalised.[50]

Applying this to the world of Rome and the Byzantine Empire, one can see that the establishment of Roman rule and its consequences for the Empire was a fundamental shift in social geography – not least because government, military authority and the recipients of taxation were newly situated miles away rather than in the hands of

[46] J. Boli and G.M. Thomas, 'World Culture in the World Polity', *American Sociological Review,* 62.2 (1997): 171-190; J. Meyer, J. Boli, G. M. Thomas and F. O. Ramirez, 'World Society and the Nation-State', *American Journal of Sociology,* 103.1 (1997): 144-181; R. Robertson, *Globalization: Social Theory and Global Culture* (London, Sage, 1992).
[47] For IR theory and the state, see: Y.H. Ferguson and R.W. Mansbach, *Polities, Authority, Identities and Change* (Columbia, University of South Carolina Press, 1996); S.D. Krasner, 'Alternative Approaches to the State: Alternative Conceptions and Historical Dynamics', *Comparative Politics* 16.2 (1984): 223-46.
[48] A. McGrew, 'Globalization and Global Politics', in *The Globalization of World Politics,* eds. J. Bayliss and S. Smith (3rd ed) (Oxford, Oxford University Press, 2005), pp. 19-40 (22-38).
[49] The emergence of a shared Christian view of the global community is charted superbly in: J. Herrin, *The Formation of Christendom* (Oxford, Blackwell, 1987). For the reconfiguration of time: M.R. Salzman, *On Roman time The Codex Calendar of 354 and the Rhythms of Urban Life in Late Antiquity,* (Berkeley and Oxford, University of California Press, 1990).
[50] J.A. Scholte, *Globalization: a critical introduction* (2nd ed.) (Basingstoke, Palgrave Macmillan, 2005), esp. p. 8.

local elites. While the consequences in institutional terms may have been different, it would be hard to deny that both positive and negative impacts on local populations resulted from them. However, once again the best fit is not the early Roman period but rather Late Antiquity, when the spread of Christianity led to non-state governance (by the Church), non-national identity (as Christians) and what Scholte calls 'non-rationalist knowledge' (for example, in the Late Antique focus on saints and their relics).[51]

One might even see clear-cut non-state supra-territorial security threats in Late Antiquity. Hunnic raiders of the Roman, Persian and East Asian worlds alike, famine and plague all seem to be major factors in sixth-century politics and economics.[52]

Conclusion

If the concept of globalization is relevant to the Roman world at all, it is most apposite to that world in Late Antiquity, including the sixth century. This is not because external contacts were especially extensive then compared to the earlier Roman period (although they may not have been greatly reduced), but because globalization requires the existence of transnational links and identities that connect local behaviour with global norms, problems and aspirations, and governance. Such beliefs transcend political boundaries and longstanding allegiances. While the Roman world may satisfy those economic and even cultural criteria proposed as indicators of globalization, it is probably only with the rise of Christianity, and perhaps not until large parts of the system concerned have a truly Christianised population, that we can see the transnational governance, concerns and identities that globalization requires. This may be first apparent in the sixth century and, as such, one might consider a case for this being the first phase of globalization.

[51] P. Brown, *The Cult of the Saints: Its rise and function in Latin Christianity* (Chicago and London, SCM Press, 1981); E.D. Hunt, *Holy Land pilgrimage in the Later Roman Empire AD 312-460* (Oxford, Clarendon Press, 1982); Gillett; M. Dietz, *Wandering Monks, Virgins and Pilgrims: Ascetic Travel in the Mediterranean World AD 300-800* (Philadelphia, Pennsylvania State University Press, 2005); J. Wilkinson (ed. and trans.), *Egeria's Travels* (3rd ed.) (Warminster, Aris and Phillips, 1999). On the universalism of the Church: C. Buck, 'The Universality of the Church of the East: How Persian was Persian Christianity?' *Journal of the Assyrian Academic Society* X.1 (1996): 54-95. See also: O.R. Constable, *Housing the stranger in the Mediterranean World* (Cambridge, Cambridge University Press, 2003).

[52] P. Heather, 'The Huns and the end of the Roman Empire in western Europe', *English Historical Review* 110, (1995): 4-41; W. Pohl, 'The role of steppe peoples in eastern and central Europe in the first millennium A.D.', in *Origins of Central Europe*, ed. P. Urbanczyk (Warsaw, Scientific Society of Polish Archaeologists, 1997), pp. 65-78; E.A. Thompson (rev. by Peter Heather), *The Huns* (Oxford, Blackwell, 1996); T. Barfield, *The Perilous Frontier: Nomadic Empires and China, 221 BC to AD 1757* (Cambridge and Oxford, Blackwell, 1989); M. Todd, *Migrants and Invaders. The Movement of Peoples in the Ancient World* (Stroud, Tempus, 2001), pp. 61-2, 97-102. For a re-statement of the argument that these movements were a major threat to the Late Roman Empire: P. Heather, *The Fall of the Roman Empire. A New History* (London, Macmillan, 2005). For plague as a perceived 'transnational' threat in Late Antiquity: P. Sarris 2007 *Economy and Society in the Age of Justinian* (Cambridge University Press, Cambridge, 2006), pp. 217, 224; P. Horden 'Mediterranean Plague in the Age of Justinian' in *The Cambridge Companion to the Age of Justinian* ed. M. Maas (Cambridge University Press, Cambridge, 2005), pp. 134-160; D.C. Stathakopolous, *Famine and Pestilence in the Late Roman and Early Byzantine Empire* (Aldershot, Ashgate, 2004); P. Allen, 'The Justinianic Plague', *Byzantion* 49 (1979): pp. 5-20; J. Durliat, 'La peste du VIe siècle. Pour un nouvel examen des sources byzantines', *Hommes et Richesses dans l'Empire byzantin. IVe-VIIe siècle (Réalités Byzantines)* (Paris, Lethielleux, 1989), pp. 107-12; K.-H. Leven, 'Die "Justinianische" Pest', in *Jahrbuch des Instituts für Geschichte der Medizin der Robert Bosch Stiftung*, ed. W.F. Kümmel (Stuttgart, Hippokrates, 1989), pp. 137-161; R. Sallares, *Malaria and Rome: A History of malaria in Ancient Italy* (Oxford, Oxford University Press, 2002).

Using bracteates as evidence for long-distance contacts

Charlotte Behr

Roehampton University

Introduction

The study of golden pendants, so-called bracteates, can contribute to the understanding of long-distance contacts in northern, western and central Europe in the 5th and 6th centuries. It is well known from the extensive archaeological record that the countries north and east of the Roman Empire were far from being isolated from the networks of trade and exchange in the Roman Empire and beyond, links that often survived the end of the western Roman Empire in the 5th century. Among the numerous finds made in northern and central Europe that belonged predominantly to a sphere of wealth and luxury were Roman coins, glass vessels, bronze pots, precious and semi-precious stones, even a Buddha statue was found on the island of Helgö in the Mälaren area.[1] Bracteates allow the reconstruction of a different type of long-distance network because they were not objects of trade and commerce but belonged to a sphere of gift exchange and diplomatic contacts.[2] The distribution pattern of these precious objects that were characterised by their intricate and sophisticated iconography leads to the recognition of contacts over long distances crossing political and ethnic boundaries. The study of the meaning and function of the bracteates that were worn as amulets showing images of Germanic gods and myths can also contribute to the discussion of the nature of distant contacts and of the people who were responsible for establishing and maintaining them in the late and post-Roman periods.

Bracteates are round pendants made of gold foil that were stamped on one side with a die showing a figurative image.[3] They were worn on necklaces, either singly or together with other bracteates, other pendants or beads.[4] With more than 900 finds they form one of the largest find groups in migration-period northern European archaeology. Currently about 620 different die images are known mostly from one bracteate but also from series with up to 14 die-identical bracteates.[5] The central images of the pendants have always a diameter of between 2 and 2.5 cm. Some were stamped on a larger disk and the central image was surrounded by one or more concentric rings that were decorated with individual stamps usually with geometric designs and sometimes small images of animals or anthropomorphic heads. In some instances it is possible to show that the same stamp was used in the border zone on two different bracteates.[6] The edge of the disk was surrounded with gold wire and a loop was attached. On some bracteates the loop attachment is strengthened with a triangular sheet of gold that is decorated with filigree and occasionally with some human masks.

To identify long-distance contacts between the people who owed or at least who deposited bracteates different aspects of the distribution pattern of bracteate finds are significant. There are bracteates that were connected because they were made with the same tools, be they the same dies with which the central image was punched or the same stamps used to decorate the concentric border zones around the central image. Then there are clusters of bracteates that are related because of the stylistic similarities in the central image and in other decorative features that are so close that the craftsmen involved must have seen other examples of the same cluster and copied them. Finally, the high level of standardisation in bracteate iconography suggests that the images represented stories and ideas that were shared by people living over a wide area in northern and central Europe.

---

[1] E. Bakka, 'Scandinavian Trade Relations with the Continent and the British Isles in Pre-Viking Times' in *Antikvariskt arkiv* 40 / *Early Medieval Studies* 3 (1971): 37-51 (39); U. Lund Hansen, *Römischer Import im Norden: Warenaustausch zwischen dem Römischen Reich und dem freien Germanien während der Kaiserzeit unter besonderer Berücksichtigung Nordeuropas*, Nordiske Fortidsminder Serie B: 10 (København, 1987); B. Gyllensvärd, 'The Buddha found at Helgö' in *Excavations at Helgö XVI: Exotic and Sacral Finds from Helgö*, B. Gyllensvärd et al. (Stockholm, 2004).
[2] A. Andrén, 'Guld och makt – en tolkning av de skandinaviska guldbrakteaternas funktion' in *Samfundsorganisation og Regional Variation. Norden i romersk jernalder og folkevandringstid*, eds. C. Fabech and J. Ringtved, Jysk Arkæologisk Selskabs Skrifter XXVII (Aarhus, 1991) 245-256; M. Gaimster, 'Scandinavian Gold Bracteates in Britain. Money and Media in the Dark Ages', *Medieval Archaeology* 36 (1992): 1-28 (21f.).
[3] All bracteate finds before 1989 are published with photos, drawings and descriptions in the iconographical catalogue *Die Goldbrakteaten der Völkerwanderungszeit*, ed. K. Hauck, et al., 1-3, Münstersche Mittelalter-Schriften 24, 1 - 3 (München, 1985-1989) [IK].

[4] N. L. Wicker, 'Display of Scandinavian Migration Period Bracteates and Other Pendant Jewelry as a Reflection of Prestige and Identity' in *De Re Metallica. The Uses of Metal in the Middle Ages*, eds. R. Bork, et al., AVISTA Studies in the History of Medieval Technology, Science, and Art 4 (Aldershot, 2005) 49-61 (54f.).
[5] Fourteen die-identical bracteates have been found in a hoard in Øvre Tøyen, Akershus, Norway (IK 479). They have been made with the same central die but the border zones were decorated differently.
[6] M. Axboe, 'The Scandinavian Gold Bracteates: Studies on their Manufacture and Regional Variations', *Acta Archaeologica* 52 (1981): 1-100 (52-55).

15

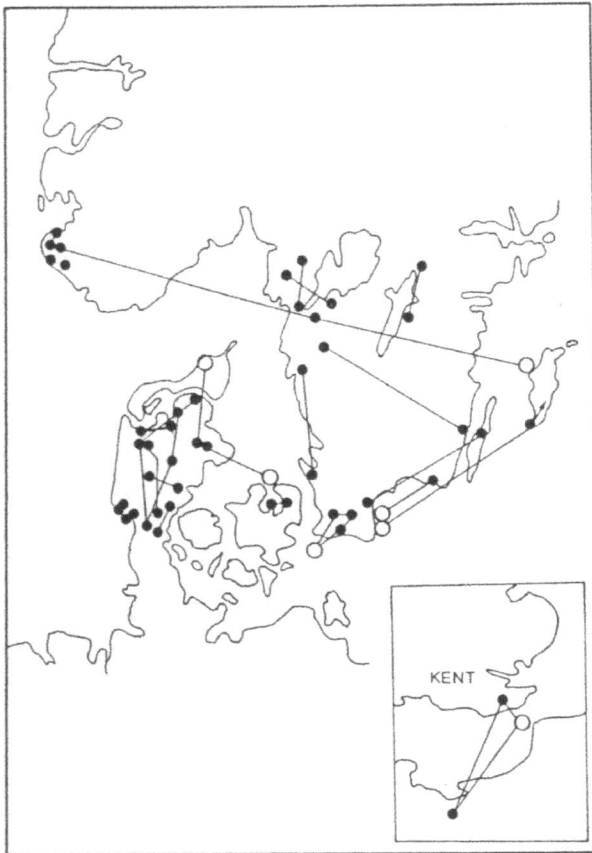

Fig. 1. Distribution map of die- and stamp-linked bracteates (without links within Gotland and Funen). Uncertain findplaces are marked with an open symbol (Axboe, 'Guld og guder', 197).

It has long been recognised that the inspiration for the bracteate images came from the image of the Roman emperor on Roman medallions and coins of the Constantinian period.[7] Soon the northern bracteate designers developed their own iconographic concepts to express their ideas. The interpretation of the images is controversial but there can be no doubt that the exceptional level of uniformity in the iconography was used to represent the same god and the same stories relating to this god.

Bracteates were made for a relatively short period between the mid 5th and the mid 6th century.[8] The largest concentrations of bracteate finds are in southern Scandinavia, especially on the Danish islands, Seeland

and Funen, in Jutland and in south-western Sweden, on the Baltic islands, Gotland, Öland and Bornholm, and in south-western Norway. On the periphery of these areas bracteates have also been found in eastern Sweden, central Norway, eastern Britain, and along the North Sea coast in northern France, Frisia and Germany. There are also some finds further south and east in Germany, Poland, Austria and even Hungary. Whereas bracteates were deposited in southern Scandinavia always in hoards, they were also put into graves in the other areas of distribution. Hoards could consist of a single bracteate or of several bracteates or of bracteates together with other precious metal objects. Many were found in close proximity to or even in settlements.[9] Graves with bracteates belonged mostly to women.[10]

Fig. 2. C-bracteate from Hult, Dalsland, the example with the broadest rim (IK 283, 1)

---

[7] Christian Jürgensen Thomsen who published the first academic study about gold bracteates in 1855 made this observation, C. J. Thomsen, 'Om Guldbracteaterne og Brakteaternes tidligste Brug som Mynt', *Annaler for Nordisk Oldkyndighed* (1855): 265-347 (270).

[8] M. Axboe, 'The chronology of the Scandinavian gold bracteates', in *The pace of change: studies in early medieval chronology*, eds. J. Hines, K. Høilund Nielsen, F. Siegmund (Oxford, 1999). pp. 126-147; M. Axboe, *Die Goldbrakteaten der Völkerwanderungszeit – Herstellungsprobleme und Chronologie*, Ergänzungsbände zum Reallexikon der Germanischen Altertumskunde 38, (Berlin, 2004), pp. 203ff.

[9] H. Geisslinger, *Horte als Geschichtsquelle dargestellt an den völkerwanderungs- und merowingerzeitlichen Funden des südwestlichen Ostseeraumes*, Offa-Bücher 19 (Neumünster, 1967), pp. 50ff.; J. Hines, 'Ritual Hoarding in Migration-Period Scandinavia: A Review of Recent Interpretations', *Proceedings of the Prehistoric Society*, 55 (1989): 193-205 (198); C. Fabech, 'Samfundsorganisation, religiøse ceremonier og regional variation', *Samfundsorganisation og Regional Variation. Norden i romersk jernalder og folkevandringstid*, eds. C. Fabech and J. Ringtved, Jysk Arkæologisk Selskabs Skrifter XXVII (Aarhus, 1991), pp. 283-303, 292ff.; L. Hedeager, 'Sacred Topography. Depositions of wealth in the cultural landscape', in *Glyfer och arkeologiska rum – en vänbok till Jarl Nordbladh*, eds. A. Gustafsson, H. Karlsson (Göteborg, 1999), pp. 229-252 (234ff.).

[10] C. Behr, 'The origins of kingship in early medieval Kent', *Early Medieval Europe* 9,1 (2000): 25-52 (35, 47ff.); M. Gaimster, 'Gold Bracteates and Necklaces. Political ideals in the sixth century', in *Roman Gold and the Development of the Early Germanic Kingdoms. Aspects of technical, socio-political, socio-economic, artistic and intellectual development, A.D. 1-550. – Symposium in Stockholm 14-16 November 1997*, ed. B. Magnus, Konferenser 51 (Stockholm, 2001), pp. 143-155 (143ff.).

Little is known about the manufacture of bracteates.[11] No workshop that can be clearly linked to the production of bracteates has ever been identified. Only two bracteate dies have been found so far, in 1990 in Postgården in northern Jutland and in 2005 in Essex, but there are no bracteates known that were made with these dies.[12] That is why any conclusions about their manufacture have to be drawn from the objects themselves.[13] Some bracteates were linked by the use of the same tool, either a die or a stamp. They are offering the possibility to recognise more or less distant contacts even if it remains debatable how they ended up in their different locations (Fig. 1).[14] The longest distance between die-linked bracteates has been observed in a group of four bracteates showing an anthropomorphic head following the model of the imperial head on Roman medallions placed over a quadruped, probably a horse. One of them was found in a large hoard containing 15 bracteates and several other gold objects in Madla in Rogaland in south-west Norway, one in an unknown findspot on the Baltic island of Gotland and two in a small hoard in Hult in Dalsland in western Sweden, more or less halfway between the two other finds. (Fig. 2)[15]. The central images are identical but there are some variations between them in the border decoration and the loops. The three find spots were located in three different political entities that had social and economic links as an analysis of their archaeological record from the migration period demonstrated.[16]

Another group of die-linked bracteates from fairly distant sites included two finds from Kent, grave 90 in the cemetery of Sarre and an unknown find location, and one cross-Channel find from Normandy, grave 39 in the cemetery of Hérouvillette (Fig. 3).[17] They show an interlaced quadruped animal in profile with its head turned backwards and a snake-like S-shaped body. Here too the border decorations and the shape of the loops vary. The bracteate from Hérouvillette belonged to a number of metal finds from graves in northern France that are described as Anglo-Saxon and which suggest cross-Channel Anglo-Saxon colonies from settlers that may have come either directly from northern Germany or from Britain.[18]

How did tool-linked bracteates arrive at their distant places of deposition? There are various models to explain this observation. Die- or stamp-linked bracteates may have been made in one workshop and then given to various people who lived in distant locations but were connected by a common donor, be it a relation or a lord who used these objects as gifts to express relationships, possibly forms of dependency with the recipients.[19] Or, the people who transported the pendants afar may have travelled to the place where the bracteates had been made to visit or to attend a special occasion and were given here the pendants.[20] Alternatively, the people who received the bracteates may have lived originally in close proximity to where they had been made but some then moved further away taking their jewellery with them. One obvious possibility was exogamy.[21] In this model women were establishing or reinforcing through marriage links between families and distant communities and can be traced through the jewellery with which they were buried or that they deposited in a hoard. Even assuming that die-linked bracteates were made in one location it

[11] The most recent summary of the state of research Axboe, *Goldbrakteaten*, 1-30; see also M. Axboe, 'Probleme der Brakteatenherstellung. Eine Übersicht über die Forschung', *Frühmittelalterliche Studien* 22 (1988): 158-169.

[12] M. Axboe, 'A Die for a Gold Bracteate' in *Sources and Resources. Studies in honour of Birgit Arrhenius*, eds. G. Arwidsson, et. al., Pact 38 (Strasbourg, 1993); Axboe, *Goldbrakteaten*, 3; C. McDonald, 'Essex/Hertfordshire', *Medieval Archaeology* 50 (2006): 281f.; M. Axboe, *Brakteatstudier*, Nordiske Fortidsminder, Serie B: 25 (København, 2007), p. 14f.

[13] N. L. Wicker, 'On the Trail of the Elusive Goldsmith: Tracing Individual Style and Workshop Characteristics in Migration Period Metalwork', *Gesta* 33, 1 (1994): 65-70; N. L. Wicker, 'Production Areas and Workshops for the Manufacture of Bracteates' in *Runeninschriften als Quellen interdisziplinärer Forschung. Abhandlungen des Vierten Internationalen Symposiums über Runen und Runeninschriften in Göttingen vom 4. – 9. August 1995*, eds. K. Düwel and S. Nowak, Ergänzungsbände zum Reallexikon der Germanischen Altertumskunde 15 (Berlin – New York, 1998), pp. 253-267; M. Axboe, 'Probleme', 158-169.

[14] K. Hauck, 'Gudme in der Sicht der Brakteaten-Forschung (Zur Ikonologie der Goldbrakteaten, XXXVI)' in *Frühmittelalterliche Studien*, 21 (1987): 147-181 (166ff.); M. Axboe, 'Guld og guder i folkevandringstiden. Brakteaterne som kilde til politisk/religiøse forhold' in *Samfundsorganisation og Regional Variation. Norden i romersk jernalder og folkevandringstid*, eds. C. Fabech and J. Ringtved, Jysk Arkæologisk Selskabs Skrifter XXVII, (Aarhus, 1991) pp. 187-202 (196ff.).

[15] IK 283, 1-3 with further literature.

[16] B. Myhre, 'Chieftains' graves and chiefdom territories in South Norway in the Migration Period', *Studien zur Sachsenforschung*, 6 (1987): 169-187; P. H. Ramqvist, 'Über ökonomische und sozio-politische Beziehungen der Gesellschaften der nordischen Völkerwanderungszeit', *Frühmittelalterliche Studien*, 25 (1991): 45-72 (46ff.) described these entities as 'petty kingdoms'.

[17] IK 492, 1-3. J. Decaëns, 'Un nouveau cimetière du Haute Moyen Age en Normandie. Hérouvillette (Calvados)', *Archéologie Médiévale*, 1 (1971): 1-125 (39ff., 74ff.); E. Bakka, 'Scandinavian-type gold bracteates in Kentish and continental grave finds' in *Angles, Saxons and Jutes. Essays presented to J. N. L. Myres*, ed. V. Evison (Oxford, 1981), pp. 11-35 (14, 18, 23f.); S. Chadwick Hawkes, M. Pollard, 'The gold Bracteates from sixth-century Anglo-Saxon Graves in Kent, in the Light of a new Find from Finglesham', *Frühmittelalterliche Studien*, 15 (1981): 316-370 (328, 340, 343); Behr, 'The crigins', 49.

[18] E. James, *The Franks* (Oxford, 1988), p. 103.

[19] A. Y. Gurevich, 'Wealth and Gift-Bestowal among the Ancient Scandinavians', *Scandinavica* 7,2 (1968): 126-138 (134ff.); Andrén, 'Guld og makt', 252ff.; Gaimster 'Scandinavian Gold Bracteates', 17.

[20] K. Hauck, 'Gudme als Kultort und seine Rolle beim Austausch von Bildformularen der Goldbrakteaten (Zur Ikonologie der Goldbrakteaten, L)' in *The Archaeology of Gudme and Lundeborg*, eds. P. O. Nielsen, K. Randsborg and H. Thrane, Arkæologiske Studier 10 (Kopenhagen, 1994), pp. 78-88 (83).

[21] B. Arrhenius, 'Smycken som diplomati' in *Föremål som vittnesbörd. En festskrift till Gertrud Grenander Nyberg på 80-årsdagen den 26 juli 1992*, ed. K. Ågren, (Stockholm, 1992), pp. 18-25 (22ff.); but see also B. Magnus, 'Brooches on the move in Migration Period Europe', *Fornvännen*, 99 (2004): 273-283 (280f.) discussing the difficulties in identifying exogamy through female grave goods.

**Fig. 3. D-bracteate from Hérouvillette,
Normandy (IK 492, 2).**

is not obvious where this workshop was located. The common archaeological practice to use comparisons of style or technique to identify regional or local relationships between objects and thus locate the origin of objects is particularly difficult when discussing these golden pendants. Bracteates were quite unique objects and the iconography of the central image and the stamp decoration of the border zones had no apparent parallels on other contemporary objects that would allow an unambiguous regional or local attribution. It is only on the basis of a comparison with stylistically closely related bracteates and their predominant area of distribution that it is probable to assume that the first example of bracteates with the head over the quadruped originated from south-west Norway and the second example of bracteates with the animal from Kent.[22]

Not only the circumstances under which bracteates were manufactured are little known also the role or status of the craftsmen who were involved in designing and making bracteates cannot be assessed with certainty.[23] Most probably migration period goldsmiths were working for a lord who had access to raw materials and provided them with the gold. They may have worked either permanently or temporarily close to the seat of those who commissioned the bracteates. Archaeological evidence about early medieval metal-working craftsmen suggests that they were at least intermittently itinerant workers.[24]

That means that tool-linked bracteates were not necessarily made in the same location but could have been manufactured in different locations because the craftsman or, another possibility, the tool had travelled.[25] Whatever the scenario tool-linked bracteates indicate some forms of contact over long distances. Other groups of tool-linked bracteates have been found in more or less distant locations. No obvious patterns in terms of distance, direction or density are evident but links appear to connect all Scandinavian regions that had any bracteate finds at all. This dense network suggests at the very least intense exchange of objects and ideas. Whereas no tool-linked bracteates connected Scandinavia with the more peripheral distribution areas, bracteate finds in Britain, Frisia, Germany or Pannonia were stylistically closely related to Scandinavian finds.[26]

Since the 19th century bracteates have been divided into four different categories according to the image in the centre.[27] Almost all bracteates that have ever been found belong to one of these categories. Within these groups, as has long been observed, are clusters of bracteates that are stylistically particularly closely related.[28] Pesch has recently defined these clusters as 'Formularfamilien'.[29] Bracteates belonging to a cluster were characterised by such close correspondences of iconographic details that it

---

pp. 40ff.; K. Leahy, *Anglo-Saxon Crafts* (Stroud, 2003), pp. 167ff. Archaeological evidence for goldsmiths and their work in the migration period include the study of objects, tools, models, casting moulds and also smith graves like the one that was found next to the bracteate grave in Hérouvillette (grave 10) see Decaëns, 'Un nouveau cimetière', 12ff.

[25] Wicker, 'On the Trail', 69.

[26] Axboe, 'Guld og guder', 196ff.

[27] O. Montelius, *Från järnåldern* (Stockholm, 1869). According to him A-bracteates are those that show an anthropomorphic head in profile, B-bracteates show one or more complete anthropomorphic figures and C-bracteates have an anthropomorphic head in profile over a quadruped. They all can be accompanied by additional animals, most commonly birds, graphic symbols and/or inscriptions, often in runes. D-bracteates are defined as only showing one or more animals, usually interlaced, but no anthropomorphic features. C- and D-bracteates form by far the largest groups among the bracteates.

[28] Already B. Salin, 'De nordiska guldbrakteaterna', *Antiqvarisk Tidskrift för Sverige*, 14,2 (1895): 1-111 (24ff., 99ff.) grouped the bracteates in clusters of stylistically related pendants and named the clusters according to their predominant areas of distribution. His work was continued, among others, by M. Mackeprang, *De nordiske Guldbrakteater*. Jysk arkæologisk Selskabs Skrifter 2, (Århus, 1952). However the allocations of bracteates to clusters was often based on rather impressionistic ideas. For a critique and discussion of the methodological implications of forming clusters see M. P. Malmer, *Metodproblem inom Järnålderns Konsthistoria* (Bonn – Lund, 1963), pp. 76ff. and E. Bakka, 'Methodological Problems in the Study of Gold Bracteates' in *Norwegian Archaeological Review*, 1 (1968): 5-35, 45-56.

[29] A. Pesch, 'Uppåkra im Licht der Formular-Familien der völkerwanderungszeitlichen Goldbrakteaten' in *Central Places in the Migration and the Merovingian Periods*, eds. B. Hårdh and L. Larsson (Stockholm, 2002), pp. 55-78 (56ff.) where she developed a conceptual framework for describing 'Formularfamilien'; a comprehensive study of the whole bracteate corpus is forthcoming, A. Pesch, *Die völkerwanderungszeitlichen Goldbrakteaten – Formularfamilien der Bilddarstellungen. Die Goldbrakteaten der Völkerwanderungszeit* 4,3: Auswertung, eds. K. Hauck. K. Düwel and W. Heizmann, Ergänzungsbände zum RGA 38,3, (Berlin – New York, in press). (I am grateful to Alexandra Pesch for her permission to include some of her unpublished distribution maps in this article.)

---

[22] C. Behr, *Die Beizeichen auf den völkerwanderungszeitlichen Goldbrakteaten* (Frankfurt am Main, 1991), pp. 186f.; Behr, 'The origins', 48ff.

[23] Wicker 'On the Trail'.

[24] J. Werner, 'Zur Verbreitung frühgeschichtlicher Metallarbeiten (Werkstatt – Wanderhandwerk – Handel – Familienverbindung)', *Antikvariskt Arkiv* 38 / *Early Medieval Studies* 1 (1970): 65-81; H. Roth, *Kunst und Handwerk im frühen Mittelalter. Archäologische Zeugnisse von Childerich I. bis zu Karl dem Großen* (Stuttgart, 1986),

is inconceivable that they were designed independently but instead must belong to one workshop-context.[30] The craftsman, or –men, who designed them must have known the other images of bracteates belonging to the same cluster. Clusters that are defined as 'Formularfamilien' can be mapped. The emerging patterns differ significantly as the following examples illustrate.

The first example comprises a cluster of 34 C-bracteates from sixteen different dies (Fig. 4 a-d).[31] The designs of the central images show close stylistic similarities in the shape of the anthropomorphic head, its particular hairstyle ending in a knot and being framed with a dotted band, the oval shape of its eye and the attachment of mouth and nose to the neck of the quadruped. The animals too have many stylistic details that are closely comparable, including the shape of the body, the position and shape of the legs, the beard, the horns, the eye and the mouth. Seven images show only the head and the animal whereas on eight images they are accompanied either by a bird or a cross, a swastika, a rosette or three dots forming a triangle.[32] Most find spots of bracteates from this cluster were in Scania in southern Sweden usually containing one bracteate only;[33] others came from the Danish islands of Funen,[34] Zealand[35] and Bornholm[36], an unknown find spot in Schleswig-Holstein,[37] from Pomerania in Poland[38], the island of Gotland[39] and Västergötland[40] in Sweden and one find is unprovenanced.[41] They included series of six or seven die-identical bracteates. Despite all the congruencies between the different versions of this cluster there appear to be some regional variation.[42] Only on finds from Scania and Bornholm the additional symbols of a cross, a swastika or a circle were inserted,[43] whereas the bracteates outside Scania had mostly no additional symbols, except for the one from Zealand with three dots forming a triangle.[44] This cluster was concentrated around the Oresund. The distribution of the find spots points towards the importance of sea travel to link these places in Scania, the Danish islands and across the Baltic Sea on its southern coast.[45]

Again it is not obvious where the bracteates forming this particular cluster were first designed or made. As the largest number of different dies has been found in Scania, it is most probable that this cluster was originally linked to one workshop in Scania. A likely candidate is Uppåkra in south-west Scania where the most detailed version of this cluster has been found.[46]

The site of Uppåkra has been researched intensively since 1996 first through systematic field-walking with metal-detectors and later through excavations.[47] A wealth of material finds dating from the early Roman imperial period to the 10th century has been found.[48] Throughout this period Uppåkra stood out in comparison with other sites in Scania because the settlement was larger and the finds richer than anywhere else.[49] The outstandingly rich metal finds and unusual house structures were signs of a so-called central place. The concept of 'central places' has been adopted in Scandinavian archaeology in the 1980s to explain sites in which the exceptional archaeological record suggests that they held some form of economic, political, religious and social pre-eminence on a local or regional level.[50] Among many different crafts, evidence for metal-working has been found in Uppåkra, if not specifically bracteate manufacture.[51] Uppåkra can be compared with a number of other 'central places' in migration-period southern Scandinavia.[52] Particularly well explored is Gudme close to the south-east coast of the island of Funen with its adjacent harbour

[30] Pesch, 'Uppåkra', 59.
[31] C. Behr, 'Beizeichen auf formularverwandten Goldbrakteaten, exemplarisch erörtert' in Der historische Horizont der Götterbild-Amulette aus der Übergangsepoche von der Spätantike zum Frühmittelalter, ed. K. Hauck, Abhandlungen der Akademie der Wissenschaften in Göttingen. Phil.-hist. Kl. Dritte Folge Nr. 200 (Göttingen, 1992), pp. 111-142 (119ff.); Pesch, 'Uppåkra', 66ff.
[32] Only a fragment of IK 606 from Smørengegård, Bornholm has been found, too small to be certain about accompanying animals or signs.
[33] IK 4 Åkarp, 272 Hermanstorp, 587 Uppåkra, 235 Dybäck, 379 Ven, 53 Fjärestad (with two die-identical bracteates).
[34] IK 30 Bolbro (with seven die-identical bracteates).
[35] IK 179 Stenholts Vang (with seven die-identical bracteates).
[36] IK 592 Sorte Muld and 606 Smørengegård.
[37] IK 325 Schleswig (uncertain).
[38] IK 100 Körlin (with six die-identical bracteates).
[39] IK 321 Near Roma.
[40] IK 138 Olovstorp.
[41] IK 366 unknown provenance.
[42] Behr, 'Beizeichen', 119ff.; Pesch, Uppåkra, 71.
[43] IK 53 (swastika and circle), 235 (cross and circle), 379 (swastika and circle), 587 (four circles), 592 (three crosses).
[44] IK 179 Stenholts Vang.

[45] Pesch, 'Uppåkra', 70f.
[46] M. Axboe, 'En C-brakteat fra Uppåkra' in Uppåkra. Centrum och Sammanhang, ed. B. Hårdh, Uppåkrastudier 3 (Stockholm, 2001), pp. 169-174; Pesch, 'Uppåkra', 69.
[47] L. Larsson, 'The Uppåkra Project. Preconditions, Performance and Prospects' in Centrality – Regionality. The Social Structure of Southern Sweden during the Iron Age, eds. L. Larsson and B. Hårdh, Uppåkrastudier 7 (Stockholm, 2003), pp. 3-26 (9ff.)
[48] Summarised in B. Hårdh, 'The Contacts of the Central Place' in Centrality, eds. Larsson and Hårdh, pp. 27-66.
[49] Hardh, 'The Contacts', 61.
[50] H. Steuer, 'Reichtumszentrum', Reallexikon der germanischen Altertumskunde, 24 (Berlin, 2003): 343-348; H. Thrane, 'Das Reichtumszentrum Gudme in der Völkerwanderungszeit Fünens' in Der historische Horizont der Götterbild-Amulette aus der Übergangsepoche von der Spätantike zum Frühmittelalter, ed. K. Hauck, Abhandlungen der Akademie der Wissenschaften in Göttingen. Phil.-hist. Kl. Dritte Folge Nr. 200 (Göttingen, 1992), pp. 299-380; C. Fabech, 'Organising the Landscape: a matter of production, power and religion' in The Making of Kingdoms, eds. T. Dickinson and D. Griffiths, Anglo-Saxon Studies in Archaeology and History 10 (Oxford, 1999): 37-47; see also contributions in B. Hårdh, L. Larsson (eds.), Central places in the migration and Merovingian periods: papers from the 52nd Sachsensymposium, Lund, August 2001. Uppåkrastudier 6 (Stockholm, 2002).
[51] B. Hårdh, 'Uppåkra i folkvandingstiden' in Fler fynd i centrum. Materialstudier i och kring Uppåkra, ed. B. Hårdh, Uppåkrastudier 9 (Stockholm, 2003) 41-80 (64ff.).
[52] J. Ringtved, 'The geography of power: South Scandinavia before the Danish kingdom' in The Making of Kingdoms, eds. Dickinson and Griffiths, pp. 49-63.

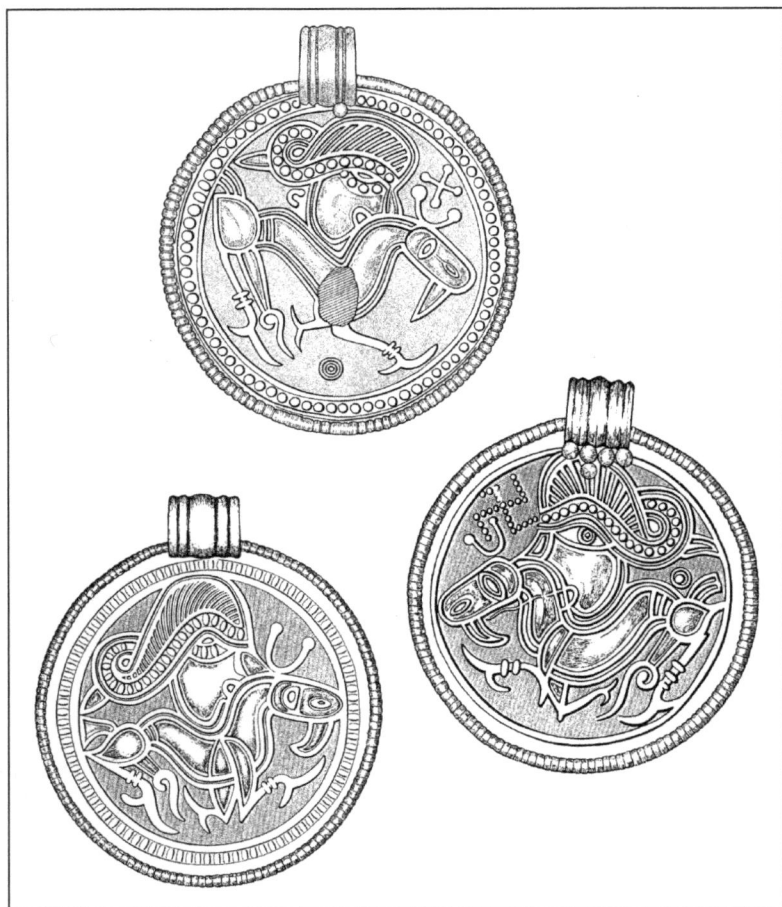

Fig. 4a-c. Three examples of workshop-related C-bracteates: 4a from Dybäck, Scania (IK 235); 4b from Fjärestad, Scania (IK 53); 4c from Bolbro, Funen (IK 30)

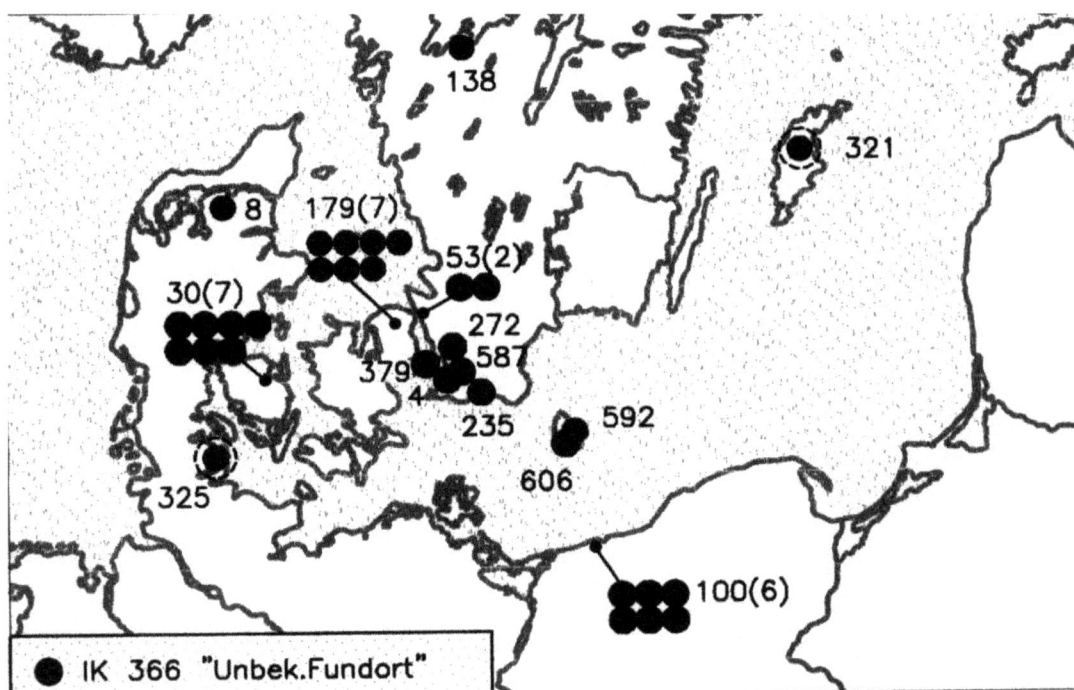

Fig. 4d. Distribution map of stylistically related bracteates (A. Pesch, *Formularfamilien*, in press)

site at Lundeborg.[53] In Gudme itself a bracteate hoard containing ten pendants has been found in a posthole of a small house and several additional bracteate finds came from the vicinity of Gudme.[54] Not only the pattern of frequent bracteate finds in or close to a central place is repeated in numerous sites but also the observation that some bracteates belonging to a cluster of stylistically related bracteates were found in and close to these places whereas others of the same cluster were found in more or less distant locations.[55] These observations suggest that bracteate production was concentrated in a few workshops in central places that were exchanging and copying iconographic formulas. A limited number of bracteate workshops – however we have to imagine that they operated in reality – would also explain more easily how it was possible to retain such a high level of standardisation of the bracteate iconography than a larger number of workshops which would have led probably to greater diversity.[56]

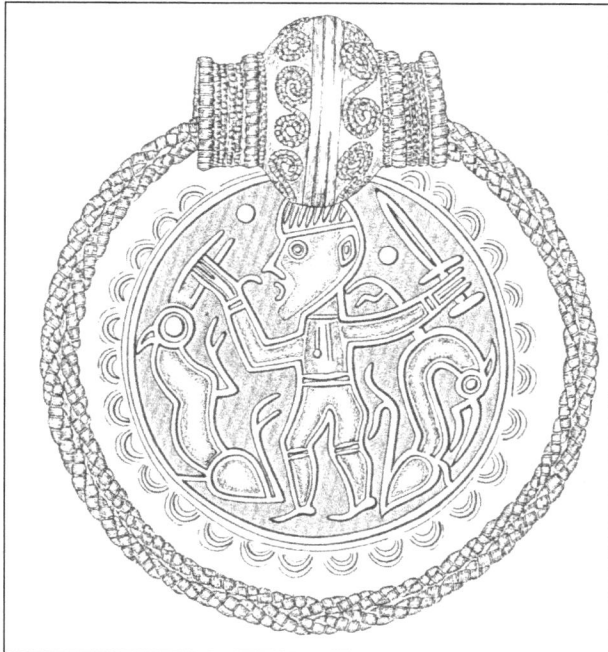

Fig. 5a. B-bracteate of unknown provenance in Schleswig-Holstein, known as 'Hamburg' (IK 71)

No focal point of distribution is apparent in the cluster of nine B-bracteates showing a male figure armed with a sword fighting two quadruped animals with impressive jaws (Fig. 5 a, b). An unambiguous interpretation of the scene is now difficult. Most probably some mythical battle between a god and hostile monsters was pictured that contemporary viewers could identify. Seven bracteates from the same die are known from an unknown find spot in Schleswig-Holstein since the 19th century.[57] In 2004 a near identical but mirror-image bracteate was discovered as a metal-detector find Near Holt in Norfolk, East Anglia and in 1999 a very similar if less artful bracteate was found in a female grave in Derenburg, in the district of Wernigerode north-east of the Harz mountains, a place that belonged to the Thuringian kingdom.[58] People wearing these pendants in East Anglia, northern Germany, then belonging to the Saxon settlement area, and Thuringia were linked in some way by these objects with their close stylistic congruencies.[59] They also shared the knowledge of the mythical story that was told in these images.

Fig. 5b. Distribution map of stylistically related bracteates (A. Pesch, *Formularfamilien*, in press)

No focal point of distribution is apparent in the cluster of nine B-bracteates showing a male figure armed with a sword fighting two quadruped animals with impressive jaws (Fig. 5 a, b). An unambiguous interpretation of the scene is now difficult. Most probably some mythical battle between a god and hostile monsters was pictured

---

[53] K. Randsborg, 'Beyond the Roman Empire: Archaeological Discoveries in Gudme on Funen, Denmark', *Oxford Journal of Archaeology*, 9 (1990): 355-366; Thrane, 'Das Reichtumszentrum'; P. O. Thomsen, et al., *Lundeborg – en handelsplads fra jernalderen. Skrifter fra Svendborg & Omegns Museum* 32 (1993), pp. 68ff.

[54] P. V. Petersen, 'Excavations at Sites of Treasure Trove Finds at Gudme' in *The Archaeology*, eds. Nielsen, Randsborg, Thrane, pp. 30-40 (34f.); M. Axboe, 'Gudme and the Gold Bracteates', in *The Archaeology*, eds. Nielsen, Randsborg, Thrane, pp. 68-77.

[55] See clusters in Behr, *Die Beizeichen*, 176ff. and 'Beizeichen', 119ff. (with maps); Pesch, 'Uppåkra', 60ff.

[56] D. A. Hinton, 'Anglo-Saxon Smiths and Myths', *Bulletin of the John Rylands University Library of Manchester* 80, 1 (1998): 6.

[57] IK 71 'Hamburg' with literature.

[58] A. Pesch, 'Und die Götter sind überall', *Archäologie in Deutschland*, 4 (2005): 6-9.

[59] These bracteates may not be the only bracteate links between Thuringia and East Anglia as H. Vierck, 'Der C-Brakteat von Longbridge in der ostenglischen Gruppe (Anhang VIII)' in *Goldbrakteaten aus Sievern*, ed. K. Hauck, Münstersche Mittelalter-Schriften 1 (München, 1970): 331-339 (337) pointed out when he suggested that the D-bracteate from grave 15 in the cemetery of Schönebeck, Sachsen-Anhalt, may have been an East Anglian import because of its rough manufacture, lacking a rim and the crudely attached loop. It was made out of silver. Only in eastern Britain bracteates made out of silver without rims and very simple loops have been found.

Fig. 6a. C-bracteate from Sievern, Lower Saxony (IK 157)

that contemporary viewers could identify. Seven bracteates from the same die are known from an unknown find spot in Schleswig-Holstein since the 19th century.[60] In 2004 a near identical but mirror-image bracteate was discovered as a metal-detector find Near Holt in Norfolk, East Anglia and in 1999 a very similar if less artful bracteate was found in a female grave in Derenburg, in the district of Wernigerode north-east of the Harz mountains, a place that belonged to the Thuringian kingdom.[61] People wearing these pendants in East Anglia, northern Germany, then belonging to the Saxon settlement area, and Thuringia were linked in some way by these objects with their close stylistic congruencies. They also shared the knowledge of the mythical story that was told in these images.

A different pattern of distribution can be recognised in a cluster of 32 C-bracteates from eighteen stylistically related dies (Fig. 6 a, b). The common design of an anthropomorphic head over a stylised quadruped was characterised by high relief. The head was bearded and

Fig. 6b. Distribution map of stylistically related bracteates (A. Pesch, *Formularfamilien*, in press)

---

[60] IK 71 'Hamburg' with literature.
[61] A. Pesch, 'Und die Götter sind überall', *Archäologie in Deutschland*, 4 (2005): 6-9.

the nose was square. The hair-style ended in a knot and a bird's head was placed above the forehead. The animal was designed with a bell-shaped head with an open mouth, a round eye and frequently a pair of horns, and a right-angled body decorated with a triangular body strap. There were never any additional animals or inscriptions on bracteates of this cluster, only occasionally some individual dots.[62] They have been found in hoards and in graves in locations spreading between south-west Norway, western Sweden, Jutland, northern Germany, Frisia and eastern Britain.[63] There is no obvious concentration of finds around a central place but the distribution pattern along the North Sea coast can be correlated with coastal travel routes along the North Sea coastline as they are known from near-contemporary written sources.[64]

Not only these two clusters of B- and C-bracteates indicated close stylistic links between Scandinavia, northern Germany and eastern Britain but also two clusters of D-bracteates that have been found in hoards in Jutland, northern Germany and Frisia, in several rich female graves in eastern Kent and in a grave and as a single find in East Anglia.[65] The nature of these contacts has been debated. The Kentish bracteate finds may express continued links with the Scandinavian and continental homelands through gift exchanges or marriages some generations after the Jutish invasion of Kent that Bede described in the 8th century.[66] Alternatively, bracteates following closely Scandinavian models may have been made locally in Kent in a particular political situation in the later 5th and earlier 6th centuries when it was important for ideological reasons to state links with Scandinavia.[67]

Apart from clusters of bracteates that were based on stylistic congruencies of the central image, other features of bracteate designs point to workshop connections. Seven bracteates from eastern Sweden and Poland were linked through a rare detail. In the triangle that was attached underneath the loop re-enforcing it were one, three, six or ten human masks in relief applied,[68] several of them framed in gold wire and associated with filigree volutes and spirals. Similar masks are known from a medallion of the Roman emperor Gratian that was mounted sometime in the 5th century as a pendant in an elaborate frame decorated with fifteen human masks. The pendant was found in a hoard at Szilágysomlyó (now Simleu Silvaniei) in Transsylvania.[69] The masks were put in oval frames of gold wire and separated by filigree double volutes. Technically and stylistically they were closely related to the masks on the bracteates.[70] Relationships between eastern Scandinavia and the lower Danube region during the later Roman and migration periods have long been observed in the material culture.[71] South-eastern European objects reached Scandinavia through trade links, tribute and loot brought back by returning Heruli and payments to northern recruits in the Roman army.[72] Several bracteate finds from graves and hoards in the lower Danube area too indicate links with southern Scandinavia.[73] Among the eleven bracteates from six different dies was one C-bracteate from an unknown find spot in Hungary[74] that belongs to a cluster of bracteates predominantly found on the Baltic islands of Gotland, Öland and Bornholm, in Scania and on the Danish island of Lolland-Falster (Fig. 7 a, b).[75] Whilst the

---

[62] Behr, *Die Beizeichen*, 185f.

[63] IK 317 Rømul, Sørtrøndelag, 275 Høyvik, Sogn og Fjordane, 109 Lille Skjør and 169 Sletner, Østfold, 137 Øvre Tøyen, Akershus, 38 Dalen, Dalsland, 363,2 Lilla Jored, Bohuslän, 64 Grumpan, Västergötland, 327 Scania (?), 274 Højbjerg, Jutland, 103 Landegge and 157, 1 and 2 Sievern, Niedersachsen, 46 Dokkum and 598 De Valom, Frisia. The British finds were from 306 Morning Thorpe, Norfolk, 602 East Leake, Nottinghamshire, 288 Kirmington, Lincolnshire and 607 Near Bridlington, East Riding. For an iconological analysis of this cluster see K. Hauck, *Goldbrakteaten aus Sievern*, Münstersche Mittelalter-Schriften 1 (München, 1970), pp. 136ff.; for an typological analysis see S. Nancke-Krogh, 'De gyldne "ryttere". En analyse og vurdering af en gruppe C-brakteater', *Hikuin*, 10 (1984): 235-246.

[64] K. Hauck, 'Völkerwanderungszeitlicher Seeverkehr, erhellt mit Schiffsresten und Fundorten von Goldbrakteaten (Zur Ikonologie der Goldbrakteaten XXXIX)' in *Trade and Exchange in Prehistory. Studies in Honour of Berta Stjernquist*, eds. B. Hårdh et al. (Stockholm, 1988), pp. 197-211 (203). Hauck illustrated sea travel in the migration period with bracteate finds in conjunction with evidence for harbours and landing points.

[65] In IK vol. 3, Text, 42ff. they are listed as Grundmuster 1, Varianten 1a and 1c. The tool-linked bracteates from Kent and Normandy, IK 492, 1-3, mentioned above, belong to Variante 1a. See map in E. Bakka, 'Scandinavian-type gold bracteates in Kentish and continental grave finds' in *Angles, Saxons and Jutes*, ed. V. Evison (Oxford, 1981), pp. 11-35 (Fig. 1).

[66] Bakka, 'Scandinavian-type', 12; Chadwick Hawkes, Pollard, 'The gold Bracteates', 325f.

[67] Andrén, 'Guld og makt', 254; L. Hedeager, 'Migration Period Europe: the Formation of a Political Mentality' in *Rituals of Power from*

Late Antiquity to the Early Middle Ages, eds. F. Theuws and J. Nelson (Leiden, 2000) 15-57 (42f.); Behr, 'The origins', 50f.

[68] One mask: IK 11 Åsum, Scania, 57,1 Fride, Gotland, 211 Wapno, Poznán, Poland, 221 Bostorp, Öland; three masks: IK 45 Dödevi, Öland; six masks: IK 62,1 Gerete, Gotland; ten masks: IK 144,1 Ravlunda, Scania (one is now missing).

[69] W. Seipel (ed.), *Barbarenschmuck und Römergold. Der Schatz von Szilógysomlyó*, Kunsthistorisches Museum (Wien, 1999), p. 186, cat. no 14.

[70] S. Lindqvist, *Vendelkulturens Ålder och Ursprung*. Kungl. Vitterhets Historie och Antikvitets Akademiens Handlingar 36.1 (Stockholm, 1926), pp. 19ff.; A. Bursche, 'Die Rolle römischer Goldmedaillone in der Spätantike', in *Barbarenschmuck*, ed. Seipel, pp. 39-53 (42) considered the possibility of itinerant goldsmiths to explain the numerous parallels with finds in the Germanic areas.

[71] B. Arrhenius, 'Skandinavien und Osteuropa in der Völkerwanderungszeit' in *Germanen, Hunnen und Awaren. Schätze der Völkerwanderungszeit*, exhibition catalogue ed. W. Menghin, T. Springer and E. Wamers (Nürnberg, 1988), pp. 441-456; B. Arrhenius, 'Connections between Scandinavia and the East Roman Empire in the Migration period' in *From the Baltic to the Black Sea. Studies in medieval archaeology*, eds. D. Austin and L. Alcock (London, 1990), pp. 118-137.

[72] Arrhenius, 'Skandinavien', 442ff.

[73] Andrén, 'Guld og makt', 254 emphasised the ideological role of bracteates in Pannonia and alluded to the Scandinavian origin myth of the Langobards in Pannonia, a parallel with the Jutish origin myth in Kent.

[74] IK 375 Ungarn.

[75] IK 62,1 Gerete, Gotland; 45 Dödevi, 115 Lundeby, 106 Lilla Istad, 186 Tjusby, 221 and 223 Bostorp, Öland; 324 Sandegård and Rønne (two fragments from the same bracteate) Bornholm, 202 and 203 Vä, 11 Åsum, Scania; 340 Sønderby, Lolland-Falster. IK 367 is from an unknown find location. Behr, *Die Beizeichen*, 181ff.

other bracteate finds from the lower Danube region were related to Scandinavian bracteates four of the dies were showing rather unorthodox images that were unique among bracteate iconography.[76]

So far groups and clusters of bracteates have been discussed that were linked through a common tool or through stylistic congruencies. However, even those bracteates that were not directly connected were all derived from a common idea. The observation that very few predominant iconographic patterns characterised these pendants makes it very unlikely that bracteates were 'invented' in more than one place. It is more probable that they were conceptualised and designed in one place from where the idea and the designs spread. The central place of Gudme has been suggested as a possible place from where bracteate iconography originated and some influence over the iconographic concepts continued to be exerted.[77] The ensuing success of the pendants with their sophisticated iconography being repeated quite unchanged for a hundred years or so, suggests that the images were telling meaningful stories that mattered to their owners.

Germanic society in the migration period has often been described as small and diverse political, military and ethnic groupings. Germanic religion too tends to be perceived as being characterised by local and regional variation.[78] Bracteates, however, are an example demonstrating that the veneration of the one god that was represented on the pendants, the knowledge of mythical stories related to him and their pictorial representations were shared widely in northern, western and central Europe during the late Roman and migration periods crossing boundaries between different groups.[79]

It is generally accepted that people in the late Roman and early medieval periods were highly mobile and that distant contacts existed throughout Europe including

Scandinavia and beyond. What can the study of bracteates add to this picture?

Fig. 7a. C-bracteate of unknown provenance in Hungary, known as 'Ungarn' (IK 375).

The distribution of this exceptionally large and homogeneous group of objects that were linked through common tools, styles and iconography shows a particularly dense network of contacts and exchanges throughout northern Europe including links with Frisia, eastern Britain, Poland, southern Germany and the lower Danube area. The distribution patterns demonstrate the special importance of coastal routes between western Scandinavia, Frisia and eastern Britain and land routes between eastern Sweden and south-eastern Europe. Concentrations of tool-linked and stylistically connected pendants around central places in southern Scandinavia emphasised the role of these newly emerging political and economic centres as places where bracteates were presumably designed, made and distributed. The religious character of these pendants highlights the role of central places for religious rituals. Bracteates were not the only objects but significant examples to demonstrate links and exchanges between central places. The analysis of stylistically linked bracteates shows that not only the objects themselves but also iconographic patterns were exchanged and copied.

---

[76] IK 491 Šaratice-D, Moravia, 484 Poysdorf-D, Lower Austria, 559 Várpalota-D, Hungary, 206 Várpalota-B.

[77] K. Hauck, 'Fünens besonderer Anteil an den Bildinhalten der völkerwanderungszeitlichen Brakteaten (Zur Ikonologie der Goldbrakteaten, XLIX)', *Frühmittelalterliche Studien,* 26 (1992): 106-148 (108); K. Hauck, 'Gudme als Kultort', 84f.

[78] A. Hultgård, 'Religion', *Reallexikon der Germanischen Altertumskunde* 24 (Berlin, 2003), pp. 429-457 (432f.).

[79] A comparable example for the knowledge, exchange and appreciation of religious images among the social elites over a wide geographical area in northern, western and central Europe can be found in the first half of the seventh century, some two to three generations after the bracteate period. The scene of a horseman throwing a spear and being aided by a small divine figure whilst his horse was fatally attacked by an enemy who was already lying on the ground was represented on four helmets and on one disk brooch. One helmet was found in mound one in the cemetery at Sutton Hoo in East Anglia, and the other helmets in graves 7 and 8 in Valsgärde and in grave 1 in Vendel, two cemeteries in Uppland in eastern Sweden. The brooch was discovered in a female grave in Pliezhausen in south-west Germany, the settlement area of the Alamans, where this part of a horse harness was used in secondary function. H. Steuer, 'Krieger und Bauern – Bauernkrieger. Die gesellschaftliche Ordnung der Alamannen' in *Die Alamannen* ed. Archäologisches Landesmuseum Baden-Württemberg (Stuttgart, 1997), pp. 275-287 (282f.).

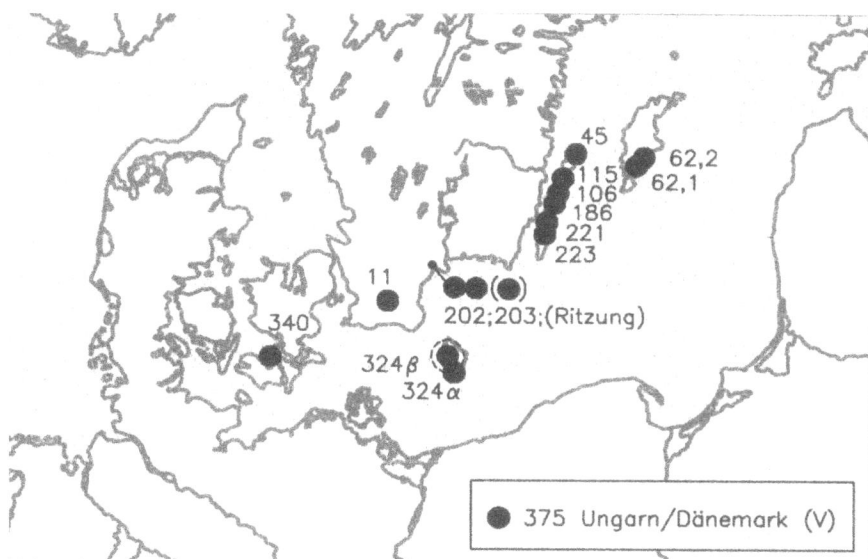

Fig. 7b. Distribution map of workshop-related bracteates (A. Pesch, *Formularfamilien*, in press)

But what does the study of connections between these pendants tell us about connections between the people who designed, made, wore or deposited them? The ways in which relationships were established and upheld cannot be identified unambiguously by using archaeological objects. Links that are apparent through the objects may have been direct or only through intermediaries. Bracteates may have been sent as diplomatic gifts through envoys. Itinerant craftsmen may have been responsible for the spread of tool- or stylistically linked clusters of bracteates. Alternatively, the owners may have travelled for various reasons taking their jewellery with them, be it to migrate to a new homeland, be it to marry outside their immediate area, and then deposited or were buried with their pendants that now appear in the archaeological record as linked. Bracteates may have been donated at the occasion of special religious festivals or political gatherings to which people travelled more or less long distances and then returned with their new pendants. We also need to take into account that only the places where bracteates were deposited are known but the owners may not even have lived close to the place where the objects have been found but went to a chosen location to offer the bracteates as a sacrifice to the gods.[80]

Still, it is possible to characterise the people who owned, wore and deposited bracteates as belonging to the elites in their societies. They had access to precious metal and objects of exquisite artistic qualities. The people who designed and made bracteates were highly educated, possibly initiated to specialised religious knowledge which enabled them to devise sophisticated pictorial narratives.[81] They were also exceptionally skilled to craft the pendants. They too may have belonged to the social elites. People linked through bracteates lived in many different political and ethnic communities but shared common knowledge and appreciation of a god and his deeds that were represented on the pendants. Contacts and exchange among them were not sporadic, isolated events but happened frequently, intensively and in many directions, whatever the precise nature of individual contacts was.

---

[80] Hoards with bracteates were most probably sacrificial depositions and not treasure hoards, see L. Hedeager, *Iron-Age Societies. From Tribe to State in Northern Europe, 500 BC to AD 700*, (Oxford, 1992), pp. 56ff.

[81] K. Hauck, 'Methodenfragen der Brakteatendeutung. Erprobung eines Interpretationsmusters für die Bildzeugnisse aus einer oralen Kultur (Zur Ikonologie der Goldbrakteaten, XXVI)' in *Zum Problem der Deutung frühmittelalterlicher Bildinhalte*, ed. H. Roth (Sigmaringen, 1986), pp. 273-296 (280).

Menas ampullae: a case study of long-distance contacts

Susanne Bangert

University of Oxford

Menas ampullae and Abu Mina

Menas ampullae are small (from c. 8 cm diameter) clay so-called 'pilgrim-flasks'.[1] They are characterised by a lentoid body and a narrow neck with two handles and are typically decorated with a standard depiction of Saint Menas standing between two kneeling camels. These were produced between 500-640 in considerable quantity at the main site associated with the saint, Abu Mina, which is amongst the largest pilgrim sites in the Late Antique and early Medieval world. Its importance can plausibly be related to imperial interest, including a political agenda dominated by the ecclesiastical authorities.[2]

Abu Mina is situated in the Mareotis some 45 kilometres west of Alexandria, in what is today generally a dry area, but which was fertile in the sixth century, with extensive production of, for example, wine. The site extends for one kilometre and so, in terms of size, can be classified as a town. In the fifth and sixth centuries it featured a large church complex surrounded by impressive courtyards, hostels and baths, encircled by a residential area with town-houses, a possible school and further baths. There is evidence for lavish decoration of the church with both mosaic and marble revetment and ornate floors. A severe fire laid the centre in ruins early in the seventh century, probably at the time of the Persian invasion. A rebuilding programme was begun soon after, but with the Islamic conquest of Egypt in the mid-seventh century, large-scale international pilgrimage stopped. Although Saint Menas continued to be venerated at Abu Mina, the site was reduced to a shadow of its former glory, even if still

described as impressive by contemporary writers. Abu Mina seemingly became deserted in the tenth century, and eventually became completely ruined.

Until 1906, it was known only from documentary sources and the ampullae. The first excavations began at the hill, locally known from the many ampullae found there. Excavations have now taken place continuously since the 1960s, mainly by the German institute in Cairo, and apart from the pottery the site is very well published.[3]

Fig. 1a Menas ampulla, 153 x 105 mm.
Photo Ashmolean Museum
(Bangert (Oxford, forthcoming) cat no 1).

---

[1] The ampullae are well published in recent catalogues such as Janette Witt, *Werke der Alltagskultur, Teil 1: Menasampullen* (Staatliche Museen zu Berlin - Preussischer Kulturbezits, Skulpturensammlung und Museum für Byzantinische Kunst, Bestandkataloge) (Wiesbaden, Reichert, 2000), p. 2; Gabriele Kaminski-Menssen, *Bildwerke aus Ton, Bein und Metall* (Liebieghaus Museum alter Plastik. Bildwerke der Sammlung Kaufmann) (Kassel, Druckerei und Verlag Gutenberg, 1996), III.; Catherine Metzger, *Les ampoules à eulogie du Musée du Louvre* (Paris, Editions de la Réunion des musées nationaux, 1981) and Susanne Bangert, *The Ashmolean Collection of Menas Ampullae within Their Social Context* (Oxford, British Archaeological Reports International Series, forthcoming), the latter with a listing of c. 200 ampullae in British museums, as well as some of the discussion presented here. The subject of this article also features in Susanne Bangert, 'Menas Ampullae and Saxon Britain: Coptic Objects in a Pagan Kingdom', *Minerva*, 17 (2006): 44-45.

[2] The time span is based on the archaeological evidence from Abu Mina. The imperial interest is not explicitly testified in any source. For a discussion see: Bangert, *The Ashmolean Collection of Menas Ampullae*. A discussion of church leaders controlling local cults from a later period, but with obvious parallels, will be available in Gervase Rosser and Jane Garnett, *The Moving Image: Zones of the Miraculous in Italy and the Mediterranean World 1500-2000* (forthcoming).

[3] For a description of Abu Mina, see Peter Grossmann, 'The Pilgrimage Center of Abu Mina', in *Pilgrimage and Holy Space in Late Antique Egypt*, ed. David Frankfurter (Leiden, Brill, 1998), pp. 281-302, or the catalogues mentioned in note 1. The excavation of the site has been ongoing since the 1960's and is published mainly by Peter Grossmann and other scholars from the German Institute in Cairo. The website of the modern monastery also has relevant information: www.stmina-monastery.org [accessed 9th January 2007].

27

Fig. 1b Variety of ampullae from Abu Mina. From Oskar Wulff, *Altchristliche und mittelalterliche byzantinische und italienische Bildwerke*, Teil I: Altchristliche Bildwerke (Berlin, 1909) Pl. LXVIII

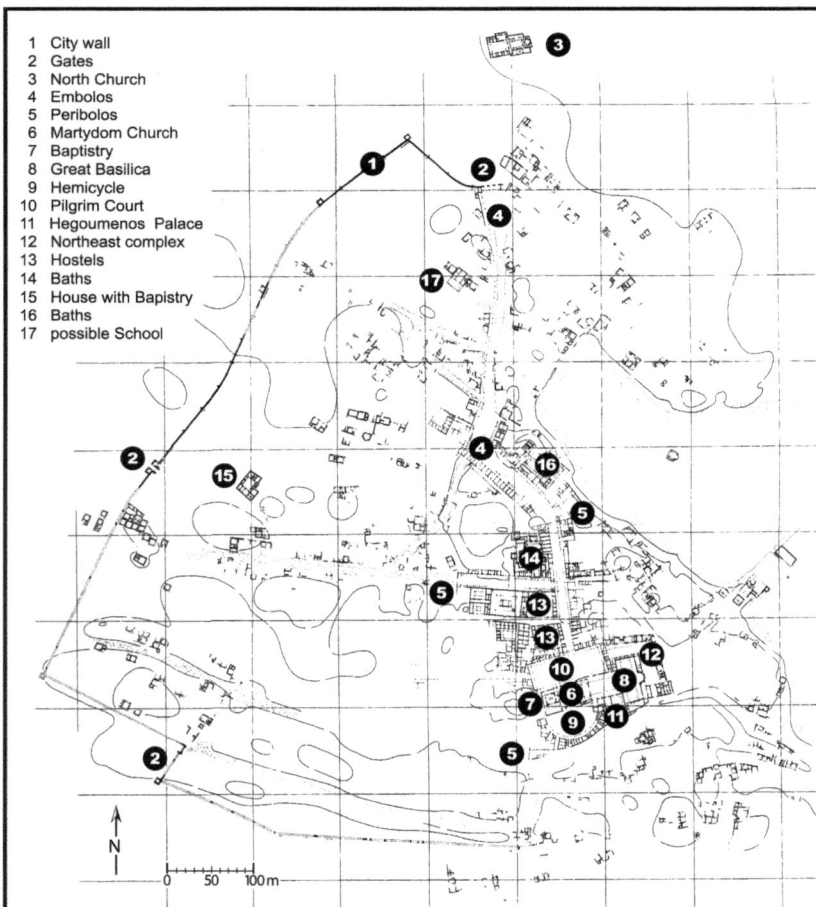

1 City wall
2 Gates
3 North Church
4 Embolos
5 Peribolos
6 Martydom Church
7 Baptistry
8 Great Basilica
9 Hemicycle
10 Pilgrim Court
11 Hegoumenos Palace
12 Northeast complex
13 Hostels
14 Baths
15 House with Bapistry
16 Baths
17 possible School

Fig. 2 Map of Abu Mina. Design by Keith Bennett. After Peter Grossmann, *Christliche Architektur in Ägypten* (Leiden, 2002) fig. 115

Various types of souvenirs were produced at Abu Mina in Late Antiquity but the ampullae are the best-known. They alone of the ceramics produced at Abu Mina have been found far and wide.[4]

Find circumstances in Europe – are they reliable?

Unsurprisingly, the ampullae are mostly found in Egypt and the Levant, but finds have also been reported from the Black Sea region and Western Europe. The finds from Western (especially Northern) Europe have, however, been queried because the find circumstances in many cases are poorly recorded. The most comprehensive research so far on the presence of ampullae in Europe was published by Chiara Lambert and Paola Demeglio, and comprises a discussion of the relation between pilgrim routes and ampullae.[5] They list the present location of ampullae, but when compiling such a list a persisting problem is the way the provenance of the object is registered by the museum in question. Most of the ampullae discussed in the article were accessioned in a period where the focus was on the objects themselves. Often little attention was paid to provenance and find circumstances, two categories of information, which anyway could be virtually impossible to obtain. Thus, a typical museum register entry for a Menas ampulla would be 'from Egypt'. This can, of course, mean 'produced in Egypt', or 'found in Egypt', or both. Indeed, such museum information was queried by Petra Lincheid, who questioned whether ampullae in collections in northern Europe can be taken as evidence for pilgrims travelling from Egypt in late antiquity.[6] Linscheid investigated ampullae reported to have been found in a local archaeological context north of the Alps, but concluded that there is no evidence for any of the finds being genuine.

G.-R. Delahaye took nearly the opposite approach to that of Linscheid, assuming that ampullae present in small numbers at a location would be ampullae from a local context.[7] Delahaye, inspired by Lambert and Demeglio, traced ampullae along the pilgrim routes in France and mentions several unpublished ampullae from France, yet did not question the quality of the information provided by the accession registers of these various museums. Neither did he conduct any further investigation into the ampullae cited by Lambert and Demeglio. As several of these ampullae were accessioned a long time ago, the *caveat* mentioned above must apply to them.

So, further investigation remains to be conducted before we can obtain a picture of how many ampullae have a North-western European archaeological context. The rest of this paper illustrates this point with reference to the ampullae in museum collections in Britain. As we shall see, we cannot assume that the presence of one or a few ampullae in a collection denote a local find.

Finds in Britain: where are the archaeological contexts?

At face value, it appears that ampullae are recorded as having been found in an archaeological context in Britain. One, for example, was published in 1951 by R. O'Ferral.[8] The ampulla was found in 1949 close to the Roman Icknield Way in Derby, Nuns' Street. Upon discovering the ampulla, staff at the British Museum were contacted, who reported back that no other ampulla had been found in Britain. O'Ferral consequently concluded that the ampulla could hardly date from the Late Antique or early Medieval period because 'Communications between the fourth and seventh centuries were bad' and the Roman-period road probably out of use. But this information can be amended: the British Museum had actually been given an ampulla in 1929, recorded as having been 'found during excavations' in Burgate, Kent in 1868. Unfortunately, neither the Canterbury Archaeological Trust nor the Society of Antiquaries is in possession of more specific information about the excavation as regards the ampulla. However, as this is not unusual for excavations of the nineteenth century, this need not mean that it is not a genuine find.

Moreover, this is not the only ampulla found in Canterbury. In recent years, another, privately-owned, ampulla has been made known to the Canterbury Archaeological Trust.[9] It was, according to family tradition, found in the Burgate area in the 1920s. Similarly, two more ampullae have been reported to the Canterbury Archaeological Trust by their present owner. These are likely to have been found in Faversham, Kent, but no further information is available.

---

[4] Discussed in Susanne Bangert, 'The Archaeology of Pilgrimage', in *Late Antique Archaeology 5*, eds. David Gwynn and Susanne Bangert (Leiden, Brill, forthcoming).

[5] Chiara Lambert and Paola Pedemonte Demeglio, 'Ampolle devozionali ed itinerari di pellerinaggio tra IV e VII secolo", *Antiquité Tardive*, 21 (1994): 205-231.

[6] Petra Linscheid, 'Untersuchungen zur Verbreitung von Menasampullen nördlich der Alpen', in *Akten des XII. internationalen Kongresses für christliche Archäologie, Bonn 1991*, ed. Ernst Daasmann and Josef Engemann, Jahrbuch für Antike und Christentum Ergänzungsband 20 (2 vols) (Münster, Aschendorfsche Verlagsbuchhandlung, 1995), vol. 2, pp. 982-986.

[7] Gilbert-Robert Delahaye, 'La diffusion des ampoules de Saint-Ménas en Gaule', *Le Monde Copte*, 27-28 (1997): 155-165.

[8] R. S. M. O'Ferral, 'A Pilgrim's Flask found in Derby', *Journal of the Derbyshire Archaeological Society*, XXIV (1951). The present whereabouts of this ampulla is not known to the Derby Museum, according to the curator, Jonathan Wallis (pers. comm.).

[9] I am grateful to Simon Pratt from the Canterbury Archaeological Trust for the information on both the ampullae and excavations in Canterbury. I also appreciate the information given to me by the present owners of the ampullae. Simon Pratt also immediately pointed to the potential of investigating St. Augustine's mission when considering Menas ampullae in Britain.

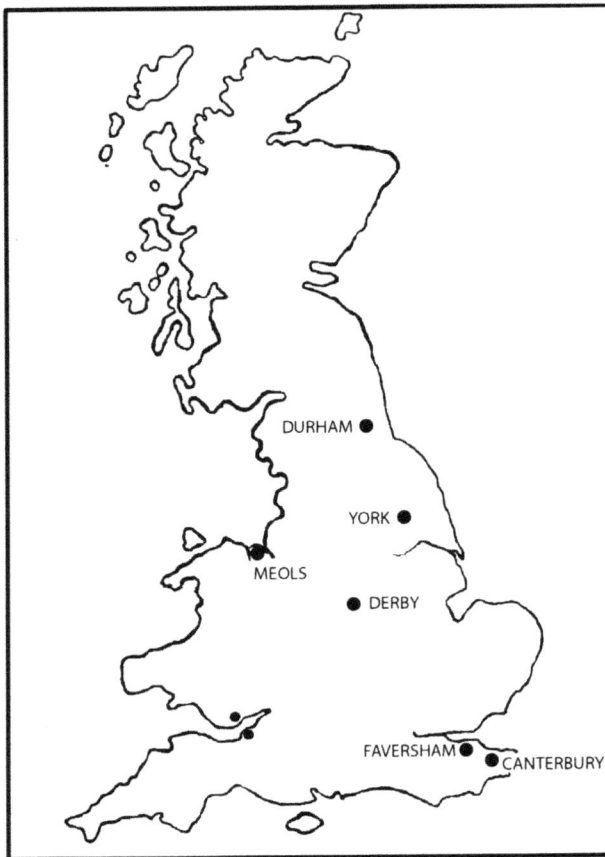

Fig. 3 Recorded finds of Menas ampullae in Britain. After Harris, 2003, fig.53

Yet another ampulla found in Britain was published in 1956.[10] The ampulla was 'found in a peat layer two feet below the sand at a point 300 yards seaward of Dove Point' at Meols in 1955, and was presented to the Grosvenor Museum in Chester. The finds from Meols are prolific and already by 1863 the first monograph on the site had been published by Abraham Hume.[11] There is a Roman phase at the site and also metalwork possibly dating to c. 400-600. Three Byzantine coins have been found subsequently, not far from where the Menas ampulla was found.[12] The archaeological context may, however, be problematic, as the site is being washed out of the escarpment and consequently many finds are made on the beach, rather than through stratigraphic excavation. It should also be mentioned that there might be another ampulla from the Meols area.[13]

A further ampulla, in The Yorkshire Museum, is recorded in the registers as having been found in York, but unfortunately without any additional information. There might, however, be more ampullae found in the north-east. In an 1891 guide to the collections of the Yorkshire Philosophical Society there is a reference to two ampullae found in 1881 at Shincliffe, near Durham (the York ampulla is also described).[14] So far, a search for further information concerning these two ampullae has been to no avail, but in the light of the other ampullae reported, it is reasonable to accept that this reference might concern a genuine find, especially as the York Archaeological Trust have reported Eastern Mediterranean amphorae from York itself.

None of the British finds, as appears from the description above, are certainly from stratigraphical excavations. When considered alone, none of them could be – nor have been – accepted unconditionally. Yet, collectively, they are worthy of further attention. As many as nine ampullae are reported from Britain. This is a significant number in relation to reported finds elsewhere in Europe. It is also, as observed by Anthea Harris, a significant total compared to the number of other types of imported objects found in Britain between the fifth and seventh centuries.[15] Consequently it is worth while to consider the context of these finds.

The British context

There appear to have been two major routes by which objects from Alexandria are likely to have reached Britain: one across continental Europe, along the Rhine corridor and eventually passing into the south-east of Britain.[16] The connection to the Mediterranean could either have been along the Rhône or through Italy and the Alps. The other route would have been by ship through the Straits of Gibraltar and up the Atlantic coast of Europe. These ships would have sailed on the high seas, only occasionally putting in at the coast for example in search of fresh water.[17] They may well have landed on the western coast of Britain: in Cornwall and Wales, and, possibly, at Meols. Ken Dark has focused attention on evidence suggesting that Byzantine Constantinople found it worthwhile to send merchants to Britain, even if the mercantile profit in itself did not justify such expeditions.[18] The more obvious non-mercantile reason could be an ideological one, and diplomatic activity is

---

[10] In 'Miscellanea', *Journal of Chester Archaeological Society*, 43 (1956): 48.

[11] Abraham Hume, *Ancient Meols; or, some account of the antiquities found near Dove Point, on the sea-coast of Cheshire* (London, 1863).

[12] Robert A. Philpott, 'Three Byzantine Coins found near the North Wirral Coast in Merseyside', *Transactions of the Historic Society of Lancashire and Cheshire 1998*, 148 (1999): 197-202. These are coins of: Justin I (518-27) follis, Maurice Tiberius (582-602) follis of regnal year 19 = 600/1 and Justinian I (527-65) deca nummium.

[13] David Griffiths, 'Great Sites: Meols', *British Archaeology*, 62 (2001): 20-25. The site will be further discussed in David Griffiths and Robert A. Philpott, *Meols: The Archaeology of the North Wirral Coast* (forthcoming).

[14] Charles Wellbeloved, *A Handbook to the Antiquities in the Grounds and the Museum of the Yorkshire Philosophical Society* (8th edn) (York, 1891).227 and Elizabeth Hartley, pers. comm.

[15] Anthea Harris, *Byzantium, Britain and the West. The Archaeology of Cultural Identity AD 400-650* (Stroud, Tempus, 2003).

[16] Harris, p. 64ff.

[17] J. Wooding, 'Cargoes in Trade along the Western Seaboard', in *External contacts and the economy of Late Roman and Post-Roman Britain*, ed. K. R. Dark (Woodbridge, Boydell, 1996), pp. 67-82.

[18] In K. R. Dark, *Britain and the End of the Roman Empire* (Stroud, Tempus, 2000), e.g. p. 230. See also Harris, p. 136. I appreciate the introduction to British trade patterns given to me by Ken Dark and Anthea Harris.

suggested as a likely reason. How can the ampullae be assessed within this framework?

One, maybe two, ampulla were found at Meols, a 'sand-dune' site and location of a coastal market town in western Britain; another is found by the Roman road in Derby, which led to the north and to Hadrian's Wall. It is possible that these ampullae could be representative of a cross-country trade, eventually ending at Meols, or further west. As noted above, at least one ampulla is from York, which was the seat of the Dux Britannica; that is, the location of the central administration of the north (as listed in the *Notitia Dignitatum* early 5th century). Another two ampullae are reported to have been found at Durham. Four are from the south-east: Canterbury and Faversham in Kent. There are secure Late Antique and early Medieval contexts in Canterbury where, at the end of the sixth century, continental missions headed by Augustine landed to promote Christianity in Britain. The archaeology of Faversham is impressive for this period, and it has been suggested as the possible location of Roman Duroleum. The finds from York are also interesting. According to the Venerable Bede, the origin of the Minster in York is a chapel of timber erected on the occasion of the baptism of the Northumbrian king, Edwin, in 627. Edwin had married Ethelburga, a Christian princess from Kent, and Paulinus, later to become bishop of York, accompanied her north, converting his host-to-be and thousands of Northumbrians.[19] This episode has been considered by many scholars (although by no means all) as a 're-Christianisation' of the country, with a very 'Roman' style of Christian worship gaining dominance over sub-Roman Christian traditions. If there were, as is also sure, sub-Roman Christians in this area Augustine's mission could be seen as a period of renewed expansion of Christianity in the region. Before discussing this further, it is relevant to outline the possible reasons behind the presence of ampullae in Britain.

Why might ampullae have been transported to Britain?

The find of a Menas ampulla does of course not prove that a person from Britain went on pilgrimage to Abu Mina and came back with an ampulla. This *could* have been the case, but ampullae might also have been traded, as was other objects from the East, perhaps as amulets. The ampullae do confirm the possibility of transport of an object from the area of Alexandria to Britain.

Fig. 4 Ampulla found at Meols (Photo David Griffiths, Grosvenor Museum Inv. No. 43.M.56, Chester)

It is plausible that the ampullae travelled these long distances from their production centre during the course of the sixth century and the first half of the seventh century. Of course, this is not certain: their properties as liquid containers are very dubious, so it is inconceivable that they could be in use because of their actual contents for long after they left Abu Mina, although their perceived contents and their former proximity to the shrine may have enhanced their value. Yet, as well as the trade in amulets, there remains the possibility that a few ampullae were traded throughout the Middle Ages, just as they were traded in Victorian times. However, as mentioned below, access to Abu Mina from Western Europe became more difficult from the eighth and ninth centuries. It therefore remains a likely scenario that, for whatever reason, people living in the sixth and seventh centuries found it worthwhile to bring Menas ampullae from Abu Mina to Britain.[20]

The British material is, as mentioned above, not plentiful, but so far comparable numerically with that from Germany and France, and certainly larger than what has been described from the Iberian Peninsula, where there

---

[19] Bede, *Ecclesiastical History*, (ed. and trans.) Judith McClure and Roger Collins, (Oxford, Oxford University Press, 1969): 97, II.xiv.

[20] An article soon to appear – William Anderson, 'Menas flasks in the West: pilgrimage and trade at the end of antiquity', *Ancient West & East*, 5 (2006): n.p. – discusses the trade context of Menas ampullae across Europe but, as pointed out by Anderson, only on the basis of the articles also mentioned here.

are very few reported finds of ampullae indeed. It can also be mentioned that, so far, no ampullae have been found in an Irish or Scottish archaeological context.[21] This leaves the ampulla/ampullae found at Meols as to date the only known ampulla in 'Celtic' Britain.

In the later sixth century, the western sea-route seems to have declined, whereas the eastern land-route expanded.[22] The implication of this development is that the Menas ampullae probably reached Meols by land if it arrived after the sixth century. If so, the Menas ampullae in Britain are found in, or have passed through, the non-'Celtic' context of the East and South. This confirms, as far as negative evidence can, that the most likely route of the ampullae into Britain was that of the Rhine system.

Still bearing in mind that the ampullae could just be representatives of a general trade in amulets, it is tempting to consider other possible explanations, suggested by the find spots of the ampullae. The ampullae in Canterbury, for example, may be related to the interest of the Papal see in Britain from the late sixth century onwards.[23] It is well known that this interest resulted in the Augustinian mission in 597, with the arrival in Britain of southern Europeans who came to promote Papal Christianity. The ampullae could have been brought to Britain in the context of the mission.

Another possibility could be that Anglo-Saxon Christians went on pilgrimage to the Mediterranean and brought the ampullae back with them. This issue leads to the discussion of how many Christians there were in these parts of Britain in the sixth and seventh centuries, to be discussed further below. However, if pilgrimage were to be envisaged only *after* the Augustinian mission, it might be argued that a very short time is left to bring perhaps (at least) nine ampullae back to Britain. Moreover, it has to be considered that Abu Mina had periods in the seventh century, such as the 'Heraclean' war (609) and the Persian invasion (619-28), when the site may have been less able to receive pilgrims. From the end of the Persian invasion to the Islamic conquest and the end of the archaeologically recorded ampullae production is little more that ten years.

If pilgrimage is envisaged *before* the Augustine mission it would presumably be from by British, rather than Anglo-Saxon Christians. If so, it is remarkable that most of the finds do not appear near the known northern and western British religious centres of the sixth century; rather the opposite, in fact.

The first option mentioned – that of the Christians from southern Europe bringing ampullae with them – is consequently a more likely scenario than Anglo-Saxon

pilgrimage to Abu Mina. The tantalizing question to ask is then why would these southern Europeans have brought Menas ampullae with them to the British Isles?

It is an interesting point that Gregory the Great preached one of his homilies in a church in Rome dedicated to Saint Menas.[24] A letter is also preserved from Pope Gregory to the (Chalcedonian) Patriarch of Alexandria, Eulogius, telling about the baptism of a considerable number of British (*"more than ten thousand Angli"*).[25] There is no reason to doubt the contact between Rome and Alexandria nor knowledge about the veneration of St Menas in Rome. This leads back to the question of Christians living or being present in south-east Britain before the Augustinian mission of 597.

The presence of Menas ampullae and Christianity in South and East Britain

Some scholars suggest that the population of eastern Britain never became de-Christianised in the fifth and sixth centuries, despite the fact that its Anglo-Saxon rulers were pagan.[26] In contrast, William Frend summed up the British situation as a 'failed promise', in which Romano-British Christianity failed to develop in fifth-century eastern Britain, compared to the development of Christianity in fifth-century Gaul.[27] According to Frend, Augustine was re-introducing Christianity, even in Kent, not simply introducing Christianity to the Anglo-Saxons. John Blair describes the situation in Kent – although Augustine did meet the cult of Saint Sixtus – as a 'clean slate'.[28] Another option, that Christianity initially declined, but was re-introduced from Gaul prior to the Augustinian mission, is raised by Ian Wood's argument that Kent had many similarities to a Christianised Frankish province in the sixth century.[29] Since 'normal' archaeological evidence for Christianity, such as churches, generally is lacking in these parts of Britain, this tends to support the opinion that no organised form

---

[24] Hom. xxxv, *In Evang.* In *Gregory the Great: Forty Gospel Homilies.* Translated by D. Hurst (Kalamazoo: Cistercian Publications 1990) pp. 301-11. For references to the location see Henri Leclercq, 'Ménas (saint)', in *Dictionnaire d'archéologie chrétienne et de liturgie*, ed. Fernand Cabrol and Henri Leclercq, 11,I (Paris, 1933), cl. 387.

[25] In Epistle XXX, David L. Edwards, *Christian England* (London, Collins, 1981), 1: Its story to the reformation. 48ff., Stephen J. Davis, *The Cult of Saint Thecla: A Tradition of Women's Piety in Late Antiquity* (Oxford, Oxford University Press, 2001), p. 112, also Ian Wood, 'The Mission of Augustine of Canterbury to the English', *Speculum*, 69 (1994), pp. 1-17.

[26] E.g. Ken Dark, *Britain and the End of the Roman Empire* (Stroud, Tempus, 2000).

[27] W. H. C. Frend, 'Roman Britain, a Failed Promise', in *The Cross goes North. Processes of Conversion in Northern Europe, AD 300-1300*, ed. Martin Carver (York, Woodbridge: York Medieval Press; Boydell, 2003), pp. 79-92 (91).

[28] John Blair, *The Church in Anglo-Saxon Society* (Oxford, Oxford University Press, 2005), p. 24.

[29] Ian Wood, *The Merovingian Kingdoms, 450-751* (London, Longman, 1994), pp. 176-80; it also appears that considerable Frankish interests were vested in the mission: Wood, 'The Mission of Augustine of Canterbury to the English'.

---

[21] Personal communication (2003) to the author by keepers of the National Museums
[22] Harris, p. 191.
[23] See above note 9.

of Christianity existed at the time of Augustine.[30] However, other forms of evidence have been compiled to the opposite effect. For example, David Howlett has shown that Latin proficiency in Britain was at distinguished level.[31] Furthermore, an analysis of the issues Augustine discussed with Pope Gregory suggests that they are points raised by audiences experienced in Christian practice.

The literature concerning Augustine's mission is extensive, and indicates that the mission had directives from Pope Gregory to the effect that the existing British Church should be subordinated to that of the incoming Papal Church.[32] Incidentally, this seems to be corroborated by Blair's argument that Saint Sixtus was adopted as a local saint, and perhaps by the case of Saint Martin's church in Canterbury, which Bede informs us predated the mission.[33] It must be remembered that the Christian church for most of its life had fought sectarians – Christians who taught falsely – and such endeavours also can be considered as 'mission'. As Martin Henig puts it, 'Contemporary records make it clear that Pope Gregory I was not really worried about paganism: he was far more concerned about a flourishing Celtic church which appeared to take little heed of Rome...'.[34]

What connection can be seen between these aspects of Christianity in Britain, Menas ampullae and long-distance contacts? Reasons for the transport of Menas ampullae are outlined above. If a religious motive is accepted behind the transportation of the ampullae, it is very tempting to see a link between this motive and the situation of Christianity in Britain.

The hypothesis is based on the suggestion that the production of Menas ampullae should be assessed in the context of the momentous debate concerning the true nature of Christ. The Abu Mina production only took place in a period where the site was under imperial, that is, pro-Chalcedonian (or diophysite), control, in what seemingly was a generally non-Chalcedonian (or monophysite) area.[35] It follows that the Menas ampullae may have had a pro-Chalcedonian connotation. The Augustinian mission was, of course, pro-Chalcedonian, as it was initiated by the Pope. This is not to say that debate in Britain concerned the Chalcedonian issue, but to suggest that the ampullae belonged in the camp of orthodoxy, in the view of Rome and Constantinople. The mission went to a country where a Church known for its stubborn adherence to non-Papal (although not monophysite) values existed, and even flourished in some areas.[36] Is the presence of the Menas ampullae in eastern Britain connected to this perception of Britain?

It will be interesting to see where Menas ampullae may be discovered in the future, and whether the hypothesis outlined above will be vindicated. If so, humble pilgrim souvenirs will provide valuable material evidence for church politics at a high level and the long-distance contacts involved.

---

[30] Martin Henig, *The Heirs of King Verica. Culture and Politics in Roman Britain* (Stroud, Tempus, 2002) p. 139.

[31] David Howlett, 'Continuities from Roman Britain' in *Pagans and Christians – from Antiquity to the Middle Ages. Papers in honour of Martin Henig*, ed. Lauren Gilmour (Oxford, BAR Publishing: 2007), pp.175-188.

[32] Clare Stancliffe, 'The British Church and the Mission of Augustine', in *St. Augustine and the Conversion of England*, ed. Richard Gameson (Stroud, Sutton, 1999), pp. 107-151.

[33] Bede *EH*, I. 26 p. 41.

[34] Henig, *The Heirs of King Verica*, pp. 128, 138-142. The quoted sentence from Martin Henig, 'Roman Britons after AD 410', *British Archaeology*, 63 (2002): 8-11.

[35] Bangert, *The Ashmolean Collection of Menas Ampullae*. See also above note 2.

[36] Harris, p. 155; Stancliffe, p. 113.

The limits of long-distance exchange: evidence from sixth-century Palaestina/Arabia

Kate da Costa

University of Sydney

Introduction

In contrast to the other papers in this volume, and as a way of putting the question of long-distance relations into deeper perspective, this paper comprises a case-study of *local* trade patterns in the sixth century. In particular, it examines the way that ceramic evidence has been used to posit a decline in long-distance trade in the Mediterranean world, and uses the Levant as an area of special focus.

There is no doubt that there is a gulf of understanding between the scholarship of Western and Eastern parts of the Roman Empire. This is in part due to the division of scholarship between the Latin- and Greek-speaking parts of the Empire which is, in turn, related to the division between Europe and the Near East.[1] More practically, it is an unfortunate consequence of the sheer volume of material which has become available during the course of the 20th century. Ironically, in scholarly terms, the distance between each end of the Mediterranean often appears to be wider in modern times that it was in antiquity. For scholars of the Western Empire, the sixth century is often seen as the century in which Roman structures were lost or discarded and European, 'mediaeval' economies and societies began to emerge. Western scholars are wont to contrast the situation with the prosperous economy they imagine persisted in the Eastern Empire (usually without citing references). Conversely, for scholars working in the sixth-century East, the western half of the Mediterranean is largely forgotten, as already effectively lost to Roman civilization, except for its undeniable role as the production centre of African Red Slip (ARS) vessels.

As scholars of long-distance change are all too aware, the data available for comparative discussion of this period is unevenly distributed, poorly published – I speak here particularly of quantitative data – and in any event, imperfect. That is the nature of the material. We must therefore be particularly rigorous in our interpretations and try harder to extract more accurate data.[2]

Let us begin by summarizing one school of thought about trade patterns in the Western Mediterranean in the sixth century. Chris Wickham's interpretation serves as an example of the minimalist position.[3] He sees the vast bulk of material that moved over long distances as being transported within the state, or fiscal system, and representing the *annona* and supply of the army. Certainly, the resulting infrastructure and networks facilitated commercial trade, of which ARS is an outstanding example. However, since the state was dominant in that mechanism, when the state and its attendant fiscal system was broken up by various invasions, such as that of the Vandals in North Africa, the commercial system also disintegrated, as there was insufficient business to support it on its own. Since the bulk of state trade was in perishables, we can trace this breakdown only through changes in the distribution and quantity of pottery, principally the various major Red Slip wares and local imitations, and particularly away from the coast.

Wickham has described the following situation in relation to Red Slip wares and their copies, focusing particularly on Italy.[4] ARS wares begin to decline in numbers from the middle of the fifth century, when regional imitations, some of them from the East, begin to replace it. The distribution of ARS in the Italian peninsula from 450 to around 570 is clearly extensive, but largely confined to the coast apart from a cluster in the south of the Apennines (possibly related to the old Via Appia) and in the western Po valley centring on Milan.[5]

A clear bias towards the eastern part of the Italian peninsula for the distribution of Phocaean Red Slip/Late Roman C (PRS) needs no explanation. At the villa di

[1] This has recently been discussed by I. Morris and J. G. Manning, 'Introduction', in *The Ancient Economy: Evidence and Models*, eds. I. Morris and J. G. Manning (Stanford University Press, Stanford, 2005), pp. 1-44 (8-14).

[2] *Ibid.*, pp. 33-35.

[3] C. Wickham, 'Overview: Production, distribution and demand', in *The sixth century: production, distribution, and demand*, eds. Richard Hodges and Will Bowden (Brill, Leiden, 1998), pp. 279-292; C. Wickham, *Framing the Early Middle Ages: Europe and the Mediterranean, 400-800* (Oxford, Oxford University Press, 2005). Wickham's substantial and important study *Framing the Early Middle Ages* (2005) was not available to me when preparing this paper for seminar presentation and publication. It, by and large, presents the same arguments as in the 1998 article used as the basis of this paper, and certainly restates his position on the relationship of commerce to state structures as reflected in the ceramic record (2005, 708-720). Any criticism here of Wickham's studies is restricted to specific points and should not be construed as a dismissal of his broader arguments, which are persuasive and backed by extensive scholarship.

[4] Wickham, *Framing*, pp. 728-41. In his later work, Wickham makes no mention of the import into Italy of Phocaean and Cypriot Red Slip, ceramics he had characterized as regional imitations of ARS in his 1998 article. In reverse, the earlier article barely mentions the extensive and localised production of Italian fine table wares.

[5] S. Tortorella, 'La sigillata africana in Italia nel VI e nel VII secolo d. C.: problemi di cronologia e distribuzione', in *Ceramica in Italia: VI-VII secolo*, ed. L. Sagui (Firenze, All'insegna del giglio, 1998) pp.41-69 (fig. 7).

Agnuli a Mattinata in coastal Apulia nearly 58% of imported fine wares are PRS, and at Otranto the proportion is 1:3 Phocaean:North African.[6] The general distribution of finds follows that of ARS – coast sites predominate except along the Via Appia route through Lucania.

John Hayes has confirmed these numbers – fifth-century Western coastal sites still have both ARS and PRS, but inland the numbers decline precipitously (1998). In the South Etruria survey the amount of ARS from 470-550 is one-third the amount known from 400-450, and one-tenth that of the fourth century.[7]

Local production of fine table-wares also existed, with increased production from the late fifth century.[8] This material, including a variety of Red Painted Wares, had fairly restricted distribution in sub-regions of the Italian peninsula.[9]

By the end of the sixth century, fine wares had completely disappeared from some Western regions.[10] In northern Gaul, which became the centre of the Frankish dominions, Wickham suggests that 'exchange can be divided into the local and regional commercial networks represented by ceramics like Argonne or Mayen ware (and, of course, smaller-scale, simpler, local agricultural and artisanal exchange networks)'.[11] In both Italy and Gaul, he also proposed that these changes in ceramic distribution were accompanied by profound changes in settlement patterns. The distribution of ARS in Italy between 550 and the seventh century is even further reduced (although some examples have been found on inland sites which did not have ARS in earlier periods) and less likely to be found in regions under Lombard control.[12]

S. Giovanni di Ruoti is a good example of the pattern of both ceramic and settlement change. There was a fair amount of imported fine ware in the early fifth century, abundant local versions largely replaced imports in the late fifth/early sixth century, the site was abandoned by the middle of the sixth century, however regional or local wares were still known in the area until the seventh or, perhaps even the eighth century.[13]

All this, Wickham contrasts with 'the liveliest and most articulated exchange patterns' in the East.[14] His argument from these data is that ARS represents long-distance trade which piggy-backed on the *annona*. As a marker of the Roman infrastructure, its decline means the corresponding decline of the state structures. Further proof of the removal of the Roman state is the increasing self-sufficiency of regions, as represented by regional or local imitations of ARS – presumably the lack of supply stimulated regional/local production.

It is therefore pertinent to examine the patterns of distribution of ARS, PRS and other regional and local fine wares in the East, and this article takes as its case study the situation in the southern Levant.[15] Unfortunately, the assembling of data is handicapped by the state of publication. Few sites could be found which quantified the total amount of recovered pottery, the amount of Late Roman red wares, and provided sufficient information to calculate the difference between fifth, sixth and early seventh material. Landgraf's publication of material from Tel Keisan set the standard for quantitative publication (regrettably still rarely met) but Byzantine occupation at the site appears to have begun as late as 520, so that changes from the fifth century cannot be documented.[16] The same problem applies for the fort at Upper Zohar, which began no earlier than the late fifth century.[17]

The figures provided therefore in Table 1 are not in any way statistically robust, nor, regrettably, as extensive as the data for Italy, but some information can be extracted and trends, if not patterns, identified. What is not clear for the figures from Italy, and what could not be controlled for in the Levantine data is the effect of amphorae on ratios. Hayes has suggested that since amphorae are often very frequent at coastal sites, we should leave them out of investigations such as this, and compare the amounts of table wares alone, which might produce a quite different picture.[18] This certainly seems to be the case for coastal sites in Palaestina, as is detailed below.

[6] A. Martin, 'La sigillata focese (Phocaean Red-Slip/Late Roman C ware)', in *Ceramica in Italia: VI-VII secolo,* ed. L. Sagui (Firenze, All'insegna del giglio, 1998) pp. 109-122.

[7] J. Hayes, 'The Study of Roman Pottery in the Mediterranean: 23 years after *Late Roman Pottery'*, in *Ceramica in Italia: VI-VII secolo,* ed. L. Sagui (Firenze, All'insegna del giglio, 1998) pp. 9-21 (13).

[8] Wickham, *Framing,* p. 729.

[9] Wickham, *Framing,* pp. 731-39.

[10] Wickham, ('Overview', p. 292) includes parts of the Po valley in this, but Tortorella's figures suggest otherwise.

[11] Wickham, 'Overview', p. 283.

[12] Tortorella, fig. 8.

[13] Hayes, 'The Study of Roman Pottery', pp. 13-14.

[14] Wickham, 'Overview', p. 291. Wickham's lack of references to Eastern economic patterns to support his statement presumably represents a widely held conviction that the statement is self-evident and needs no extensive substantiation. Of the two works he cites in 1998 (although see the much more extensive data on the East in 2005 (759-794)), one study deals with amphorae alone and the other with the Aegean, an area which from the Levantine perspective is practically part of the Western empire. As it happens, I agree with his statement, and recent, epigraphically based survey treatments simply reinforce an impression of the volume of private trade at all levels in the East. For an example of that latter, see B. Levick, 'The Roman Economy: Trade in Asia Minor and the Niche Market', *Greece & Rome,* 51 (2004): 180-198.

[15] C.f. Wickham, *Framing,* 770-80.

[16] J. Landgraf, 'Byzantine Pottery', in *Tell Keisan (1971-1976): une cite phenicienne en Galilee,* ed. J. Briend and J.-B Humbert (Fribourg, Switzerland, Editions Universitaires Fribourg Suisse, 1980) pp. 67-80.

[17] R. Harper, *Upper Zohar: An Early Byzantine Fort in Palaestina Tertia: Final Report of Excavations in 1985-1986* (Jerusalem/Oxford, BSAJ/Oxford University Press, 1995).

[18] Hayes, 'The Study of Roman Pottery', p. 17.

Site	LRRW % (where available)	ARS quantity	CRS quantity	PRS quantity	Egyptian RS quantity
Caesarea Maritima	Riley's figures in text	11.8%	23%	25.2%	rare
	Recalculated from lists (appears to be 1-3% of total ceramics)	19.8%	38.3%	40.7%	1.2%
	From Oleson harbour, 14.9% is ARS and Byzantine misc. fine wares	14.9%			
Sumaqa	Total qty: 5505 (or 55000) 755 sherds LRRW= 13.7%	6%	59%	26%	0
Tell Keisan	500-550 (55 datable sherds)	1 2%	4 7%	49 89%	
	550-650 (29 datable sherds) Total site pottery 4881, (not including lamps; LRRW = 4.7%)	5 17%	8 28%	16 55%	
Jalame	Half the ARS is mid-4th, site should end in late 5th, LRRW N=988 (9.6 - 13.4%) Pottery N=7559-10334 depending on amphora counts (not including 400+ lamps)	84 8.5%	742 75.1%	162 16.4%	
Kh Cana	46.58% total ceramics is EByz LRRW = 15.4% of EByz pottery = 7% site pottery	Yes, ?	Yes, ?	Yes, ?	No
Jezreel	0.87% pottery in Area E 1992	?	?	?	0
Jerusalem	81	39 48%	5 6%	37 46%	0
Upper Zohar	43692 (or 43699), LRRW = 2.9%, only 132 sherds published	58 44%	21 16%	53 40%	0
En Boqeq	1098 (may have some forms counted twice if rim joined base); not <1120 as Hayes has as total	110 10%	438 40%	550 50%	0
Capernaum	Only 1 deposit gave actual counts, and in summary Loffreda is clear that the greatest number in later deposits is CRS	75+ ~22%	98+ ~29%	165+ ~49%	0
Hippos	2 pieces CRS in city centre, more in NW church	Some	Some	Most common	0
Pella	LRRW (715/699) must be <1% of site total	16% of 6th – 7th LRRW	16%	67%	1%
Jarash	Macellum data only	Main import	Some	Some	Jerash bowls most common fine ware
Kh. Nakhil	No figures	?	?	Most common	No ERS or Jerash bowls
Aqaba	130,000 760 LRRW = 0.58%	Most common	Small	Small	2nd to ARS

Table 1: Quantities of Late Roman Red Wares (LRRW) as proportion of site pottery, and amounts of African (ARS), Cypriot (CPS) and Phocaean Red Slip (PRS) out of the LRRW corpus at each site.

Caesarea

Caesarea Maritima was the capital of Palaestina Prima, principal port and administrative centre of all Palaestina.[19] Riley's figures come from the excavations at the Hippodrome and show that the Late Roman Red Wares (LRRW) appear to comprise only 1-3% of the total corpus, which includes significant amounts of amphorae.[20] If all fine wares, including Pompeiian Red and Eastern Terra Sigillata A are included, the LRRW account for just over 37% of fine wares. PRS and Cypriot Red Slip (CRS) are nearly equally abundant, while ARS falls from 50% of the pre-fifth-century fine ware material to 20% of the later corpus. Other excavations at Caesarea have produced different results, although the actual figures are not published. Magness' work on the material from the Temple platform suggests a predominance of CRS, and Oleson found not one sherd of PRS in underwater excavations.[21]

Sumaqa

Sumaqa lies on a watershed of the Carmel range, not far south of Haifa, and can therefore be considered a coastal site. It is described as a small village, with an estimated population of 900 – 1000 inhabitants.[22] Significant processing installations are found in the immediate agricultural hinterland and within the settlement some with massive 750kg crushing weights. Several of the 'workshops' can be confidently identified as either wine or oil presses, but several used grooved columns to crush the products. Dyeing, nut oil production or tanning are suggested purposes, but none have been conclusively identified.[23] It would be reasonable to assume that the village produced an agricultural surplus. The coinage profile ranged from the fourth to the seventh centuries. The diagnostic pottery was discussed by Kingsley.[24] This comprised 5505 sherds, predominantly from a range of amphorae, but including 755 sherds of imported fine ware bowls, representing 13.7% of the diagnostic pottery. However, the actual ratio is unclear: Dar estimates that the diagnostic sherds on which Kingsley worked represented about 10% of excavated ceramics and there is

no indication that any of the unpublished 50,000 sherds were identified in any way.[25] Nor is there any information on whether only diagnostic LRRW sherds (i.e. rims, bases, decorated fragments) were kept, or whether, as is the case at Pella and the early seasons at Tel Keisan all LRRW, even undecorated body sherds, are considered diagnostic and therefore kept.[26] If the former, we might assume that the 755 come from some 7550 LRRW sherds. In the more likely case that every LRRW sherd was considered a diagnostic, the ratio of LRRW at the site falls to about 1.4%, similar to Caesarea. Whatever the case, at Sumaqa CRS seems dominant.

Tel Keisan

The predominantly Bronze Age and Phoenician site of Tel Keisan is just north of the Carmel sites, about four kilometres from the coast and eight kilometres from Akko.[27] There is a clear break in occupation after the Hellenistic period, and the church and associated Byzantine levels appear to begin in around 520.[28]

The vast bulk of recovered Byzantine pottery was of amphorae: 70% of the 4906 vessels sherds recovered were storage jars. The LRRW comprised 4.7% of the corpus.[29] Amongst the LRRW (229 sherds) PRS was clearly dominant with 80% overall. However, when differentiated by date, an interesting pattern occurs, with PRS falling to 55% in the period 550-650. Hayes, in contrast, considered all the PRS to date before 550, which would leave only late CRS and ARS in the late sixth – seventh century.[30]

Jalame

Jalame lies on the inland side of Mt. Carmel and is best known as a glass manufacturing centre of the Late Roman period.[31] As we now know, the excavators' coin-based dating of the site tightly to the third quarter of the fourth century conflicts with the evidence of the pottery, which can be dated up until the late fifth century.[32] Depending on how the material is counted, LRRW comprise just over 9 – 13% of the site total, with CRS predominating. Total figures for each class or ware of pottery were not

[19] L. Levine and E. Netzer (eds.), *Excavations at Caesarea Maritima 1975, 1976, 1979 - Final Report* (Jerusalem, Hebrew University, 1986) (= *QEDEM* 21); K. Holum et al., *King Herod's Dream: Caesarea on the sea*, (London, W.W. Norton and Co., 1988); R. L. Vann (ed.), *Caesarea Papers: Straton's Tower, Herod's harbour, and Roman and Byzantine Caesarea* (Ann Arbor, Journal of Roman Archaeology, 1992); A. Raban and K. Holum (eds.), *Caesarea Maritima: A Retrospective after Two Millennia* (Brill, Leiden, 1996).
[20] J. A. Riley, 'The Pottery from the First Session of Excavation in the Caesarea Hippodrome', *Bulletin of the American Schools of Oriental Research*, 218 (1975): 25-63
[21] J. Magness, 'Late Roman and Byzantine pottery, preliminary report, 1990' in Vann, pp. 129-153; J. Oleson, 'Artifactual Evidence for the History of the Harbors of Caesarea' in Raban and Holum, pp. 359-377.
[22] S. Dar, *Sumaqa: A Roman and Byzantine Jewish village on Mount Carmel, Israel* (Oxford, British Archaeological Reports International Series 815, 1999).
[23] Dar, p. 94.
[24] S. Kingsley, 'The Pottery', in Dar, pp. 263-329.

[25] Dar, p. 263 n. 1
[26] Landgraf, pp. 67-68.
[27] J. Briend and J.-B. Humbert (eds.), *Tell Keisan (1971-1976): une cite phenicienne en Galilee* (Fribourg, Editions Universitaires Fribourg Suisse, 1980).
[28] *Ibid.*, table 1.
[29] Landgraf.
[30] J. Hayes, 'Late Roman Fine Wares and their Successors: a Mediterranean Byzantine Perspective' in *La céramique byzantine et proto-islamique en Syrie-Jordanie (IVe-VIIIe siècles apr. J.-C.) Actes du colloque tenu à Amman, 3-5 Dec. 1994*, eds. P. Watson and E. Villeneuve (Beyrouth: Institut français d'archéologie du Proche-Orient, 2001), pp. 275-282 (281) (figures in table are incorrect).
[31] G. D. Weinberg (ed), *Excavations at Jalame: site of a glass factory in late Roman Palestine* (Columbia, University of Missouri Press, 1988).
[32] G. D. Weinberg, 'Chronology and Stratigraphy', in *Jalame*, ed. G. D. Weinberg, pp. 1-4 for the pottery; Hayes, 'The Study of Roman Pottery', pp. 11-12; Hayes, 'Late Roman Fine Wares', p. 278.

given in the publication, although the 400+ lamps from the site are definitely not included in the counts examined here. Some classes have exact figures, others are uncertain because the published examples are said to represent unspecified numbers of other examples (e.g. 59 jugs are catalogued with no indication of how many each form represents).[33] Although amphorae predominate at the site, there are significant numbers of cooking, local serving and fine wares. It is likely that the true proportion of LRRW is much less than the 9% calculated here.

Kh. Cana

Kh. Cana, one of three sites associated with the miracle of water into wine, lies eight kilometres north-west of Nazareth and a few kilometres north of Sepphoris.[34] It is an inland site. Pottery dates from the Early Bronze age to the 15th century, although the only substantial architectural remains uncovered during excavations have been Byzantine.[35] At Kh. Cana we know only that all three wares (ARS, PRS, CRS) were present at the site, but that together they formed 7% of the site pottery.[36] The dating of the contexts assigned to the Early Byzantine period is not clear, given that the following period, 'Early Arab', is said to date from 640 and is characterized by Kh. Mefjer ware, which is otherwise considered a characteristically Abbasid fabric.[37]

Tel Jezreel

Further inland, Tel Jezreel in the Esdraelon Valley (more or less on the main Roman road from Arabia to the coastal harbours, a road carrying significant trade traffic) has a relatively limited amount of Roman material excavated, compared to the significant Iron Age deposits there. Final cataloguing of the late period pottery is still underway, so that only the material from the 1992 season could be used to estimate proportions.[38] Less than 1% of the pottery recovered in that season from the Roman and Byzantine areas could be identified as LRRW. Grey identified, even within this limited sample, ARS, CRS, LRC, a possibly Late Roman/Asia Minor Light-coloured ware, and locally produced fine wares. The local wares were approximately equal in number to the Red Slip wares in Area E. No Egyptian Red Slip was identified.

Jerusalem

This religiously significant city was not a regional administrative capital during the Roman period. It was raised to a patriarchy in 451 at Chalcedon and its role as both Jewish and Christian religious capital meant that it was a major market in the Late Roman and Byzantine periods. The early limited soundings in the city have been revised in the light of more modern Israeli excavations by Jodie Magness, but principally to assess reliability and revise chronologies.[39] Limited pottery from the Jewish Quarter excavations by Nahman Avigad were published by Magness in that study but since only diagnostic sherds were included in her catalogue, quantities are difficult to establish. However, she noted that there was no CRS in the excavated areas, suggesting that none was imported to Jerusalem before the mid- sixth century.[40]

Hayes catalogued the fine wares from Tushingham's excavations in the Armenian Garden, which produced only 81 sherds of LRRW.[41] Of these, 6% were CRS, the rest divided evenly between ARS and PRS.

Upper Zohar

Upper Zohar is a small fort on the west side of the Dead Sea.[42] The dating of the site is disputed: the excavator considers it to have begun in the late fifth century, while Magness has re-dated both Upper Zohar and the fort at En Boqeq to not earlier than the sixth century.[43] Although figures were given both for the total amount of sherds at the site (43692 (or 43699 based on figures in text)) and the proportion of LRRW (1,251 sherds, 2.87%) and local fine wares (29, 0.7%), a problem of identification remains. Only 132 of the LRRW were listed in the catalogue, of which 16% were CPS, and around 40% each of ARS and PRS. There is no indication of the wares of the other 1119 sherds of LRRW. No Egyptian Red Ware was found at the site.

[33] B. L. Johnson, 'The Pottery' in *Jalame*, ed. G. D. Weinberg, pp. 137-226 (203-209).
[34] D. R. Edwards, 'Cana of the Galilee', www2.ups.edu/community/cana/sitepg.htm, [accessed 26 July 2006].
[35] J. Olive, 'Field Director's Preliminary Report' in *Excavations at Khirbet Cana: 1998 Preliminary Report*, ed. D. R. Edwards, 1998, http://nexfind.com/cana/fielddirector.html [accessed 26 July 2006].
[36] D. Avshalom-Gorni and A. Shapiro, 'Pottery Report' in *Excavations at Khirbet Cana: 1998 Preliminary Reports*, ed. Douglas R. Edwards, 1998, http://nexfind.com/cana/ceramic.html, [accessed 26 July 2006]
[37] A. Walmsley, 'Turning East. The Appearance of Islamic Cream Ware in Jordan: The "End of Antiquity"?' in Watson and Villeneuve, pp. 305-313.
[38] A. D. Grey, 'The Pottery of the Later Periods from Tel Jezreel: an Interim Report', *Levant*, 26 (1994): 51-62.

[39] J. Magness, *Jerusalem ceramic chronology circa 200-800 CE* (Sheffield Academic Press, Sheffield, 1993).
[40] Magness, *Jerusalem ceramic chronology*, pp. 119-152.
[41] J. Hayes, 'Hellenistic to Byzantine Fine Wares', in *Excavations in Jerusalem 1*, ed. A.D. Tushingham (Toronto, Royal Ontario Museum, 1985), pp. 179-194; Hayes, 'Late Roman Fine Wares and their Successors'.
[42] Although Wickham (2005) stresses the inland penetration of RS in Syria and Palaestina (pp. 716 and 771), it should be remembered that Upper Zohar and En Boqeq lie closer to the main port of Gaza (ca. 85 km as the crow flies) than do the cluster of sites in southern Italy lie to any major port. Those Italian sites, at least 100kms from a port, seem to have been supplied overland, perhaps by the Via Appia route. The Jordan River/Dead Sea was used for shipping in antiquity, as was the Orontes in Syria. Overland trade routes were also extensive. RS did not penetrate inland in the East any further than it had in the West.
[43] Harper, p. 115; J. Magness, 'Redating the forts at Ein Boqeq, Upper Zohar and other sites in SE Judaea, and the implications for the nature of the Limes Palastinae', in *The Roman and Byzantine Near East vol 2: Some Recent Archaeological Research* ed J. H. Humphreys (Ann Arbor, JRA Supplementary Series 31, 1999), pp. 189-206.

General ware	Loffreda	Hayes	Contexts	total	% LRRW (340)
ESA*	6			6	
PRS	19	24 +70 stamps	+71(+)	165	49%
CRS	31	30 + 5 stamps	+63(+)	98	29%
ARS	28	31 + 27 stamps	+17(+)	75	22%

* Eastern Sigillata A

Table 2. Quantities of LRRW at Capernaum based on Loffreda (1974) counts in section 1, Hayes' recalculations

En Boqeq

There are various structures at En Boqeq, on the south western shore of the Dead Sea, of which we are concerned with the excavations of the small fort.[44] The forts at Upper Zohar and En Boqeq are roughly similar in size, so that the 1098 (revising Hayes' count of <1120) sherds of LRRW are comparable.[45] At En Boqeq PRS accounts for half the LRRW while ARS is only 10%.

Capernaum

Capernaum, at the northern end of the Sea of Galilee, was a major pilgrimage centre by the fourth century, as Egeria's itinerary makes clear.[46] Ceramics from that part of the site owned and excavated by the Franciscans have been relatively well published.[47] Unfortunately, Loffreda gave no counts of the ceramics by type or ware. Hayes attempted to improve the statistics by re-examining the illustrated pottery sherds and stamps. However, it is not clear from his table what overlap there is between illustrated pieces and stamped pieces.[48] Even combing through the second part of the report where important contexts are discussed, and where the pottery is contextualized, cannot generate accurate counts. The best that can be attempted is to sum the numbers illustrated by Loffreda in the type section, the figures obtained by Hayes from illustrated sherds in the second part of the book and from the stamp illustrations and counts made from the text references in the second part of the book (Table 2).

PRS seems to dominate at the site, and ARS is only 22% of the LRRW. Loffreda is clear that in the latest levels (sixth century) CRS occurs in the greater numbers.

Hippos

Lying on the east shore of the Sea of Galilee, Hippos was one of the Decapolis cities. Excavations have been undertaken since 2000, and are continuing. Impressions here are taken from the on-line pottery reports, which do not give exact figures, and which by and large discuss the LRRW in terms of the dating evidence they provide for critical loci.[49] PRS is reported as the most common of the LRRW fabrics, with all ARS forms (dating from the first half of the third century to the third quarter of the seventh century) less common. In the upper city few sherds of CRS were found. In contrast, in the North West Church, destroyed in the earthquake of 749, all three wares were found, and the latest in date were the CRS.

Pella

Situated along side a permanent spring, occupation at Pella (ancient Semitic name: Fahel/Pihel, modern name: Tabaqat Fahl) dates from the Neolithic to the Hashemite period.[50] The most extensive habitation occurred during the late Roman/Byzantine period (approx. fourth – seventh centuries). At Pella, the available figures reflect the situation up until the early 1990s. Although total pottery figures were not provided by Watson, experience at the site suggests that 699 sherds would be less than 1% of recovered pottery.[51] Pella's dominant LRRW fabric is PRS.

[49] Anon. 'Pottery report 2001', 2001, http://hippos.haifa.ac.il/excavationReport/2001/potteryReport.htm [accessed 26 July 2006]; J. Mlynarczyk, 'Pottery report: Sussita 2002', in *Hippos: Third Season of Excavations, July 2002*, Arthur Segal et al. (Zinman Institute of Archaeology, Haifa, unpublished manuscript), pp. 38-59; J. Mlynarczyk, 'Pottery report', in *Hippos-Sussita: Fourth Season of Excavations, June-July 2003*, Arthur Segal et al. (Zinman Institute of Archaeology, Haifa, 2003), pp. 50-88.
[50] i.e. R. H. Smith, *Pella of the Decapolis I: The 1967 season of the college of Wooster Expedition to Pella* (The College of Wooster, Wooster, 1973); R. H. Smith and L. P. Day, *Pella of the Decapolis II: Final Report on the College of Wooster Excavations in Area IX, the Civic Complex, 1979-1985* (College of Wooster, Wooster, 1989); A. W. McNicoll, R. H. Smith and J. B. Hennessy, *Pella in Jordan 1* (Australian National Gallery, Canberra, 1982); A. McNicoll et al., *Pella in Jordan 2* (Sydney, Mediterranean Archaeology Supplement 2, 1992).
[51] P. Watson, 'Change in foreign and regional economic links with Pella in the seventh century AD: the ceramic evidence', in *La Syrie de Byzance a l'Islam VIIe-VIIIe siecles: Actes du Colloque international (Lyon - Maison de l'Orient Mediterranee, Paris - Institut du Monde*

[44] M. Gichon, *En Boqeq: Ausgrabungen in einer Oase am Toten Meer* (Mainz am Rhein, von Zabern, 1993).
[45] Hayes, 'Late Roman Fine Wares and their Successors', p. 282.
[46] J. Wilkinson (ed. and trans.), *Egeria's travels* (3rd. ed.) (Warminster, Aris and Philips, 1999).
[47] S. Loffreda, *Cafarnao II: La ceramica* (Jerusalem, Studium Biblicum Franciscanum, 1974).
[48] Hayes, 'Late Roman Fine Wares and their Successors', p. 282

Jarash

Although several teams have or are working at Jarash, none have published their pottery in such a way as to be usable for this table, with the exception of the Spanish *macellum* material, which is a relatively small corpus.[52] The majority of LRRW sherds are of 'Jerash bowls', the main identified local imitation of ARS, which as the name suggests, were made in Jarash. Of the imported material, ARS was the greatest, which may suggest why Hayes and Watson consider this ware to be the inspiration for the first generation of Jerash bowls.[53]

Kh Nakhil

Lying 25 kilometres south of Kerak, parts of the 1000 acres site of Kh. Nakhil were excavated in 1993.[54] Trenches revealed part of a Nabataean temple compound and a Byzantine church which was used as domestic premises in the Ayyubid through to Ottoman period. Surface collection of sherds previous to the excavations suggests that habitation began in the Early Bronze Age. No figures were provided, but PRS appears to be the main imported fine ware, and no Jerash bowls were identified at the site.

Aqaba

Roman Aila has been under excavation since 1994, revealing a settlement concentrated about one kilometre north-west of Islamic Ayla, due to silting up of the earlier shoreline. Settlement at the site ranges from the Nabataean to Byzantine, while sites in the area date from at least the Chalcolithic. The port was the beginning of the ancient King's Highway which led to Damascus via Amman/Philadelphia. The final report is not yet available, so that figures have been taken from the data in the 1996 season report, which provides excellent quantifiable figures.[55] The general trend has not fundamentally changed, although more, and earlier, Egyptian Red Slip has been found.[56] In 1996 the team excavated 130,000 sherds of which around 0.5% were LRRW (760 sherds). These were mainly ARS, followed

in second place by Egyptian Red Slip. A few sherds of PRS and CRS were found from the fifth century and all four wares were present in deposits of the seventh century.

Locally made fine wares

The only class of fine wares produced in the Southern Levant which has received systematic scholarly study is the 'Jerash bowl', which is predominantly a group of plates, decorated with paint, and explicitly Christian in its iconography.[57] Inspiration for the forms comes from ARS and for the painted and stamped decoration from Egyptian Red Slip and Coptic painted pottery.[58] Their place of manufacture is certain, based on kiln wasters, unfired examples and distribution.[59] 'Jerash bowls' date from 500/525 to the mid-seventh century, although production seems to be considerably reduced after the early seventh century.[60] They are found principally in Jordan, north of the Wadi Mujib, and the three sites with the greatest concentrations are, in order, Jerash, Kh. Samra and Pella.

Other local fine wares, such as Rouletted Rim bowls and Fine Byzantine ware, although discussed by Magness, who suggests Jerusalem for their place of manufacture, need more comprehensive study to determine their correct dating and distributions.[61] Nonetheless, locally produced fine table wares did exist in the southern Levant from the later fifth century through to at least the end of the seventh century.

Although a very crude statistical analysis, we can see that LRRW decrease as a proportion of the site pottery with distance from the coast. The exceptions appear, paradoxically, to be the absolute waterfront sites of Caesarea and Aqaba, both major ports (one Mediterranean the other on the Red Sea) where no doubt the very high levels of amphorae are diminishing the proportion of fine wares.

Within the fine ware corpus, it seems as if ARS and CRS are less popular away from the Mediterranean coast. The distribution of CRS might be explained by weight; its

Arabe) 11-15 Septembre 1990, eds. P. Canivet and J-P Rey-Coquais (Damascus, Institut français de Damas, 1992), pp. 233-248.

[52] A. Uscatescu and M. Martin-Bueno, 'The Macellum of Gerasa (Jerash, Jordan): From a Market Place to an Industrial Area', *Bulletin of the American Schools of Oriental Research*, 307 (1997): 67-88.

[53] P. Watson, 'Jerash bowls. Study of a provincial group of Byzantine decorated Fine ware', in 'Jerash Archaeological Project 1984-1988 II', ed. F. Zayadine, *Syria* 66 (1989): 223-261; Hayes, Late Roman Fine Wares and their Successors', p. 279.

[54] J. Kareem, 'The pottery from the first season of excavations at Khirbet Nakhil', Villeneuve and Watson, pp. 77-93.

[55] S. T. Parker, 'The Roman Aqaba Project: The 1996 Campaign', http://www.chass.ncsu.edu/history/rapweb/1996.htm [accessed 26 July 2006]

[56] S. T. Parker, 'Review of Estelle Villeneuve and Pamela M. Watson, eds.: *La céramique byzantine et protoislamique en Syrie-Jordanie (IVe –VIIIe siècles apr. J.-C.). Actes du colloque tenu à Amman les 3, 4 et 5 décembre 1994'*, *Bulletin of the American School of Oriental Research*, 341 (2005): 78-80 (79).

[57] P. Duerden and P. Watson, 'PIXE/PIGME Analysis of a series of Byzantine Painted Bowls from Northern Jordan', *Mediterranean Archaeology*, 1, (1988): 96-111; Watson, 'Jerash bowls. Study of a provincial group'. P. Watson, *Jerash Bowls: Byzantine Decorated Fine Ware from Jordan*, University of Sydney, unpublished PhD, 1991; P. Watson, 'Ceramic Evidence for Egyptian Links with Northern Jordan in the sixth-eighth Centuries', in *Trade, Contact, and the Movement of Peoples in the Eastern Mediterranean: Studies in Honour of J. Basil Hennessy*, eds. S. Bourke and J.-P. Descoeudres (Sydney, Meditarch, 1995), pp. 303-320.

[58] Watson, *Jerash Bowls: Byzantine Decorated Fine Ware*.

[59] E. Lapp, 'A Comparative Clay Fabric analysis of Fired and Unfired Jerash Bowl Fragments by Means of Petrography and Direct Current Plasma (DCP) Spectrometry', in Watson and Villeneuve, pp. 129-137.

[60] Watson, *Jerash Bowls: Byzantine Decorated Fine Ware*, pp. 195-196.

[61] Magness, *Jerusalem ceramic chronology*.

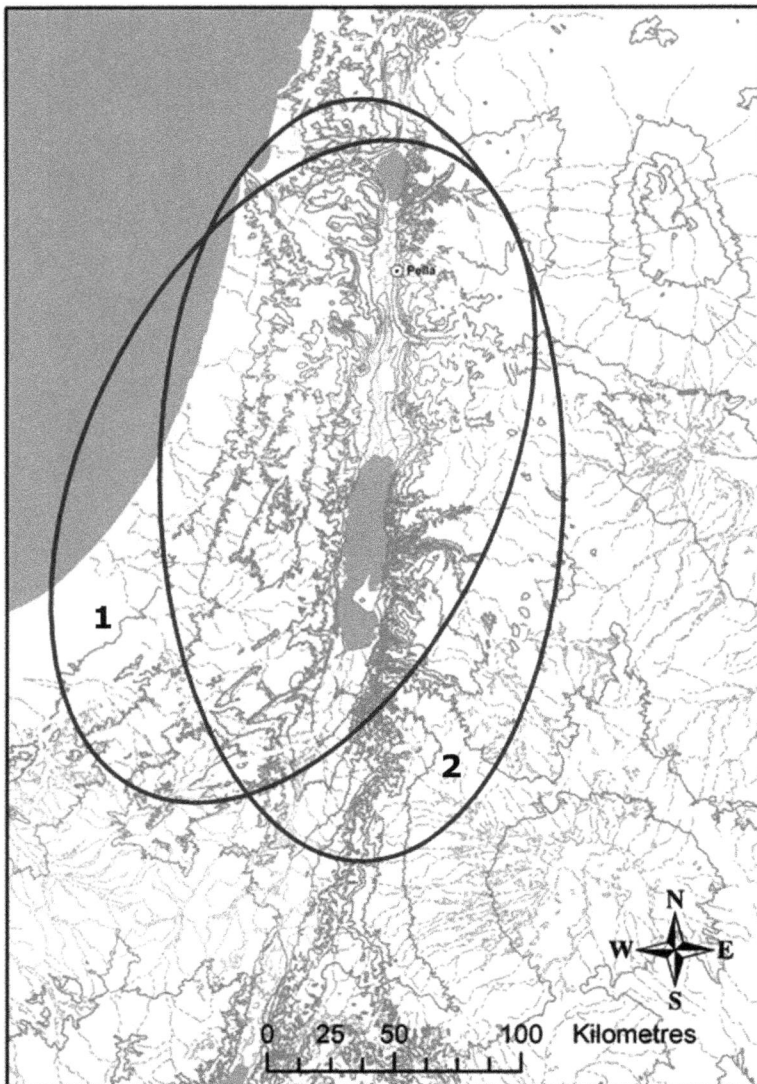

Map 1. First – third century distribution:
1: Darom, 2: Roundbodied no discus lamps

forms are generally hefty basins rather than fine plates.[62] Jerusalem, Upper Zohar and Jarash do not fit this pattern, all having relatively high proportions of ARS. However, the sample numbers at all three sites are low, and the *macellum* as a special market place at Jarash might be expected to have anomalous sampling.

It is unlikely that the patterning is a factor of date, although in Hayes' summary of the apparent situation in the southern Levant, he notes that ARS is predominant until the late fourth century, when the regional imitators of CRS and PRS begin substantial production.[63] CRS seems to be most popular in the fifth century. After 550 there is a split between Syria and Palaestina: in the south between 450-550 we have lots of PRS, then CRS

increases again, with some ARS coming back into the region.

This pattern, the decrease of ARS, the increase in regional and local 'imitations', the decline of regional wares from the end of the sixth century – and PRS does seem to fall away rapidly by the end of the sixth – and the continued presence of ARS, even in diminished amounts throughout the sixth century, seems to match fairly closely the situation Wickham described in Italy.

One other class of ceramics in the southern Levant has been quantified in more detail than locally made fine wares. Mould made lamps provide excellent evidence for changes in local and regional trade patterns and can be

---

[62] J. Hayes, *Late Roman Pottery* (Rome, British School at Rome, 1972), pp. 371-386.
[63] Hayes, 'Late Roman Fine Wares and their Successors', p. 279.

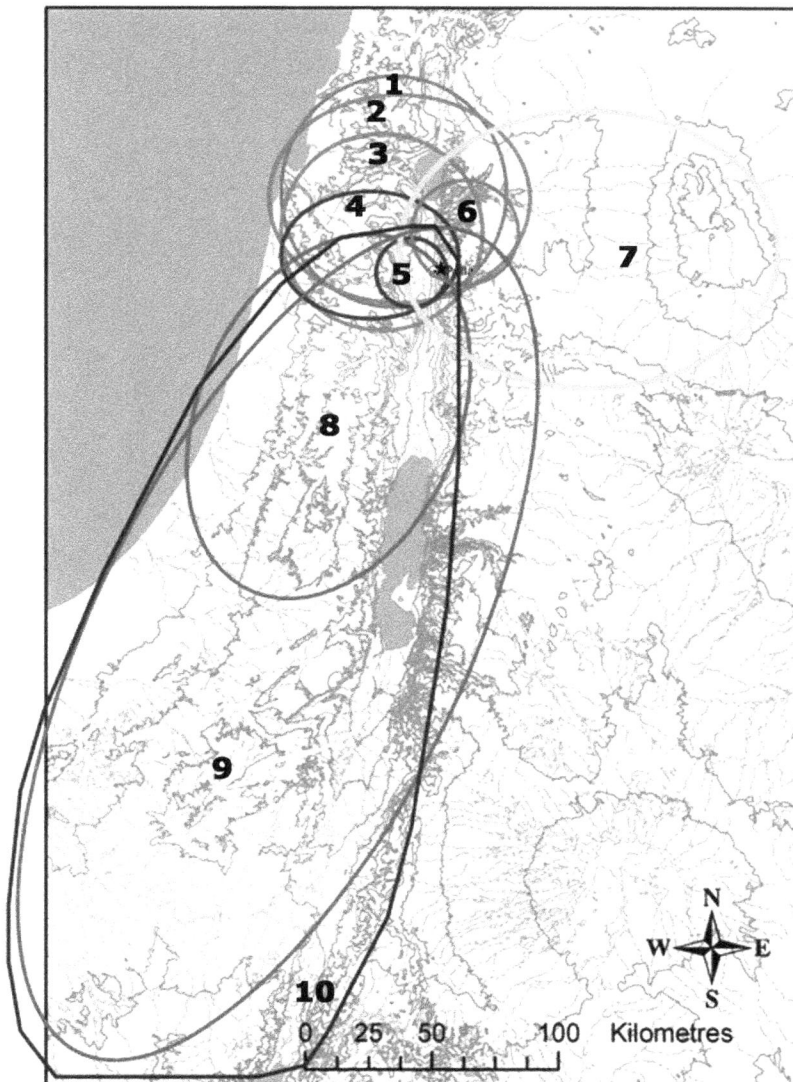

**Map 2. Fifth-sixth-century distributions:
1: Bilanceolate, 2: Galilean, 3: Bowshaped
nozzle, 4: Pear shaped fan handled,
5: Broad nozzle, 6: North Jordan,
7: 'Hauran', 8: Small Candlestick,
9: Byzantine Wheelmade, 10: Negev
Wheelmade**

used to examine the sixth century.[64] The figures show clearly that from the mid-fifth throughout the sixth century in the southern Levant is the period of most intense regionalism, i.e. the greatest number of workshops distributing over relatively small areas. Three maps of the distribution of lamp types in the earlier Roman, Byzantine and late Byzantine/early Islamic period show this phenomenon (maps 1-3). The lamp types used for these maps are those considered indigenous, so that the ubiquitous early Roman discus lamp has been excluded, and are based only on lamp types found at Pella, in order to reduce complexity.[65]

From the first to the third centuries two main types (map 1) were distributed very widely in the regions, although the indications are that each was manufactured at more than one site.[66] In marked contrast, during the fifth to sixth centuries (map 2), many distinctive lamp types existed, most restricted to relatively small areas and probably only manufactured at one place.

The contraction of production at the end of the sixth century is illustrated in map 3. Here we see much more widespread distribution of fewer types. In this case, as in the earliest cycle, manufacture of some types is known at

---

[64] K. da Costa, 'Byzantine and early Islamic lamps', pp. 241-257; K. da Costa, 2001, 'More Evidence from Ceramic Lamps for Local Trade Patterns in the Byzantine and Umayyad Periods', in *Australians Uncovering Ancient Jordan: Fifty Years of Middle Eastern Archaeology*, ed. A. Walmsley, (University of Sydney, Research Institute for the Humanities and Social Sciences, 2001), pp. 259-270.
[65] The southern Levant has a distinct lamp tradition which, although related to other mould made lamps in the Mediterranean, is conspicuous by the avoidance of a discus, and the orientation of the lamp to be viewed with the nozzle 'up'. Roman discus lamps were important prototypes for the later Roman through to Umayyad locally made

lamps, but their figured discuses set them apart from the local tradition, even when they were undoubtedly manufactured in the southern Levant. See K. da Costa, *Byzantine and early Umayyad ceramic lamps from Palaestina/Arabia (ca 300 - 700 AD)*, unpublished PhD, University of Sydney, 2003.
[66] da Costa, *Byzantine and early Umayyad ceramic lamps*; K. da Costa, 'The Byzantine lamps from Pella: their trade relationships', *Acts of the ILA/IFPO Roundtable Ancient Lamps of the Bilad esh-Sham Nov. 2005, Amman Jordan*, (International Lychnological Association/Institute Français de Proche Orient, forthcoming) for quantities and more detailed discussion.

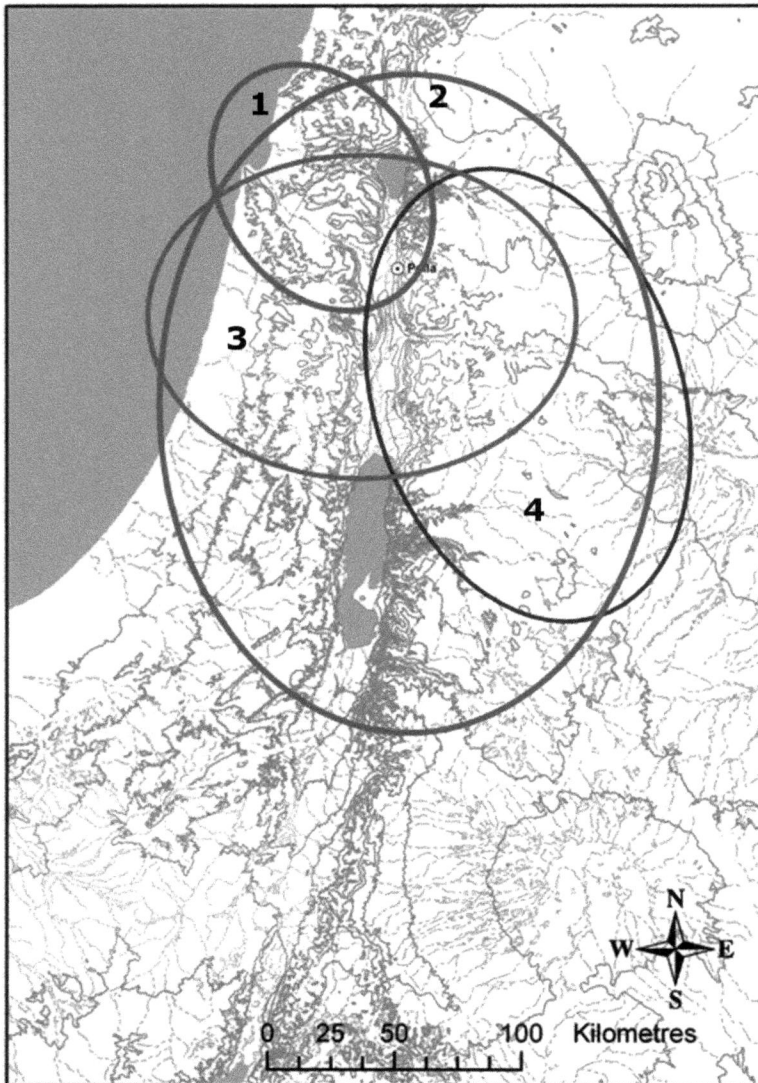

Map 3. Late sixth-mid eighth-century distribution: 1: Phoenician Slipper, 2: Large Candlestick, 3: Samaritan 4, 4: Jerash

more than one site, although to date it has not been possible to visually distinguish these. Lamps of this time period were also distributed across the Palaestina/Arabia/Phoenicia borders, unlike the types shown in map 2.

The lamp data has been interpreted as showing an increase in prosperity in the late fourth – later sixth centuries.[67] It appears, and it is not clear whether demand led the way or not, that more people lit lamps after dark and more lamps were put into tombs during funerals. This encouraged new manufacturers to open shop in a field where the profit margins were possibly quite small. A downturn or structural change in the economy over the second half of the sixth century caused these small manufacturers to go out of business, leaving only the larger concerns afloat in the seventh century.

In summary, in Palaestina and Arabia we have decreasing amounts of fine wares on inland sites, we have regional

imitations of ARS – that is CRS and PRS – which largely disappear by the end of the sixth century, there are locally produced fine table wares in use during the sixth century, there is a slight pick up in ARS in the seventh century, and we have extremely localized production and distribution of locally produced lamps, especially in the fifth and sixth centuries.

Here is the paradox. The sixth century is usually seen as a prosperous period in the East. Certainly, its 'lively' economy is often contrasted with the supposed situation in the West in that period. However we seem to be observing the same ceramic pattern in East and West. Although today many would hesitate to describe the Western situation as a 'decline', there seems no doubt that during that century, despite Justinian's best efforts, the Roman Empire effectively disappeared in the western end of the Mediterranean. There is equally no argument that the Empire remained the political and therefore fiscal power in the eastern half of the Mediterranean. We must therefore reinterpret the ceramic patterning Wickham used to support his interpretation. Our figures, both in

---

[67] *Ibid.*

east and west are insufficient to determine whether in fact long-distance trade fell away, or whether the products of regional and local workshops simply supplanted our distinctive identifiers, ARS above all.

The rise of regional and local trade, not necessarily at the expense of long-distance trade, may be an indicator of a change in overall economic structures in the entire Mediterranean basin. This may not have to do with the presence or absence of the Roman state, but the changes in long-distance relations other papers in this volume examine, possibly with areas beyond the Graeco-Roman world.

The Importation of Byzantine and Sasanian Glass into China during the fourth to sixth centuries

Mei-Ling Chen

School of Oriental and African Studies, University of London

Introduction

Long-distance contacts involving China, Persia and the Roman world started in Antiquity, but the most well-known set of contacts, involving the so-called Silk Road, thrived for much of the medieval period. The Silk Road, as is well-known, started at Xian, the capital city of China's T'ang dynasty (618-907), went through Baghdad and Antioch, before reaching Egypt, Constantinople and Rome. In recent years, work by Chinese archaeologists has established that a demand and curiosity for exotic goods in China had actually been developing at least since the fourth century. This is clear from the discoveries of foreign commodities in recent Chinese archaeological excavations.

Finds of Eastern Roman and Sasanian glass not only provide good evidence for the inflow of foreign cultures and commodities into China during this period, but also well reflect the political situation of contemporary Chinese society.

Fourth- to sixth-century China was in a fragmentary state: it was unstable politically and one of the major problems it confronted was the constant threat and invasions of the barbarians from the north. Coincidently, this was an analogous situation to that faced by its western neighbour, the Roman Empire, confronting the invasions of Germanic tribes into southern and western Europe. In the second half of the third century, the Han Chinese had established an empire known as the Western Jin (Map 1). This polity was ended by the Xiongnu in 316 and their successors established a new authority in the south of China, known as the Eastern Jin (centred around modern-day Nanjing). This heralded the beginning of a period of antagonism between North and South which lasted from the fourth to the sixth century (Map 2). In the throes of such territorial change, Han Chinese control of the overland trade route between northern China and

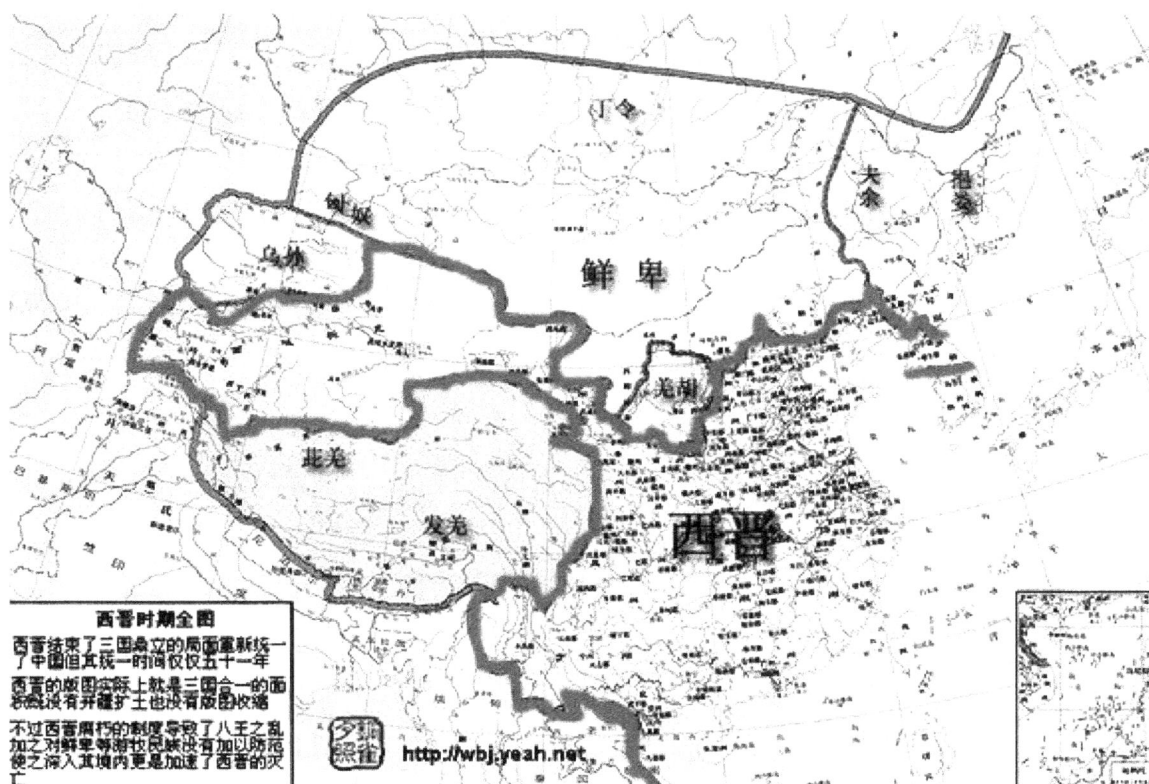

Map 1. China in the second half of the third century.
Thick grey encircled areas relate to the territory of the Western Jin Dynasty (265-316AD)
Source: http://www.21class.com/resource/library/text.asp?id=857

Map 2. China in the fourth century: the beginning of the antagonism between North and South
(Thick dark encircled areas relate to the territory of the Eastern Jin Dynasty)
Source: http://www.21class.com/resource/library/text.asp?id=857

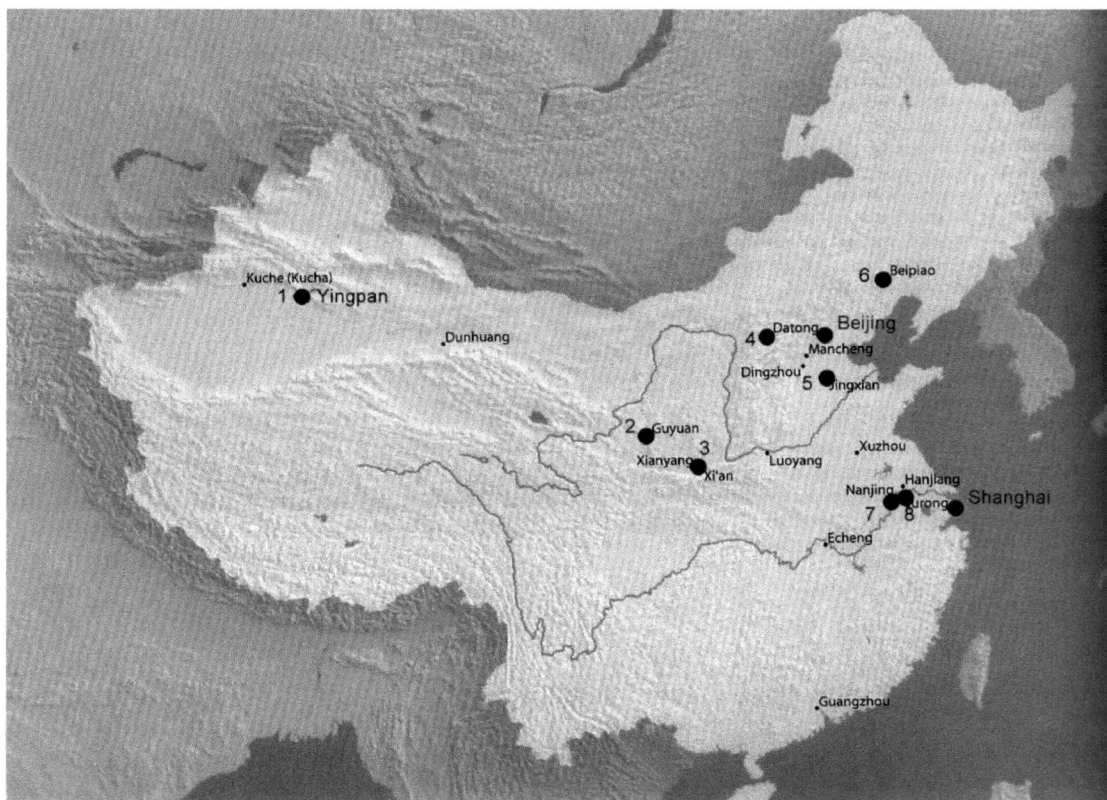

Map 3. Distribution map showing sites where Eastern Roman and Sasanian glass has been found in China
(After Watt, 2004, p.56).

the Western Region (Chinese Turkistan) was lost to the non-Han Chinese people who had close contact with the Central Asian traders. The Eastern Jin polity, which had established itself in the South in order to survive, had to maintain its foreign contacts through a maritime trade route instead. Therefore, the competition between North and South further stimulated the development of both overland and maritime trade routes in the early medieval history of China.

Interestingly, the distribution of finds of Byzantine and Sasanian glass in China also reflects such this dual phenomenon.[1] In this paper, I take the imported glassware as a point of focus and discuss the sites where this glass is found, starting with the western-most sites and proceeding in an eastwards direction (Map 3).

Yingpan, Xinjiang Autonomous Region

Glass sherds have been found at several sites in Xingjiang Autonomous Region, along the Southern and Northern Silk Routes. For example, a glass beaker 8.8 cm in height and 10.8 cm in diameter (rim) was found at Yingpan in Weili county (Fig.1).[2] This beaker, dating to the Eastern Jin period, has effloresced and the colour has become yellowish-white. However, as An Jiayao has observed from an analysis of the broken rim, the original quality of the glass is fine and it was transparent with a yellowish hue. The wall of the beaker was decorated with two horizontal rows of curvilinear facets, with 12 oval facets in the first row and 7 round facets in the second. This is a typical Sasanian glass design, favouring such cut facet decoration. A similar glass beaker of the same size was uncovered from a Partho-Sasanian tomb at Shimam on the south-west of the Caspian Sea coast[3].

Fig. 1. Glass beaker uncovered from Yingpan, Xinjiang (After Fuxi Gan, 2005, p. 16, pl. 8.9).

Guyuan, Ningxia Autonomous Region

Moving east to the Central Plain of China along the Yellow River from Xingjiang, a transparent glass bowl with pale green hue was excavated from the tomb of Li Xian (dated 569) in Guyuan, Ningxia in 1983 (Fig. 2).[4] Li Xian (503-569) was the Grand General and Commander of the Northern Zhou dynasty (part of the Northern Dynasties) which was established by the sinicized Xianbei people.

The height of this bowl is 8cm and the diameter at the mouth is 9.5cm. This vessel is different from the Yingpan glass beaker insofar as it is a typical Sasanian hemispherical bowl shape and was decorated with concave circular facets in relief. There are 8 circular facets in relief in the upper row and 6 in the lower row, and one in high relief served as a foot.

According to An Jiayao, this bowl was made in the mould-blown technique on the basis of the uneven thickness of the walls and the presence of tool marks.[5]

Fig. 2. Glass bowl uncovered from Guyuan, Ningxia (After Watt, 2004, p. 258) Xianyang, Shaanxi Province, cat. 158).

A transparent dish with cut-facet decoration was excavated from the tomb of Wang Shiliang and his wife, in Xianyang, near Xian, Shaanxi Province (Fig. 3).[6] The tomb was dated to 583. Wang Shiliang was Duke of Guang-chang and Grand General of the Northern Zhou Dynasty.

The height of this dish is 3cm, and the diameter of the rim is 10.8cm. This dish has a thick wall and was decorated with 2 rows of circular facets. Although the dish has a yellowish tinge, and is partially covered with a layer of efflorescence, it still retains a high quality of transparency. An Jiayao regards this as a Roman or Early Byzantine glass because a dish with similar shape and decoration was uncovered in Iraq and was believed to

---

[1] In this paper I use the term 'Byzantine' to describe the Eastern Roman world from the reign of Constantine I onwards.

[2] Jiayao An, 'Wei, Jin, Nanbeichao shiqi de boli jishu' (Glass Technology of Wei, Jin, Northern and Southern Dynasties), in *Zhongguo gudai boli jishu de fazhan (Development of Chinese Ancient Glass*, ed. Fuxi Gan, ch. 8 (Shanghai, Shanghai kexue chubanshe, 2005).

[3] Shinji Fukai, *Persian Glass* (New York and Tokyo, Weatherhill / Tankosha, 1977), p.29.

[4] James C. Y. Watt. (ed.), *China: Dawn of a Golden Age, 200-750 AD* (New York, The Metropolitan Museum of Art, 2004), p.258.

[5] Watt, p.258, cat. 158.

[6] Watt, pp.258-259, cat. 159.

have been inherited by the Sasanians from the Byzantine Empire[7]. However, Roman and Byzantine glass tends to have thinner walls, whereas this dish has thicker walls, and so some doubt has been cast on this interpretation.

Fig. 3. Glass dish uncovered from Xianyang, Shaanxi (After Watt, 2004, p. 258, cat. 159)

Datong, Shanxi Province

Another transparent glass bowl with cut facet decoration was excavated from a tomb in the suburb of Datong, Shanxi Province (Fig.4).[8] The dating is no later than mid-fifth century. The diameter of the rim is 10.3cm. Different from the previous Sasanian cut-facet glass vessels, this bowl was decorated with 4 interlaced rows of small oval facets and a row of 6 circular facets as well as one circular facet at the bottom. This colourless glass has good quality of transparency. Its thick wall clearly shows its Sasanian characteristic when being compared to the thin Roman glass bowl with similar decoration uncovered from a late third-century grave at Leuna in Saxony.[9]

Fig. 4. Glass bowl uncovered from Datong, Shanxi (After Watt, 2004, p. 156, cat. 65).

Jingxian, Hebei Province

A light green transparent glass bowl decorated with wave pattern but covered with a layer of efflorescence on the surface of both inside and outside was excavated from the tomb of Madame Zu, at the Feng family cemetery in Jingxian, Hebei Province (Fig. 6).[10] The Feng family served in the Northern Wei court and the tomb was dated to the fifth to sixth centuries.

Quite different from the previous thick Sasanian glass vessels, the wall of this bowl is only 0.2cm and the diameter of the rim is 10.3cm. The body of the bowl was decorated with applied thick trails forming a wave or net pattern, and at the bottom, the bowl was attached with a short ring foot and left with a pontil mark. According to An Jiayao and Yoshimizu, some glass vessels with applied wave pattern were also found in Southern Russia and northern coast of Black Sea region.[11] Therefore, this is likely to be a Byzantine glass bowl.

Fig. 6. Glass bowl uncovered from Jingxian, Hebei (After Watt, 2004, p. 157, cat. 66).

Beipiao, Liaoning Province

Then in the northeast of China, a special zoomorphic glass sprinkler was uncovered from the tomb of Feng Sufu in Beipiao, Liaoning Province, dating to 415 (Fig. 7).[12] Feng Sufu was the younger brother of the ruler of the Northern Yan of the Sixteen Kingdoms period (309-439).

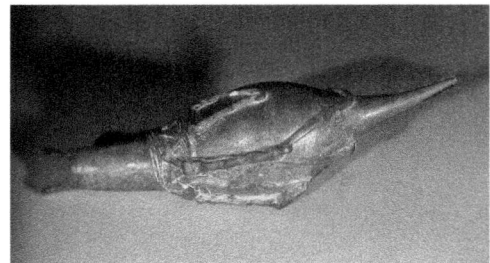

Fig. 7. Glass sprinkler uncovered from Beipiao, Liaoning (After Watt, 2004, p. 59, fig. 48).

---

[7] Watt, pp.258-259, cat. 159.

[8] Watt, p.156, cat. 65.

[9] Hugh Tait (ed.), *Five Thousand Years of Glass* (London, British Museum Press, 1991).

[10] Watt, pp.156-157, cat. 66.

[11] Watt, pp.156-157, cat. 66. Also, see Tsuneo Yoshimizu, *Toyo no garasu:Chugoku, Chosen, Nihon (Oriental glass: China, Korea, Japan)* (Tokyo, Sansaisha, 1977).

[12] Jiayao An, 'Glass Vessels and Ornaments of the Wei, Jin and Northern and Southern Dynasties Periods' in *Chinese Glass*, ed. Cicilia Braghin (Firenze, Leo S. Olschki, 2002), pp.49-50.

This sprinkler was apparently a Roman glass produced by free-blowing technique. It has been generally described as a duck-shape water dropper with trailed threads of glass around the neck and upper body, which were taken as wings of the duck.[13] However, it does not seem to be convincing to describe it as a duck form since there are no clear indications of a duck head, beakers and wings. Instead, it is more likely to be a slug because on one hand, in Greek and Roman art tradition, the representation of images and objects were usually concrete and explicit. In other words, it is unlikely to represent a duck. On the other hand, as aquatic themes play an important role in Roman art, it is not unusual to see Roman glass objects made in the forms of fish, molluscs and crustaceans, and the like. A beautiful Roman glass sprinkler blown in the shape of a snail, dating to the fourth century, provides a good reference (Fig. 8). This sprinkler is now in the collections of Bristol City Museum and Art Gallery.[14]

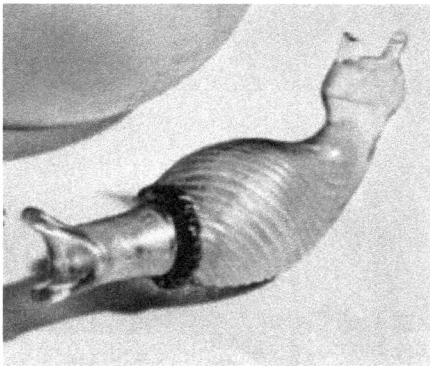

Fig. 8. Snail sprinkler (After Bristol Museum, cat. 174).

Xiangshan, Nanjing, Jiangsu Province

Finally let us look at the find-spots in Southern China. A few imported glass vessels dating to the Eastern Jin period have been uncovered in Nanjing, Jiangsu Province. One is a Roman beaker excavated from Tomb 7 at Xiangshan, Nanjing, dating to 322 (Fig. 9).[15] The tomb belongs to the cemetery of an influential noble family, Langyewang, of the Eastern Jin.

Unlike the previous glass vessels, this beaker was not that well preserved. Not only it is covered with a layer of efflorescence but also has cracks and damage all over the vessel. This beaker, originally transparent, was decorated with horizontal lines, seven vertical oval facets, and a round circular facet at the bottom. Its height is 10.4 cm and the diameter of the rim is 10.8cm.

Fig. 9. Glass beaker uncovered from Xiangshan, Nanjing, Jiangsu (After Watt, 2004, p. 210, cat. 116).

Jurong, Jiangsu Province

An exquisite colourless glass bowl was excavated from Chuncheng in Jurong county, Jiangsu province, dated to 439 (Fig. 10).[16] The height of this bowl is 6.3cm and the diameter of the mouth is 8.5cm. The body is decorated with six rows of hexagonal facets just like a honeycomb, one of the well-known Sasanian glass styles. When taking a closer look, it is amazing to see a small honeycomb gleaming inside each hexagonal facet, which makes the play of light more appealing. At the bottom, the bowl is decorated with more rows of facets. Since this bowl contains few air bubbles, it has high quality of transparency and crystal-like colourless-ness. Based on the thin wall and regular shape, the bowl was likely to be made in mould-blown technique, then ground and polished.

Fig. 10. Glass bowl uncovered from Jurong, Jiangsu (After Watt, 2004, p. 211, cat. 117).

According to Fukai, both mould-blowing and free-blowing techniques were used in Persia during the Partho-Sasanian period, both thick-walled and thin-walled vessels were produced.[17] With the help of mould, the execution of complex forms can be facilitated. Therefore, this is again an excellent piece of Sasanian glass.

---

[13] An, pp.49-50. Ellen J. Laing. 'A Report on Western Asian Glassware in the Far East', *Bulletin of the Asia Institute*, 5 (1995): 109-110.
[14] Nicholas Thomas, *Ancient Glass –The Bomford Collection of Pre-Roman & Roman Glass on loan to the City of Bristol Museum & Art Gallery* (Bristol, City of Bristol Museum and Art Gallery, 1976).
[15] Watt, pp.210-211, cat. 116.

[16] Watt, p.211, cat. 117.
[17] Fukai, p.31.

Concluding remarks

From the above finds, it is clear to see that good quality, transparent, and decorated glassware was imported into China during the fourth to sixth centuries from both the Persian and Eastern Roman empires. However, whereas in the West, glass was mass produced and trade in glass widespread, especially after the invention and spread of the blowing technique around the Mediterranean region during the first centuries BC and AD, glassware was, in contrast, very rare in China. Thus, the owners of this high-quality imported glassware were mainly aristocrats. The distribution of the find-spots clearly demonstrates direct contacts between Chinese Turkistan and the Central Plain area, which are likely to have been mediated along the middle and lower Yellow River which stood against the power in Nanjing in the Lower Yenzi River.

In addition, analysis of this assemblage reveals that Chinese aristocrats had a taste and a preference for crystal-like, colourless glass, particularly that where the cut facets were arranged in a geometric pattern and further enhanced the light effect. As these vessels were executed so finely, it seems that the Chinese believed them to be made of real crystal and called them 'shui jing wan', which means 'crystal bowl'. Ge Hong (283-343), a well-known contemporary Daoist philosopher with an expertise in alchemy left an important information in his work 'Baopuzi' that 'the crystal bowls made in foreign countries, are in fact prepared by compounding five sorts of (mineral) ashes. Today this method is being commonly practiced in Jiao and Guang (that is, Annam and Guangdong). Now if one tells this to ordinary people, they will certainly not believe it, saying that crystal is a natural product belonging to the class of rock crystal'.[18]

In conclusion, the impact of luxurious Early Byzantine and Sasanian glassware imports in China encouraged the Chinese craftsmen in today's Vietnam and Guangdong region to imitate it. This suggests close contact between Nanjing and the seaports in Indo-China, which served as gates of inflow of foreign cultures, commodities and even possibly technology. The East-West trade routes, both overland and maritime, were apparently in rapid development during this period.

---

[18] Joseph Needham, *Science and Civilization in China, vol.15, Alchemy and Chemistry* (Taibei, Taiwan Commercial Press, 1985), p.108.

'Byzantine' and 'oriental' imports in the Merovingian Empire from the second half of the fifth to the beginning of the eighth century

Jörg Drauschke

Römisch-Germanisches Zentralmuseum, Mainz

Introduction: recent developments in 'Byzantine' finds

Interest in 'Byzantine' and/or 'Mediterranean' finds in Western Europe has increased noticeably in recent years. The material in question has usually been examined by archaeologists of the early medieval barbarian kingdoms of the Franks, Lombards, Anglo-Saxons and so on, as well as those of equestrian nomads like Huns, Avars and Bulgars, also at the periphery of the Byzantine world.[1] Much of this debate has taken place in the German-speaking literature, where the emphasis has been on typical 'Byzantine' small finds and their possible provenance, for example, the early Merovingian-period swords (spathae) with gilt handles, belt buckles and fittings, as well as helmets of the 'Baldenheim' type.[2]

This research has taken place against a background of an intensified interest in the archaeological study of Late Antiquity and the Early Byzantine Empire. The discovery of production centres for amphorae, for example, has permitted the reconstruction of exchange patterns and discussion on the role of particular settlements and sub-regions in the Mediterranean trade-network.[3] The preoccupation with Mediterranean amphorae and fine-wares has prompted a discussion about the exchange of goods and the character of the late antique and early medieval Mediterranean economy.[4] This has renewed the debate on the entire range of Byzantine material culture and also on problems concerning the history of individual settlements and broader landscapes both in the Mediterranean and in Western and Central Europe.[5] As a result, a rapidly rising quantity of archaeological material in Central and Western Europe has been identified as having an origin in the Mediterranean area and/or in the Byzantine Empire.

The purpose of this contribution is to examine a sample of this material from a critical perspective and to rethink its assumed provenance. The focus is on the eastern and northern Merovingian kingdom, although there is no claim that this comprises a complete survey of the possible Mediterranean objects identified in the region. The discussion centres on the question of which forms can be deduced at all reliably to be from the Mediterranean area and whether a provenance within the Mediterranean region can be identified. It raises the question of whether the term 'Byzantine' (as a descriptor for this material) requires a critical re-definition, and whether alternative designations for some objects would not be more meaningful. Finally, this paper turns to the problem of how Mediterranean goods may have arrived in the Frankish kingdom in the first place.

Aspects of interaction between the Early Byzantine Empire and the West are well-documented in texts and in archaeology. The imitation of Byzantine court ceremonial within the barbarian kingdoms, for example, is well-known. The attraction of the imperial court in Constantinople to elite Westerners is beyond doubt and imperial-style court ceremonies were imitated in the West

[1] For recent publications with an overview character, see: C. Pause, 'Die Franken und der Orient', *Rheinisches Landesmuseum Bonn* 2 (1996): 41-49; Cs. Bálint, 'Byzantinisches zur Herkunftsfrage des vielteiligen Gürtels', in *Kontakte zwischen Iran, Byzanz und der Steppe im 6.-7. Jahrhundert*, ed. Cs. Bálint (Varia Archaeologica Hungarica 10; Budapest, Naples and Rome, 2000), pp. 99-162; F. Daim, '"Byzantinische" Gürtelgarnituren des 8. Jahrhunderts', in *Die Awaren am Rand der byzantinischen Welt*, ed. F. Daim, (Monographien zur Frühgeschichte und Mittelalterarchäologie, 7; Innsbruck, 2000), pp. 77-204; É. Garam, 'Funde byzantinischer Herkunft in der Awarenzeit vom Ende des 6. bis zum Ende des 7. Jahrhunderts', *Monumenta Avarorum Archaeologica*, 5 (Budapest 2001); D. Quast, 'Byzantinisch-gepidische Kontakte nach 454 im Spiegel der Kleinfunde', in *International Connections of the Barbarians of the Carpathian Basin in the 1st-5th centuries A.D.*, eds. E. Istvánovits and V. Kulcsár (Konferenz Aszód, Nyíregyháza 1999; Aszód, Nyíregyháza, 2001), pp. 431-452; J. Drauschke, 'Funde ostmediterraner / byzantinischer Herkunft im merowingerzeitlichen Südwestdeutschland', *Archäologische Informationen*, 25 (2002): 151-156; A. Harris, *Byzantium, Britain and the West. The Archaeology of cultural identity AD 400-650* (Stroud, 2003).
[2] J. Werner, 'Neues zur Herkunft der frühmittelalterlichen Spangenhelme vom Baldenheimer Typus', *Germania*, 66, 2 (1988): 521-528; D. Quast, 'Die merowingerzeitlichen Grabfunde aus Gültlingen' (Stadt Wildberg, Kreis Calw). (Forschungen und Berichte zur Vor- und Frühgeschichte in Baden-Württemberg 52; Stuttgart, 1993); H.-W. Böhme, 'Der Frankenkönig Childerich zwischen Attila und Aëtius. Zu den Goldgriffspathen der Merowingerzeit', in *Festschrift für Otto-Herman Frey zum 65. Geburtstag*, ed. C. Dobiat (Marburger Studien zur Vor- und Frühgeschichte 16; Marburg, 1994), pp. 69-110.
[3] P. Reynolds, *Trade in the Western Mediterranean, AD 400-700: The ceramic evidence* (British Archaeological Reports, International Series 604; Oxford, 1995); J.-P. Sodini, 'Production et échanges dans le monde protobyzantin (IVe-VIIe s.): Le cas de céramique', in *Byzanz als Raum. Zu Methoden und Inhalten der Historischen Geographie des östlichen Mittelmeerraumes*, eds. K. Belke et al. (Österreichische Akademie der Wissenschaften, Philosophisch-Historische Klasse, Denkschriften 283 / Veröffentlichungen der Kommission für die Tabula Imperii Byzantini 7; Vienna, 2000), pp. 181-208.
[4] For a list of different models, see: J.-M. Carrié, 'Les échanges commerciaux et l'État antique tardif', in *Économie antique. Les échanges dans l'Antiquité: le rôle de l'État* (Entretiens d'Archéologie et d'Histoire 1; Balma, Fonsegrives, 1994), pp. 175-211.
[5] For a summary, see: J.-P. Sodini, 'La contribution de l'archéologie à la connaissance du monde byzantin (IVe-VIIe siècles)', *Dumbarton Oaks Papers* 47 (1993): 139-184; A. E. Laiou (ed.), *The economic history of Byzantium. From the seventh to the fifteenth century* (Dumbarton Oaks Studies 39; Washington D.C., 2002).

in order to legitimise the barbarian kings' own rule.[6] An *imitatio* in more everyday contexts can also be recognised in material culture terms – for example, in the fashions of female costumes and in the turned furniture in some sixth-century graves.[7] The adoption of Mediterranean styles also resulted, inevitably, in the imitation of Mediterranean objects as well as the importation of them.[8]

Some of the objects produced in the area north of the Alps would have required raw materials that were not available in Western Europe. Amongst other things, mercury was necessary for the gilding of objects and mineral soda was used in glass production until the eighth century.[9] At least some evidence about the goods imported into Central and Western Europe can be inferred from the written sources.[10] Except for a few examples (spices and textiles), the Mediterranean products known from archaeology and those known from historical sources do not overlap.

However, this contribution deals mainly with objects that derived from the Mediterranean area and/or the Byzantine Empire and that made their way somehow to north-west Europe. They are mainly found as component parts of the furnishing of graves.

Franks, Alamanni and 'Byzantine' imports in the early Merovingian period (fifth to sixth centuries)

We begin our discussion in the early Merovingian period, where most of the available archaeological evidence comes from the so-called 'Reihengräber', which dominate the funerary landscape from the second half of the fifth century onwards. One should bear in mind the limitations of grave-goods as evidence for reconstructing past processes; nevertheless, early Merovingian-period grave-goods are of vital importance in the debate over Byzantine influence in north-western Europe.

Spathae

One of the key categories of objects thought to have a Mediterranean origin are *spathae* with gilt handles, elaborate swords with gilt handles (Fig. 1). The starting point for any discussion of their origin is Childeric's grave at Tournai, a very high-status weapons grave of the late-fifth century. Byzantine craftsmen, their Frankish pupils, Ostrogoths and Huns from southern Russia and/or Hungary were all, at some point, considered as possible producers of the swords.[11] Once a typology of Frankish and Alamannic *spathae* had been undertaken, however, it was generally accepted that they had been manufactured in Central Europe.[12] B. Arrhenius was one of the few to argue against this consensus, suggesting in her 1985 study on Merovingian garnet jewellery that the swords had a Constantinopolitan provenance. Her argument was based on the identification of a cement containing gypsum as a constituent part of the cloisonné ornaments. This, in her opinion, could only have been used in a central workshop in Constantinople.[13] H.W. Böhme, expanding on Arrhenius's work, then postulated a Mediterranean origin for most swords of this type. He suggested that a possible contract between Childeric and

---

[6] See, for example, the events at Tours in 508: K. Hauck, 'Von einer spätantiken Randkultur zum karolingischen Europa', *Frühmittelalterliche Studien* 1 (1967): 3-93, esp. 30-37; M. McCormick, 'Clovis at Tours, Byzantine public ritual and the origins of medieval ruler symbolism', in *Das Reich und die Barbaren*, eds. E. K. Chrysos and A. Schwarcz (Veröffentlichungen des Instituts für Österreichische Geschichtsforschung 29; Vienna and Cologne, 1989), pp. 155-180, esp. 163-171.

[7] H. Vierck, 'Werke des Eligius', in *Studien zur vor- und frühgeschichtlichen Archäologie. Festschrift J. Werner*, eds. G. Kossack and G. Ulbert (Münchner Beiträge zur Vor- und Frühgeschichte, Ergänzungsband 1, II; Munich, 1974), pp. 309-380; M. Schulze, 'Einflüsse byzantinischer Prunkgewänder auf die fränkische Frauentracht', *Archäologisches Korrespondenzblatt* 6 (1976): 149-161; H. Vierck, 'La "Chemise de Sainte Bathilde" à Chelles et l'influence byzantine sur l'art de cour Mérovingien au VIIᵉ siècle', in *Centenaire de l'Abbé Cochet. Kolloquium Rouen 1975* (Rouen, 1978), pp. 521-570; H. Vierck, '*Imitatio imperii* und *interpretatio Germanica* vor der Wikingerzeit', in *Les pays du nord et Byzance (Scandinavie et Byzance). Kolloquium Uppsala 1979*. ed. R. Zeitler (Uppsala, 1981), pp. 64-113; H. Schach-Dörges, '*Imitatio imperii* im Bestattungsbrauch?' *Germania* 83, 1 (2005): 127-150.

[8] For example, see: M. Schulze-Dörrlamm, 'Byzantinische Knebelverschlüsse des frühen Mittelalters', *Germania* 80, 2 (2002): 571-594; M. Schulze-Dörrlamm, 'Gleicharmige Bügelfibeln der Zeit um 600 aus dem byzantinischen Reich', *Archäologisches Korrespondenzblatt* 33 (2003): 437-444.

[9] H. Roth, 'Handel und Gewerbe vom 6. bis 8. Jh. östlich des Rheins', *Vierteljahrschrift für Sozial- und Wirtschaftsgeschichte* 58 (1971): 323-358, esp. 356; K.H. Wedepohl, 'Mittelalterliches Glas in Mitteleuropa: Zusammensetzung, Herstellung, Rohstoffe', (Nachrichten der Akademie der Wissenschaften Göttingen II, Mathematisch-Physikalische Klasse, 1998, 1, Göttingen, 1998).

[10] A. Verhulst, 'Der Handel im Merowingerreich: Gesamtdarstellung nach schriftlichen Quellen', *Antikvarisk Arkiv 39 / Early Medieval Studies* 2 (1970): 2-54, esp. 24; D. Schwärzel, 'Handel und Verkehr des Merowingerreiches nach den schriftlichen Quellen' (Kleine Schriften aus dem Vorgeschichtlichen Seminar Marburg 14; Marburg, 1983); D. Claude, 'Der Handel im westlichen Mittelmeer während des Frühmittelalters', *Untersuchungen zu Handel und Verkehr der vor- und frühgeschichtlichen Zeit in Mittel- und Nordeuropa II. Kolloquium Göttingen 1980* (Abhandlungen der Akademie der Wissenschaften Göttingen, Philologisch-Historische Klasse, 3. F. 144; Göttingen, 1985), pp. 83-95.

[11] H. Arbmann, 'Les épées du tombeau de Childéric', *Årsberättelse* (Lund) (1947/48): 97-137, esp. 124 ff. with a summary of earlier publications.

[12] K. Böhner, 's. v. Childerich von Tournai III. Archäologisches', *Reallexikon der Germanischen Altertumskunde IV* (Berlin and New York, 1981), pp. 441-460; I.P. Zaseckaja, 'Klassifikacija polihrommnyh izdelij gunnskoj epohi po stilisticeskim dannym', in *Drevnosti epohi velikogo pereselenija narodov V-VIII vekov* (Moscow, 1982), pp. 14-30; 246-248. For division into Frankish and Alamannic types, see: H. Ament, *Fränkische Adelsgräber von Flonheim in Rheinhessen* (Germanische Denkmäler der Völkerwanderungszeit B 5; Berlin, 1970), pp. 51 ff. fig. 4; W. Menghin, 'Das Schwert im frühen Mittelalter' (Wissenschaftliche Beibände zum Anzeiger des Germanischen Nationalmuseums 1; Stuttgart, 1983), pp. 155 ff. (types IIIa,b and IVa-c); K. Böhner, 'Germanische Schwerter des 5./6. Jahrhunderts', *Jahrbuch des Römisch-Germanischen Zentralmuseum* 34, 2 (1987): 411-490, 421 ff. (types B and C2-6); M. Martin, 'Bemerkungen zur chronologischen Gliederung der frühen Merowingerzeit', *Germania* 67, 1 (1989): 121-141, esp. 125 ff. (types B1-3).

[13] B. Arrhenius, *Merovingian Garnet Jewellery. Emergence and social implications* (Stockholm, 1985), pp. 98 ff.

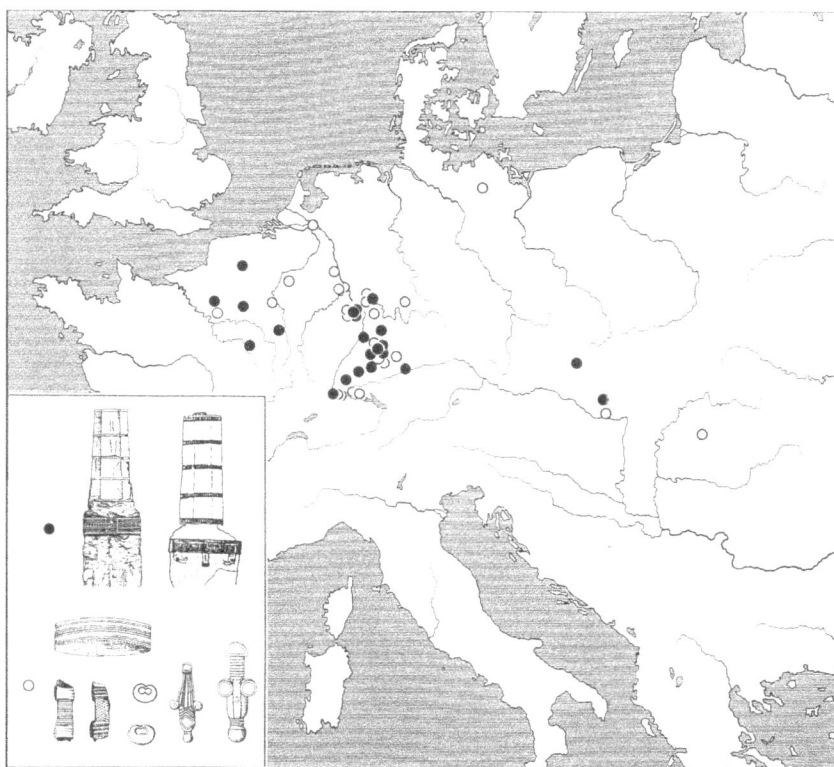

Fig. 1: Distribution of *spathae* with gilt handles and other splendour swords (after Böhme, 'Der Frankenkönig Childerich', p. 81 fig. 7 with additions).

the Byzantine Emperor of 476-477 (and arranged by Odoacer) had prompted an inflow of Mediterranean goods. Since subsidies were also being paid by the Byzantines to Gepid and other Germanic leaders, goods may also have been mediated through Central Europe.[14]

However, doubts about a Byzantine origin for all gilt-handled *spathae* remain. The assignment of the cloisonnés of the Childeric weapons to a workshop from Constantinople remains speculative because a workshop processing gypsum-cement could have been situated elsewhere – for example, in Italy or Carthage. Doubts have also been expressed about the assumed agreement between Childeric and the Byzantine emperor, since an alternative interpretation of the text might imply that the contract was between the Frankish leader and a Saxon noble named Adovacrius.[15]

P. Périn and M. Kazanski interpret the cellular cloisonné-style decoration on the weapons and further objects as a fashion of the 'barbarised military aristocracy' of the Western Roman Empire in the second half of the fifth century. They had a good reputation with Danubian barbarian kings and were sought after at the imperial court in Constantinople, but the origin of this development, they argue, is to be looked for in the

Western Mediterranean, rather than the Byzantine Empire.[16] Yet, while the workshops in the West should not be underestimated, some objects in the Childeric burial, for example the ornament with round garnet crystals, are analogous to those found, among other objects, in the complexes at Apahida, Olbia and Kerč. This might suggest an eastern Mediterranean origin.[17] Thus a Mediterranean provenance for most high-status *spathae* remains quite plausible, although manufacture in the workshops of the Byzantine Empire is under no circumstances secured.

---

[14] K. Böhner, 'Die frühmittelalterlichen Spangenhelme und die nordischen Helme der Vendelzeit', *Jahrbuch des Römisch-Germanischen Zentralmuseum*, 41, 2 (1994): 471-549.

[15] D. Quast, 'Les Francs et l'Empire Byzantin. L'horizon des épées à poignée en or', *Les Dossiers de l'Archéologie*, 223 (1997): 56-63, esp. note 3.

[16] P. Périn and M. Kazanski, 'Das Grab Childerichs I', in *Die Franken – Wegbereiter Europas. Ausstellungskatalog Mannheim 1996-97*, eds. A. Wieczorek et al. (Mannheim and Mainz 1996), pp. 173-182; M. Kazanski and A. Mastykova, 'Le Caucase du Nord et la région méditerranéenne aux 5e-6e siècles', *Eurasia Antiqua* 5 (1999): 523-573, esp. 539; M. Kazanski, A. Mastykova and P. Périn, 'Byzance et les royaumes barbares d'Occident au début de l'époque mérovingienne', in *Probleme der frühen Merowingerzeit im Mitteldonauraum*, ed. J. Tejral (XI. Internationalen Symposium 'Grundprobleme der Frühgeschichtlichen Entwicklung im Nördlichen Mitteldonaugebiet', Kravsko 1998. Spisy Archeologického Ústavu AV CR Brno 19; Brno 2002), pp. 159-193, esp. 160.

[17] C. v. Carnap-Bornheim, 'Eine cloisonnierte Schnalle mit wabenförmigem Zellenwerk und Almandinrundeln aus Olbia', *Germania* 73, 1 (1995): 151-155. For a reply to the opinion of Périn and Kazanski, see: M. Schmauder, 'Die Oberschichtgräber und Verwahrfunde Südosteuropas und das Childerichgrab von Tournai. Anmerkungen zu den spätantiken Randkulturen', *Acta Praehistorica et Archaeologica* 30 (1998): 55-68.

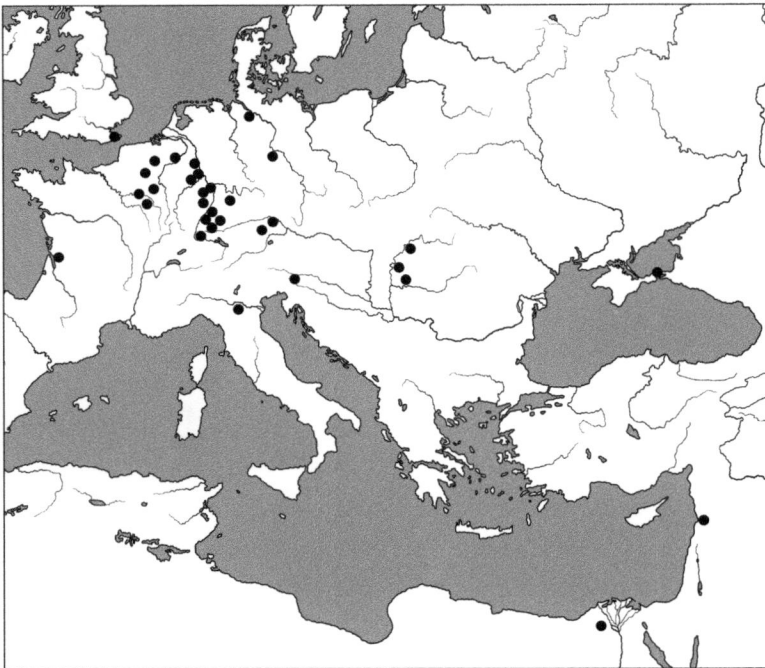

Fig. 2: Distribution of crystal buckles (after Quast 'Byzantinisch-gepidische Kontakte', p. 436 fig. 4).

Scramasaxes

The grave of Childeric contained not only a *spatha* with a gilt handle, but also a small, narrow *scramasax*. Scramasaxes were common in the region between the lower Danube and eastern France in the second half of the fifth century. Their development in an equestrian nomadic environment is certainly not out of question and they may have been mediated through the activities of the Huns.[18] There is a parallel from Sardis in Asia Minor and it is quite possible that some originate within the Byzantine Empire, particularly since the narrow small *scramasax* became part of the armament of the Byzantine army.[19] It is interesting that both the weapon of Childeric and the one from Sardis are classical *scramasaxes*, which occur particularly in the Transcaucasus and in Central Asia during the fourth and fifth centuries, and not in Central Europe. It is possible that the *scramasax* found in Childeric's grave originated there, and was brought to Western Europe via the Byzantine Empire. It must be distinguished from a longer, also one-edged, sword type ('sabre'), which is known more frequently from graves of the equestrian nomads in the Eurasian steppes and whose

manufacture in Byzantine workshops cannot be assumed at present.[20]

Buckles

The literature dealing with the different types of early Merovingian belt buckles and fittings with a probable Mediterranean origin has increased enormously in recent years.[21] In addition, the publication of the collection of Römisch-Germanischen Zentralmuseum Mainz by M. Schulze-Dörrlamm has introduced a new typological classification.[22] Thus, the state of knowledge concerning

---

[18] H. Schach-Dörges, *Das frühmittelalterliche Gräberfeld bei Aldingen am mittleren Neckar* (Materialhefte zur Archäologie in Baden-Württemberg 74; Stuttgart, 2004), p. 68.

[19] D. Quast, 'Auf der Suche nach fremden Männern. Die Herleitung schmaler Langsaxe vor dem Hintergrund der alamannisch-donauländischen Kontakte der zweiten Hälfte des 5. Jahrhunderts', in *Germanen beiderseits des spätantiken Limes*, eds. Th. Fischer et al. (X. Internationales Symposium 'Grundprobleme der Frühgeschichtlichen Entwicklung im Nördlichen Mitteldonaugebiet', Xanten 1997. Spisy Archeologického Ústavu AV CR Brno 14; Cologne, 1999), pp. 115-128; for their distribution see also: U. Koch, *Das alamannisch-fränkische Gräberfeld bei Pleidelsheim* (Forschungen und Berichte zur Vor- und Frühgeschichte in Baden-Württemberg 60; Stuttgart, 2001) p. 279 with fig. 113 and list 31.

[20] Kazanski, Mastykova and Périn, pp. 172 ff.

[21] Riegl was the first to ascribe a Mediterranean origin to the belt-buckle from Apahida: A. Riegl, *Spätrömische Kunstindustrie* (Vienna, 1901), pp. 339 f. For other important publications on early Merovingian belt-buckles of this provenance, see: J. Werner, 'Zu den donauländischen Beziehungen des alamannischen Gräberfeldes am alten Gotterbarmweg in Basel' in *Helvetia Antiqua. Festschrift E. Vogt*, eds. R. Degen et al. (Zürich, 1966), pp. 283-292; Ament, pp. 30 f.; J. Werner, 'Archäologische Bemerkungen zu den dendrochronologischen Befunden von Oberflacht', *Fundberichte aus Baden-Württemberg* 1 (1974): 650-657; V. Bierbrauer, *Die ostgotischen Grab- und Schatzfunde in Italien* (Biblioteca 'Studi Medievali' 7; Spoleto 1975), p. 160; Quast, *Die merowingerzeitlichen Grabfunde aus Gültlingen*, p. 54 and list 3; Böhme, 'Der Frankenkönig Childerich', p. 82 and list 1; M. Kazanski, 'Les plaques-boucles méditerranéennes des Ve-VIe siècles', *Archéologie Médiévale* 24 (1994): 137-198; D. Quast, 'Schmuckstein- und Glasschnallen des 5. und frühen 6. Jahrhunderts aus dem östlichen Mittelmeergebiet und dem Sasanidenreich', *Archäologisches Korrespondenzblatt* 26 (1996); 333-345; D. Quast, 'Garnitures des ceintures méditerranéennes à plaques cloisonnées des Ve et début VIe siècles', *Antiquités Nationales* 31 (1999): 233-250; M. Herdick, 'Vom Mineral zum Prestigeobjekt. Überlegungen zur Fertigung und kulturhistorischen Bedeutung der Meerschaum- und Magnesitschnallen', *Concilium medii aevi* 3 (2000): 327-347; Quast, 'Byzantinisch-gepidische Kontakte', pp. 444-446, lists 1-3, fig. 3-6.

[22] M. Schulze-Dörrlamm, *Byzantinische Gürtelschnallen und Gürtelbeschläge im Römisch-Germanischen Zentralmuseum I. Kataloge vor- und frühgeschichtlicher Altertümer 30, 1* (Mainz, 2002).

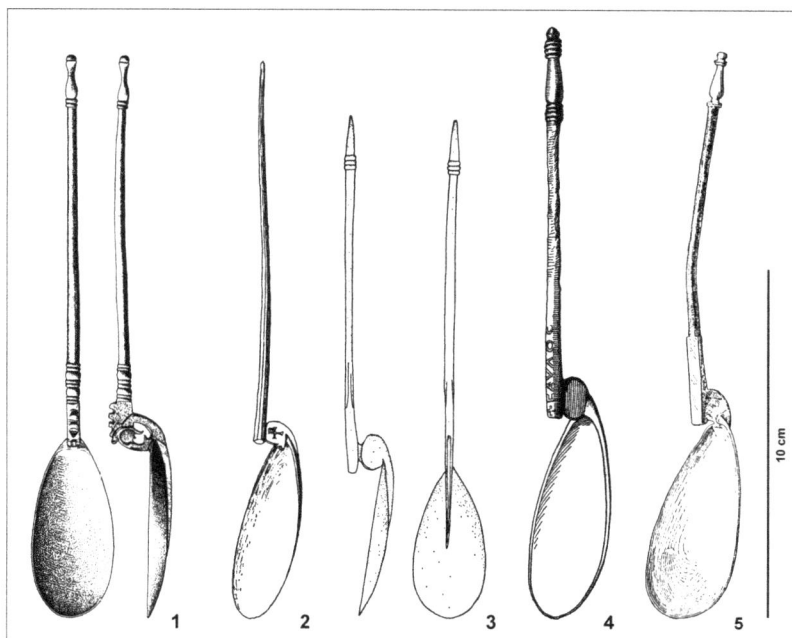

Fig. 3: Early Byzantine silver spoons of the types Isola Rizza, Desana, Barbing-Irlmauth, Lampsakos C var. 1 und 2. 1: Krefeld-Gellep (Germany) grave 1782, 2: Lausanne - Bois de Vaux (Switzerland) woman's grave, 3: Barbing-Irlmauth (Germany) grave 19, 4: Sutton Hoo (Britain) ship-burial, 5: Erfurt-Gispersleben (Germany) woman's grave (1-3.5 after Hauser, *Spätantike und frühbyzantinische Silberlöffel*, pl. 4a; 8a; 14a; 22c; 4 after Kitzinger, 'The Sutton Hoo ship-burial: The silver', p. 55 fig. 5).

the spectrum of Mediterranean buckles from the second half of the fifth century to the first half of the sixth century is now excellent.

Buckles found in the Frankish and Alamannic territories are usually of gold or gilded bronze with rectangular, D- or kidney-shaped fittings in cloisonné-style, buckles from sea foam (that is, *sepiolite*, a clay mineral which can be carved) and/or magnesite, crystal buckles (Fig. 2) and heart-shaped buckles, as well as few other special forms.[23] Like some of the gilt-handled *spathae,* it is likely that some buckles were manufactured in the western Mediterranean area, although an exact localization of the actual workshops is not yet possible.[24] Other buckles and fittings from the Merovingian Empire are not Mediterranean originals and must be understood as imitations, since they do not correspond typologically to the finds available from the origin areas and/or consist of iron, which did not play a role in the manufacturing process in the Mediterranean area.[25]

Spoons

If the finds discussed so far originate almost exclusively from richly equipped warrior graves, then Byzantine silver spoons (*cochlearia*) are to be found also in the graves of women. In older research, a Christian and/or liturgical interpretation of the spoons dominated, but in recent studies a secular interpretation is favoured for those pieces found north of the Alps.[26] The silver spoons from the regions north and west of the Alps – mainly types Isola Rizza, Desana, Barbing Irlmauth and Lampsakos C (Fig. 3)[27] – were found, insofar as they have a context, in very richly furnished burials. These can be dated, with a few exceptions, to around 500. In the Mediterranean area, by contrast, especially in northern Italy, they are primarily known as components of treasure

[26] E. Kitzinger, 'The Sutton Hoo ship-burial: The silver', *Antiquity* 14, 53 (1940): 40-63, esp. 59 f.; H. Dannheimer, 'Silberlöffel aus Reihengräbern', *Bayerische Vorgeschichtsblätter* 30 (1965): 278; H. v. Petrikovits, 'Frühchristliche Silberlöffel', in *Corolla memoriae Erich Swoboda dedicata* (Römische Forschungen in Niederösterreich 5; Graz and Cologne, 1966), pp. 173-182; V. Milojčić, 'Zu den spätkaiserzeitlichen und merowingischen Silberlöffeln. Mit einem Beitrag von Hermann Vetters', *Bericht der Römisch-Germanischen Kommission* 49 (1968): 111-152, esp. 122 ff.. For 'secular' interpretations, see: H.W. Böhme, 'Löffelbeigabe in spätrömischen Gräbern nördlich der Alpen', *Jahrbuch des Römisch-Germanischen Zentralmuseum* 17 (1970): 172-200, esp. 189 f.; Bierbrauer, *Die ostgotischen Grab- und Schatzfunde in Italien*, pp. 184 ff.; M. Martin, 'Esslöffel/Weinsiebchen und Toilettgerät'. in *Der spätrömische Silberschatz von Kaiseraugst*, eds. H.A. Cahn and A. Kaufmann-Heinimann (Basler Beiträge zur Ur- und Frühgeschichte 9; Derendingen, 1984), pp. 55-132, 92; S.R. Hauser, *Spätantike und frühbyzantinische Silberlöffel* (Jahrbuch für Antike und Christentum, Ergänzungsband 19; Münster, 1992), pp. 82 ff.
[27] Hauser, *Spätantike und frühbyzantinisch? Silberlöffel*. Some new finds must be added to his catalogue. These are: Eltville a. Rhein, Rheingau-Taunus-Kreis (Hessen, Germany): Böhme, 'Löffelbeigabe in spätrömischen Gräbern nördlich der Alpen', p. 195, list IV. Mainz-Hechtsheim (Rheinland-Pfalz, Germany): A. Wieczorek et al. (eds.), *Die Franken – Wegbereiter Europas* (Ausstellungskatalog Mannheim 1996-97; Mannheim and Mainz 1996), p. 1025 with fig. Niedernai, Dép. Bas-Rhin (France): M. Zehnacker, 'Niedernai – Une necropole du 5 et 6 siècle après J.C. Fouilles recentes 4', in *À l'aube du Moyen Age: l'Alsace mérovingienne*, ed. B. Schnitzler (Les collections du Musée Archéologique 5; Strasbourg, 1997), pp. 89-137, esp. 114-118 fig. 9 f. Prittlewell, Essex (Great Britain): Museum of London Archaeology Service, *The Prittlewell Prince. The discovery of a rich Anglo-Saxon burial in Essex* (London, 2004), pp. 28 f. fig. p. 29 and 40.

[23] Schulze-Dörrlamm, *Byzantinische Gürtelschnallen und Gürtelbeschläge*; Werner, 'Archäologische Bemerkungen', pp. 650 ff.; D. Quast, 'Ein byzantinischer Gürtelbeschlag der Zeit um 500 aus Weingarten (Lkr. Ravensburg) Grab 189', *Fundberichte aus Baden-Württemberg* 21 (1996): 527-539.
[24] For example, see: Kazanski, pp. 150 f. types I.3.K, pl. 11,18; 23,5.
[25] Drauschke, 'Funde ostmediterraner/byzantinischer Herkunft im merowingerzeitlichen Südwestdeutschland', p. 152; Schulze-Dörrlamm, *Byzantinische Gürtelschnallen und Gürtelbeschläge*, p. 2, note 47 and 142.

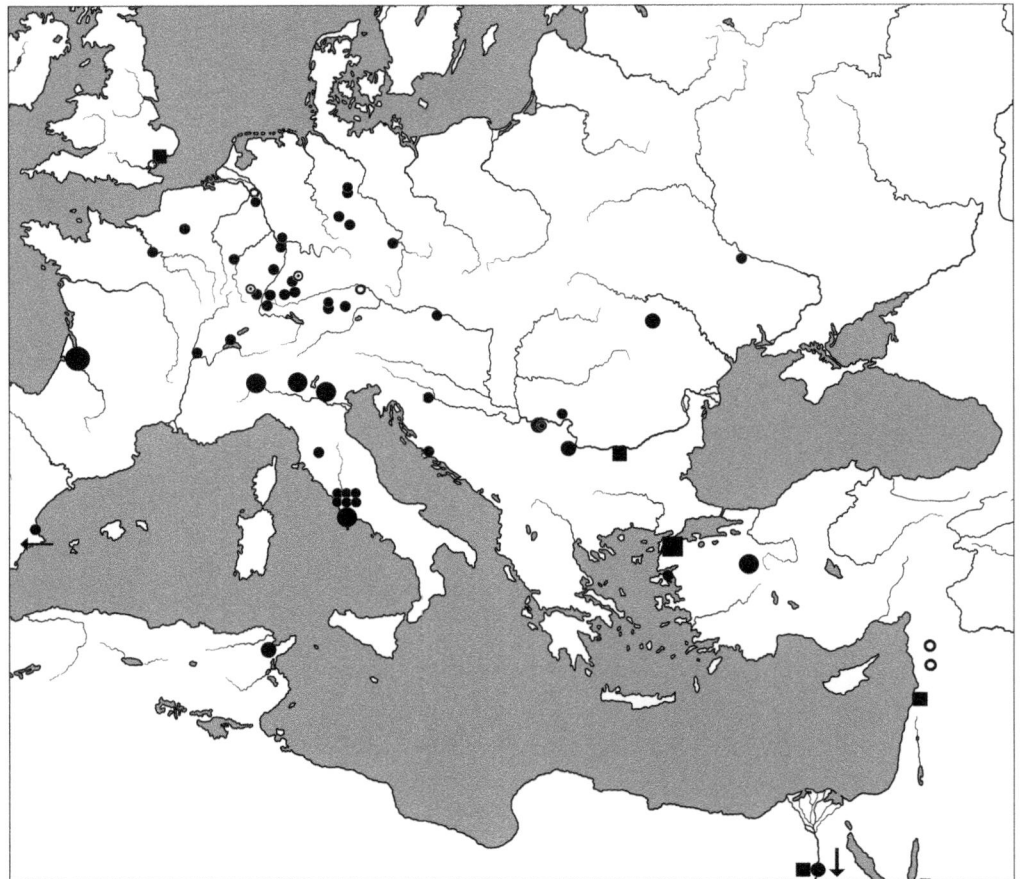

Fig. 4: Distribution of early Byzantine silver spoons in the West around 500 AD. (●) Italic or western Balkan, (■) eastern Mediterranean and (○) uncertain origin, (◉) Late Antique residual finds (arranged after Hauser, *Spätantike und frühbyzantinische Silberlöffel*, 145-146 distribution map 2-3 with additions)

troves and/or church treasures. Nearly all *cochlearia* found north and west of the Alps are thought, as a result of the careful analysis of S. Hauser, to be either of Italian or western Balkan origin (Fig. 4), or to have been produced in a Late Roman context and in a provincial workshop.[28] There are, in addition, a few spoons of uncertain origin.

Helmets

With helmets (and the remaining categories of object in this section), we are no longer concerned with objects found exclusively in fifth and early-sixth century graves, but with objects that are also found in later Merovingian contexts. Again, a variety of origins has been suggested for some of them. Helmets of the Baldenheim type, for example, had been seen as western Asiatic, Coptic, Italic-Ostrogothic and purely Frankish, until J. Werner addressed them as Byzantine officer helmets in view of new finds from the destruction layers of early Byzantine cities on the Balkans. He favoured a Byzantine provenance for the majority of these helmets, suggesting that they were perhaps even manufactured in central

fabricae in Constantinople.[29] D. Quast argued in support of this interpretation and came to the conclusion that all helmets of the Baldenheim type originated from Byzantine workshops.[30]

However, these arguments have now been challenged. After K. Böhner had already distinguished between a western and eastern type of helmet, F. Stein divided the well-known examples into five different groups (Fig. 5), arguing that only the first three groups were connected with Byzantine workshops in the East.[31] She suggested that the fifth group, which includes four helmets from Central Europe, could have been manufactured in Italy. In another recent analysis of the helmets, M. Vogt allocated individual helmets to workshops and located production both in Italy and in the Byzantine Empire.[32]

---

[29] Werner, 'Neues zur Herkunft der frühmittelalterlichen Spangenhelme vom Baldenheimer Typus', pp. 523 ff.. For previous interpretations, see: Quast, *Die merowingerzeitlichen Grabfunde aus Gültlingen*, p. 30.

[30] Quast, *Die merowingerzeitlichen Grabfunde aus Gültlingen*, pp. 36 ff. and 131 list 2.

[31] Böhner, 'Die frühmittelalterlichen Spangenhelme und die nordischen Helme der Vendelzeit', pp. 527 f. F. Stein, 'Die Spangenhelme von Pfeffingen und Gammertingen – Überlegungen zur Bestimmung ihrer Herstellungsräume', *Acta Praehistorica et Archaeologica* 35 (2003): 41-61, esp. 45 ff.

[32] M. Vogt, 'Die frühmittelalterlichen Spangenhelme – Ein Überblick zu archäologischen, kunsthistorischen und herstellungstechnischen Problemen', *Acta Praehistorica et Archaeologica* 35 (2003): 9-29, esp.

---

[28] Hauser, *Löffelbeigabe in spätrömischen Gräbern nördlich der Alpen*.

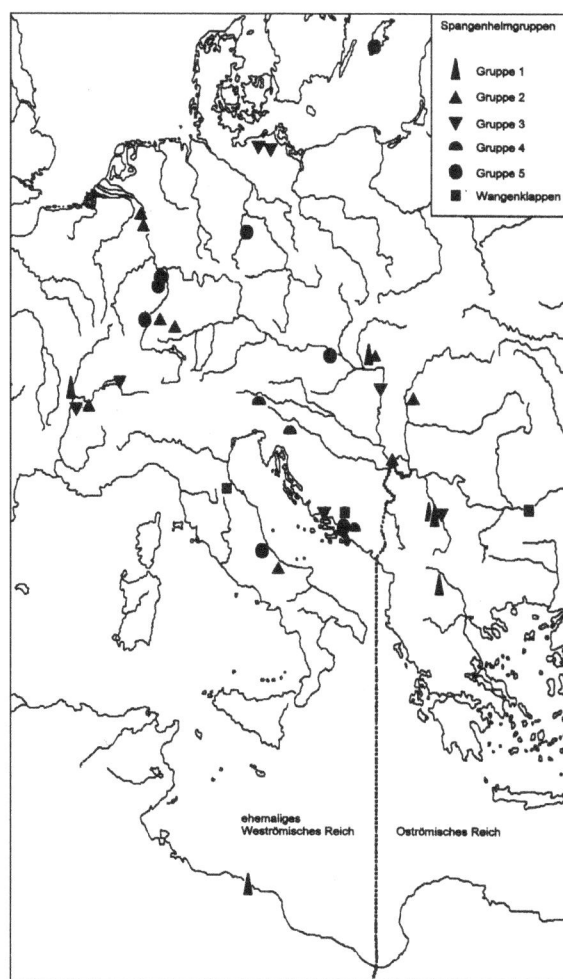

Fig. 5: Distribution of the different groups of helmets of the 'Baldenheim' type (after Stein 'Die Spangenhelme von Pfeffingen und Gammertingen', p. 52 fig. 11).

Textiles

Unsurprisingly, textiles do not occur very frequently in the archaeological record, although some rare examples of silk imports are still extant.[33] Fifth- to seventh-century Byzantine workshops were heavily influenced by Sasanian fashions, particularly in relation to design and colours. As a result, it is almost impossible to differentiate between the products of either country.[34]

Plant-remains

Again, this is a difficult category to detect archaeologically. One example of botanical evidence for exotic plants has recently been identified in the form of incense from Schaffhausen (Switzerland), but this is very rare indeed.[35]

Glass vessels

Byzantine glass vessels are also extremely rare in early Merovingian-period contexts. An outstanding, unique piece is the flask from grave 51 of Bräunlingen (Germany) that can be dated to the third quarter of the fifth century.[36] This, just under 40 cm tall, narrow glass flask with a ribbed surface can be compared quite convincingly with Syrian glass vessels, and there are also similar pieces from the northern Caucasus.[37] An eastern Mediterranean origin for these flasks is very probable.

Ivory combs

Two fragments of Mediterranean ivory combs, excavated from grave 150 at Fridingen (Baden-Württemberg, Germany) and grave 285 from Griesheim (Hessen, Germany) are almost certainly Mediterranean products of the fifth to early-sixth centuries.[38] It is likely that they

25; for a recent catalogue, see also: Quast, 'Byzantinisch-gepidische Kontakte nach 454 im Spiegel der Kleinfunde', p. 446, list 4.

[33] For example grave 974, Lauchheim, Ostalbkreis (Baden-Württemberg, Germany): I. Stork, 'Lauchheim, Ostalbkreis 1994 - frühe Phasen des großen Gräberfelds der Merowingerzeit', *Archäologische Ausgrabungen in Baden-Württemberg* (1994): pp. 212-216; J. Banck-Burgess, 'An Webstuhl und Webrahmen. Alamannisches Textilhandwerk', in *Die Alamannen* (Stuttgart, 1997), pp. 371-378; J. Banck, 'Ein merowingerzeitlicher Baumsarg aus Lauchheim/Ostalbkreis – Zur Bergung und Dokumentation der Textilfunde', in *Textiles in Europaean archaeology. 6th NESAT Symposium Borås 1996*, eds. L. Bender Jørgensen and Ch. Rinaldo (GOTARC Ser. A 1; Göteborg, 1998), pp. 115-124.

[34] H. Roth, 'Seidenstoffe des 4. bis 9. Jh. in Westeuropa', in *Geld aus China. Ausstellung Bonn 1982* (Kunst und Altertum am Rhein 108;

Cologne and Bonn, 1982), pp. 110-115; X. Liu, *Silk and religion. An exploration of material life and the thought of people, AD 600-1200* (Delhi, 1996), p. 21; A. Muthesius, 'Essential processes, looms, and technical aspects of the production of silk textiles', in *The economic history of Byzantium. From the seventh to the fifteenth century*, ed. A. Laiou (Dumbarton Oaks Studies 39; Washington D.C., 2002), pp. 147-168.

[35] Graves 626, 752 and 789 from Schleitheim, Kt. Schaffhausen (Switzerland). A. Burzler et al., *Das frühmittelalterliche Schleitheim - Siedlung, Gräberfeld und Kirche* (Schaffhauser Archäologie 5; Schaffhausen, 2002).

[36] G. Fingerlin, 'Bräunlingen, ein frühmerowingerzeitlicher Adelssitz an der Römerstraße durch den südlichen Schwarzwald', *Archäologische Ausgrabungen in Baden-Württemberg* (1997): pp. 146-148; A. Wieczorek and P. Périn (eds.), *Das Gold der Barbarenfürsten* (Ausstellungskatalog Mannheim 2001, Publikationen des Reiss-Museums 3; Stuttgart, 2001), p. 170, no. 4.15.

[37] E.M. Ruprechtsberger (ed.), *Syrien. Von den Aposteln zu den Kalifen. Ausstellungskatalog Linz, Schloss Schallaburg, Klagenfurt 1993-95* (Linzer Archäologische Forschungen 21; Linz, 1993), p. 399 no. 12; Kazanski and Mastykova, p. 560, fig. 22,5; 563 fig. 24,11 (Djurso grave 259, Sopino grave 11). I would like to thank M. Kazanski for this and other information.

[38] A. v. Schnurbein, *Der alamannische Friedhof bei Fridingen an der Donau (Kreis Tuttlingen)* (Forschungen und Berichte zur Vor- und Frühgeschichte in Baden-Württemberg 21; Stuttgart, 1987), pp. 136 f. pl. 32-34A; J. Meiner, 'Die Hochzeit zu Kana und der Hauptmann von Kafarnaum. Ein frühchristlicher Elfenbeinkamm aus Griesheim (Hessen)', *Antike Welt* 27, 5 (1996): 387-396; H. Göldner and V. Hilberg, *Griesheim, Kreis Darmstadt-Dieburg, Gräberfeld des 6. bis 8. Jahrhunderts. Ausgrabungen in dem merowinger- bis karolingerzeitlichen Reihengräberfriedhof "An der Rückgasse"* (Archäologische Denkmäler in Hessen 1; 2. Auflage, Wiesbaden, 2000), p. 12.

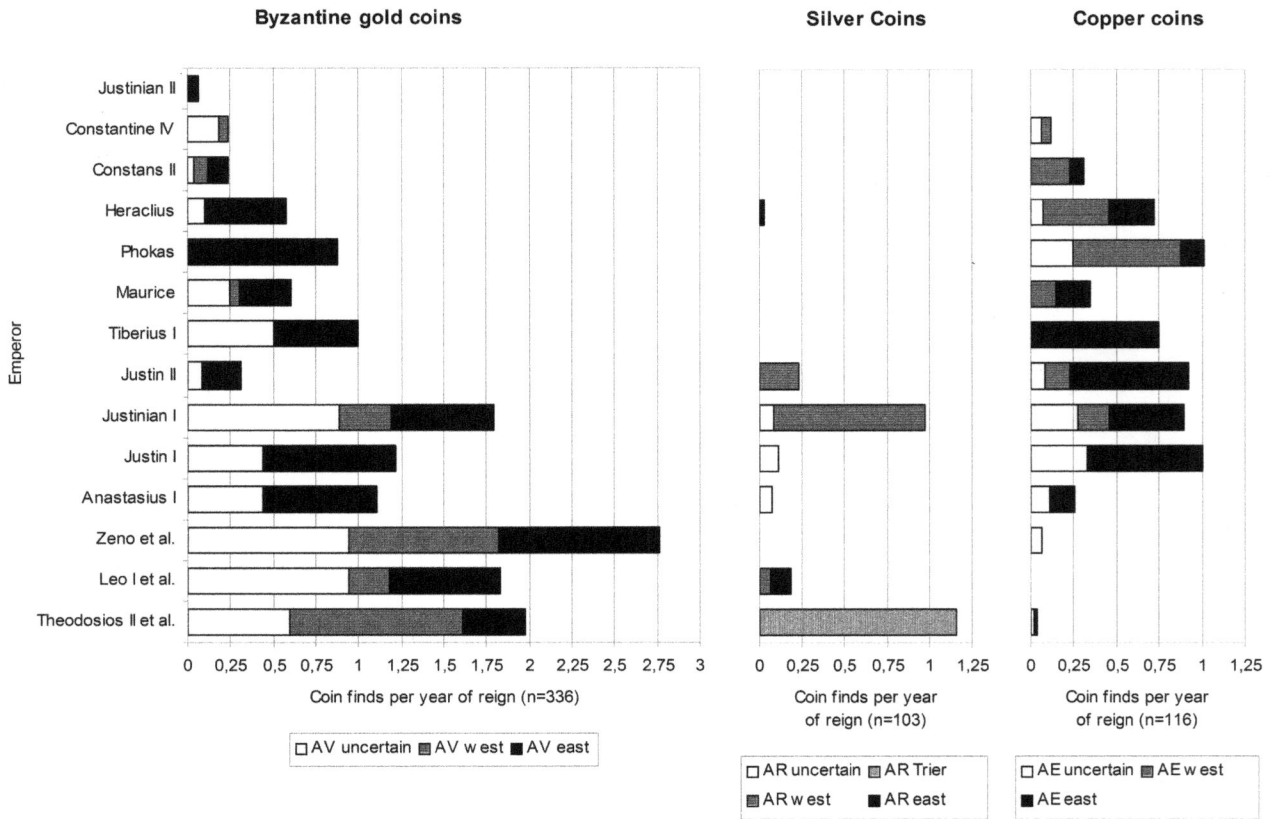

Fig. 6: Diagram showing the frequency of imperial Byzantine coins in the area of the Merovingian Kingdom, sorted in accordance with metal and mints in the eastern and western part of the empire. Deposits and coins from the Childeric-grave are not included.

were manufactured in eastern Mediterranean workshops.[39]

Coins

Finally, the coins of the Byzantine Empire must be included in this discussion. It is helpful in this to examine the number of issues from Mediterranean mints in diachronic perspective (Fig. 6), taking the total number of coins per Emperor and dividing by the number of years in that Emperor's reign, taking into account the regnal years the coins were minted in. This shows that there is a high proportion of Byzantine gold coins dating to the period before the end of Zeno's reign (474-491), perhaps suggesting some continuation in administrative structures. Thereafter, the flow of Byzantine gold coins into the Merovingian kingdoms strongly decreases.[40] By contrast, by the reign of Anastasius I, increased numbers of copper coins made their way into the Merovingian world, where they may have been used as currency. On this point, we must bear in mind that most of the gold

coins were found in contexts where they had been deposited as jewellery or used as *obolus* within the graves, and so their presence cannot be read as evidence for the use of these coins as currency. Notwithstanding, these difficulties, the finds have the potential to illuminate the general tendencies of Byzantine minting and to shed light on Merovingian contacts with the Byzantine world.[41]

In summary, a detailed analysis of the apparently 'Byzantine' objects found in the Merovingian kingdom in the fifth and early-sixth centuries shows that that the number of objects that can be demonstrated to have been actually manufactured in the eastern Mediterranean region and exported into the north and west is substantially smaller than one might assume on the basis of some of the literature available. In fact, the present state of the field suggests that many of apparently *eastern*

---

[39] For parallels, see: W.F. Volbach, *Elfenbeinarbeiten der Spätantike und des frühen Mittelalters* (Kataloge vor- und frühgeschichtlicher Altertümer 7; 3. Auflage Mainz, 1976), pp. 122 f. no. 202-205 pl. 98 f.

[40] The coinage of the Ostrogothic kingdom in Italy is not included in the analysis. See now: M.A. Metlich, *The coinage of Ostrogothic Italy* (London, 2004).

[41] See, for comparison: W. Hahn, *Moneta Imperii Byzantini 1-3* (Denkschriften der Österreichischen Akademie der Wissenschaften, Philosphisch-Historische Klasse 109; 119; 148 / Veröffentlichungen der Numismatischen Kommission 1; 4; 10; Vienna 1973; 1975; 1981); Ph. Grierson, *Byzantine coins* (Los Angeles, 1982); M.F. Hendy, *Studies in the Byzantine monetary economy c. 300-1450* (Cambridge, 1985); C. Morrisson, 'Byzantine money: its production and circulation', in *The economic history of Byzantium* ed. A. Laiou (Dumbarton Oaks Studies 39; Washington D.C. 2002), pp. 909-966.

Mediterranean objects might well originate in the *western* Mediterranean area (that is, Italy and/or the western Balkans). So, the notion of direct contacts between the Germanic leaders in the West and the Emperor in Constantinople receives little support in the archaeological evidence – or in the written sources, insofar as diplomatic legations between the empires are not often recorded.[42] Incidentally, this situation puts the eastern Mediterranean pottery evidence from Britain into sharp relief, for analogous pottery only reached Lyon (for example) (Fig. 7) as late as the sixth and seventh centuries, whereas in Britain it is found in fifth and sixth century contexts.[43] As we shall now see, different factors seem to have been at work in the second part of the Merovingian period.

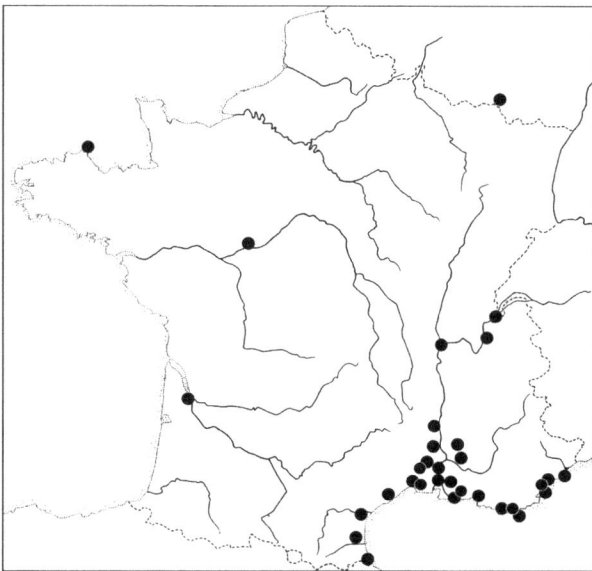

Fig. 7: **Find spots of Eastern Mediterranean amphorae in Gaul, 5th-7th century (after Bonifay/Villedieu 1989, 41, fig. 17.**

Sixth- and seventh-century 'Byzantine' finds in the Merovingian Empire

Coins

After c. 530, the range and distribution of 'Byzantine' finds in the Merovingian kingdom alters substantially. Byzantine coins are well represented in the archaeological record (Fig. 6), although their quantity

decreases after an absolute high point under Justinian I – mainly *siliquae* of Italian mints, which are found almost exclusively in the Austrasian part of the Frankish kingdom – until the last coinages of Justinian II (685-695/705-711).[44] The enormous output of coins under Justinian I is reflected in the Byzantine archaeological record, as is the concomitant decline in coinage in the seventh century, and so the Merovingian finds seem to reflect this same pattern.

Buckles

'Byzantine' buckles continue to be found in Merovingian contexts in the second part of our period. Much work has been undertaken on this assemblage and, like those buckles found in earlier Merovingian contexts, they have no single point of origin. One can find examples which almost certainly originate in the eastern Mediterranean area, examples which can be connected with workshops in Pannonia, the Balkans, Italy and/or the western Mediterranean, as well as examples which represent local imitations of imported buckles.

A detailed look at a few examples from Austrasia starts to bring clarity to this picture. A group of belt-buckles with firmly-executed, partly pierced-work fittings can now be dated primarily to the second third of the sixth century with a few later examples.[45] For most of these, parallels can be found in the Mediterranean area, mainly in Italy and/or Spain, although there are also a few parallels from further east, at sites in Slovenia and Hungary. It would seem that the western, rather than eastern, Mediterranean area must be seen as the point of origin for most of these buckles, primarily Italy and/or the Adriatic area.[46] Experiments on two buckles from the cemetery of Bopfingen, Ostalbkreis (Baden-Württemberg, Germany) appear to confirm this, suggesting that it was likely that Ossia-Sepia shells were used as moulds.[47]

'Sucidava'-type buckles (after J. Werner and/or D1 after M. Schulze-Dörrlamm) also belong to the sixth century.

[42] G. Wolf, 'Fränkisch-byzantinische Gesandtschaften vom 5. bis 8. Jahrhundert und die Rolle des Papsttums im 8. Jahrhundert', *Archiv für Diplomatik* 37 (1991): 1-13.

[43] Britain: Harris, pp. 143 ff. fig. 44; M. Bonifay and F. Villedieu, 'Importations d'amphores orientales en Gaule (Vᵉ-VIIᵉ siècles)', in *Recherches sur la céramique byzantine.*, eds. V. Déroche and J.-M. Spieser (Kolloquium Athen 1987; Bulletin de correspondance hellénique, Suppl. 18; Athens, 1989), pp. 17-46; C. Citter et al., 'Commerci nel Mediterraneo occidentale nell'Alto Medioevo', in *Early Medieval towns in the western Mediterranean. Kongress Ravello 1994*, ed. G. P. Brogiolo (Documenti di archeologia 10; Mantova, 1996), pp. 121-137.

[44] J. Drauschke, *Zwischen Handel und Geschenk – Studien zur Distribution von Waren im östlichen Merowingerreich des 6. und 7. Jahrhunderts anhand orientalischer und lokaler Produkte* (Unveröffentlichte Dissertation Freiburg, 2005), p. 117; similar in the Avaria: P. Somogyi, *Byzantinische Fundmünzen der Awarenzeit* (Monographien zur Frühgeschichte und Mittelalterarchäologie 5; Innsbruck, 1997). I would like to thank J. F. Fischer for permission to use the catalogue of his unpublished PhD thesis on coins in the Merovingian Empire.

[45] G. Fingerlin, 'Eine Schnalle mediterraner Form aus dem Reihengräberfeld von Güttingen, Ldkrs. Konstanz', *Badische Fundberichte*, 23 (1967): pp. 159-187.

[46] New finds: J. Boube, 'Eléments de ceinturon wisigothiques et byzantins trouvés au Maroc', *Bulletin d'Archéologie Marocaine* 15 (1983/84): 281-296, esp. 284-288 pl. I. 1-2; E. Riemer, 'Byzantinische Gürtelschnallen aus der Sammlung Diergardt im Römisch-Germanischen Museum Köln', *Kölner Jahrbuch für Vor- und Frühgeschichte* 28 (1995): 777-809, esp. 791 ff.

[47] R.-D. Blumer and M. Knaut, 'Zum Edelmetallguß in Ossia-Sepia-Formen im Frühmittelalter', *Fundberichte aus Baden-Württemberg* 16 (1991): 545-553.

The distribution of these buckles in the western Merovingian kingdom has not changed radically since their first mapping, and M. Schulze Schulze-Dörrlamm's distribution maps indicate that, in total, only eight examples have been found here. Individual finds are now also known in southern France, northern Italy and Asia Minor, but the numerous new finds in the lower Danube area suggests that this was their main area of circulation. It is not clear where they were produced, but the north-eastern Mediterranean area and the lower Danube region remain strong possibilities.[48]

'Syracus' buckles (after J. Werner and/or D12 after M. Schulze-Dörrlamm) are dated from the late-sixth to the middle and/or the third quarter of the seventh century and have a distribution with a different centre of gravity. They are unknown in France and there are only isolated finds in the lower Danube region. There is, however, a more intensive distribution in south-eastern England, Spain, Italy and the northern Adriatic, North Africa and Egypt, as well as Asia Minor, Greece, and on the Crimea.[49] Not all buckles of the Syracus type can be attributed to eastern Mediterranean workshops: on the contrary, some variants seem to be of a western Mediterranean origin.[50]

Other buckle forms which have sometimes been described as 'Byzantine' are found predominantly in the area of the north-west Balkans,[51] but it is more appropriate to characterize these as representatives of the 'Pannonian' types Pécs, Nagyharsány and Boly Želovce.[52] It is negligible, of course, to ask whether workshops on the border with the Byzantine Empire were responsible for their production or whether the craftsmen remained in Pannonia, and continued to work under the new Avar rulers.[53] One such example is the bronze buckle found in grave 114B at Harting (Bavaria, Germany). This is a Boly Želovce-type buckle – its pierced-work fitting can be compared with examples from Pécs-Gyárváros and Keszthely.[54]

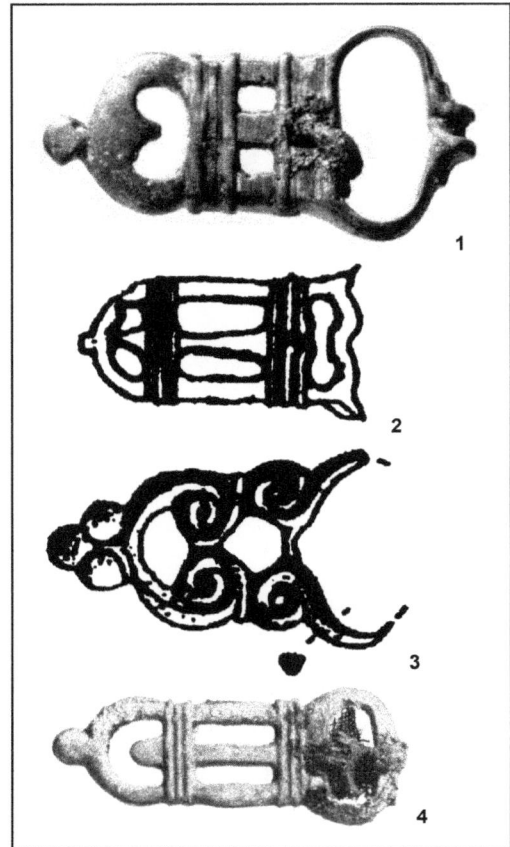

Fig. 8: 'Pannonian-byzantine' buckles from the Bavarian region:
1. Linz-Zizlau (Austria) grave 151 (Ladenbauer-Orel, *Linz-Zizlau – Das baierische Gräberfeld an der Traunmündung*, pl. 29), 2: Feldkirchen (Germany) grave 35, 3: Salzburghofen (Germany) grave 178 (Knöchlein, *Studien zur Archäologie der Merowingerzeit im Rupertiwinkel*, pl. 20A,2; 36A,2), 4: Weihmörting (Germany) grave 91 (Zeiß, 'Das Reihengräberfeld von Weihmörting', pl. 4,16).

Grave 151 at Linz-Zizlau (Oberösterreich, Austria) yielded a bronze belt-buckle with firm pierced-work (Fig. 8.1), which has been classified as a Pécs-type buckle[55], and there are analogous buckles from Salzburg-Liefering (Austria)[56], from grave 35 at Feldkirchen (Bavaria, Germany)[57] as well as from grave 91 at Weihmörting

[48] J. Werner, 'Byzantinische Gürtelschnallen des 6. und 7. Jahrhunderts aus der Sammlung Diergardt', *Kölner Jahrbuch für Ur- und Frühgeschichte* 1 (1955): 36-48, esp. 37 and map I; Schulze-Dörrlamm, *Byzantinische Gürtelschnallen und Gürtelbeschläge*, pp. 146-151 fig. 54.

[49] Werner, 'Byzantinische Gürtelschnallen des 6. und 7. Jahrhunderts aus der Sammlung Diergardt', p. 36 fig. 2, map 1; Schulze-Dörrlamm, *Byzantinische Gürtelschnallen und Gürtelbeschläge*, pp. 171-179 fig. 62. Recent collection: M. Kadıoğlu and Ph. v. Rummel, 'Frühbyzantinische Bronzefunde aus dem Theater von Nysa am Mäander', *Anadolu / Anatolia* 24, (2003): 103-114, esp. 110-113, list 1, fig. 13. New finds can be added from Kalavasos (*Kopetra*), Cyprus: M. Rautmann, *A Cypriot village of Late Antiquity. Kalavasos-Kopetra in the Vasiliskos Valley* (Journal of Roman Archaeology, Suppl. Ser. 52; Portsmouth, 2003), p. 108 no. II-19-1, fig. 3.41; and also from Poland: M. Wołoszyn, 'Die byzantinischen Fundstücke in Polen. Ausgewählte Probleme', in *Byzantium and East Central Europe*, eds. G. Prinzing and M. Salamon (Symposium Krakau 2000. Byzantina et Slavica Cracoviensia 3; Kraków, 2001), pp. 49-59, esp. 52 f. fig. 2.

[50] Ch. Eger, 'Eine byzantinische Gürtelschnalle von der Krim in der Sammlung des Hamburger Museums für Archäologie', in *Materiali po archeologii Istorii i Etnografii Taurii V* (Simferopol, 1996), pp. 343-348.

[51] D. Csallány, 'Les monuments de l'industrie byzantine des métaux II', *Acta Antiqua Academiae Scientiarum Hungaricae* 4 (1956): 261-291.

[52] V. Varsik, 'Byzantinische Gürtelschnallen im mittleren und unteren Donauraum im 6. und 7. Jahrhundert', *Slovenská Archeológia* 40, 1 (1992): 77-108; U. Ibler, 'Pannonische Gürtelschnallen des späten 6. und 7. Jahrhunderts', *Arheološki Vestnik* 43 (1992): 135-148.

[53] Garam, p. 108; Ibler, 'Pannonische Gürtelschnallen', p. 138.

[54] E. Wintergerst, *Neue reihengräberzeitliche Funde aus der Umgebung von Regensburg* (Dissertation, University of Bamberg, 1996), pp. 69-70 pl. 34.3. Ibler, 'Pannonische Gürtelschnallen', fig. 3.3.16.

[55] H. Ladenbauer-Orel, *Linz-Zizlau - Das baierische Gräberfeld an der Traunmündung* (Vienna and Munich, 1960), p. 60, pl. 15.

[56] Ibler, 'Pannonische Gürtelschnallen', p. 145 no. 13.

[57] R. Knöchlein, *Studien zur Archäologie der Merowingerzeit im Rupertiwinkel* (Dissertation, University of Munich, 1991), pl. 36A.2.

(Bavaria, Germany) (Fig. 8.2.4).[58] The best parallels for the bronze buckle with firm, pierced-work fitting from grave 178 of Salzburghofen (Bavaria, Germany)[59] (Fig. 8.3) can be seen amongst the range of the Nagyharsány-type buckles – for example, those from Kruje or Gyód.[60] A very similar buckle was recently discovered in grave 205 at Straubing-Alburg (Bavaria, Germany).[61] Altogether, 'Pannonian' buckles are concentrated more strongly in the southeastern-most region of the Merovingian Empire (that is, Bavaria), which is not surprising, in view of its proximity to the area of their apparent manufacture.

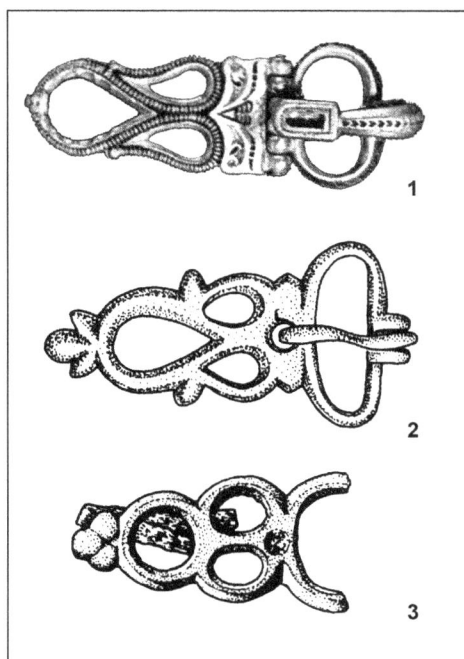

Fig. 9. 1: Golden buckle from the treasure of Mytilene (Lesbos/Greece) (Yeroulanou, 'Jewellery in the Byzantine World', p. 290 fig. 207); 9.2: Bronze buckle from Pécs (Hungary) grave 7 (Garam, pl. 64,6); 9.3: Bronze buckle from Aubing, city of Munich (Germany) grave 657 (Dannheimer, *Das baiuwarische Reihengräberfeld von Aubing, Stadt München*, pl. 67,I5).

Various imitation 'Byzantine' buckles have been found in the region north of the Alps. These include square double-buckles and buckles of the type Syracus/D 12.[62] It would seem that knowledge of Byzantine forms was spreading into Central and Western Europe in the early sixth century. Interestingly, this can be reconstructed with the help of a different type of buckle: one pierced-work gold buckle was found in the treasure trove of Mytilene on Lesbos (Fig. 9.1).[63] Almost identical pieces are also known from Avar sites (Fig. 9.2) – some of these are produced on a larger scale and some are simple bronze buckles.[64] Both can be described as 'Nagyharsány'-type buckles. Finally, in the west of the region, there are more imitation 'Byzantine' buckles, which G. Zeller categorised as 'Schwabsburg'-type.[65] Some of these can be further classified into a type that is an imitation of the 'Pannonian' type, 'Nagyharsány' (Fig. 9.3).[66]

More examples could be cited here, and a discussion of the origin and distribution of belt sets would be a useful line of further research. However, on the basis of the above analysis it is already clear that it is far too simplistic to refer simply to 'Byzantine' buckles, for they are likely to derive from several different geographical regions.[67] Yet, it is also clear that there *are* imported buckles from the Mediterranean area and the Byzantine world, in particular. Sites in the eastern Merovingian kingdom are more likely to show these connections than sites in the western part of the kingdom.[68]

[58] H. Zeiß, 'Das Reihengräberfeld von Weihmörting, B.-A. Passau', *Bayerische Vorgeschichtsblätter* 12 (1934): 21-41, pl. 4.16.

[59] Knöchlein, p. 57, pl. 20A.2.

[60] Varsik, 'Byzantinische Gürtelschnallen im mittleren und unteren Donauraum im 6. und 7. Jahrhundert', p. 103 pl. 5.3; Schulze-Dörrlamm, *Byzantinische Gürtelschnallen und Gürtelbeschläge*, p. 228, fig. 84.8.

[61] S. Möslein, 'Ein weiteres frühmittelalterliches Gräberfeld von Alburg', *Das Archäologische Jahr in Bayern* (2000): 99-102, fig. 100.

[62] Schulze-Dörrlamm, *Byzantinische Gürtelschnallen und Gürtelbeschläge*, pp. 31-33 fig. 12. and buckles of the type Syracus/D 12. G. Zeller, *Die fränkischen Altertümer des nördlichen Rheinhessen* (Germanische Denkmäler der Völkerwanderungszeit B 15; Stuttgart, 1992), pl. 69,5; H. Dannheimer, *Das baiuwarische Reihengräberfeld*

von Aubing, Stadt München (Monographien der Prähistorischen Staatssammlung München 1; Stuttgart, 1998), p. 102, pl. 19B.6.

[63] A. Yeroulanou, 'Jewellery in the Byzantine World', in *Greek Jewellery from the Benaki Museum Collections* ed. E. Georgoula (Athens, 1999), pp. 280-295, esp. 290 fig. 207.

[64] Garam, pl. 64; 65, 1-4.

[65] G. Zeller, 'Das fränkische Gräberfeld von Hahnheim', *Mainzer Zeitschrift* 67/68 (1972/73): 330-367, esp. 341 f., note 77.

[66] Dillingen (Bavaria, Germany): Th. Kersting, *Besiedlungsgeschichte des frühen Mittelalters im nördlichen Bayerisch-Schwaben* (Beiträge zur Ur- und Frühgeschichte Mitteleuropas 24; Weissbach, 2000), pp. 37-38 pl. 17A.6. Östringen-Odenheim (Baden-Württemberg, Germany), grave 8: *Badische Fundberichte* 17 (1941-47), pl. 89,9. München-Aubing (Bavaria, Germany) grave 657: Dannheimer, *Das baiuwarische Reihengräberfeld von Aubing, Stadt München*, p. 166 pl. 67. Mannheim-Straßenheim (Baden-Württemberg, Germany) grave 84: (pers. comm. Dr. U. Koch). Eltville (Hessen, Germany) grave 558: (pers. comm. Dr. M. C. Blaich). Edingen, Gde. Edingen-Neckarhausen (Baden-Württemberg, Germany): (pers. comm. Prof. Dr. G. Fingerlin). Gießen and environment (Hessen, Germany): H. Zeiß, 'Hessische Brandbestattungen der jüngeren Merowingerzeit', *Germania* 18 (1934): 279-284, esp. 281, fig. 1,4. Schwabsburg: Zeller, *Die fränkischen Altertümer des nördlichen Rheinhessen*, pl. 69.12.

[67] Drauschke, *Zwischen Handel und Geschenk*, pp. 133 ff.

[68] A discussion of origin and distribution of belt sets with many pieces would lead to far now, see for example: J. Werner, 'Nomadische Gürtel bei Persern, Byzantinern und Langobarden', in *La Civiltà dei Longobardi in Europa*, eds. E. Cerulli et al. (Kongress Rom und Cividale dei Friuli 1971. Problemi attuali di Scienza e di Cultura 189; Roma, 1974), pp. 109-139; Bálint, 'Byzantinisches zur Herkunftsfrage des vielteiligen Gürtels'; M. Schmauder, ,Vielteilige Gürtelgarnituren des 6.-7. Jahrhunderts: Herkunft, Aufkommen und Trägerkreis', in *Die Awaren am Rand der byzantinischen Welt*, ed. F. Daim (Monographien zur Frühgeschichte und Mittelalterarchäologie 7; Innsbruck, 2000), pp. 15-44.

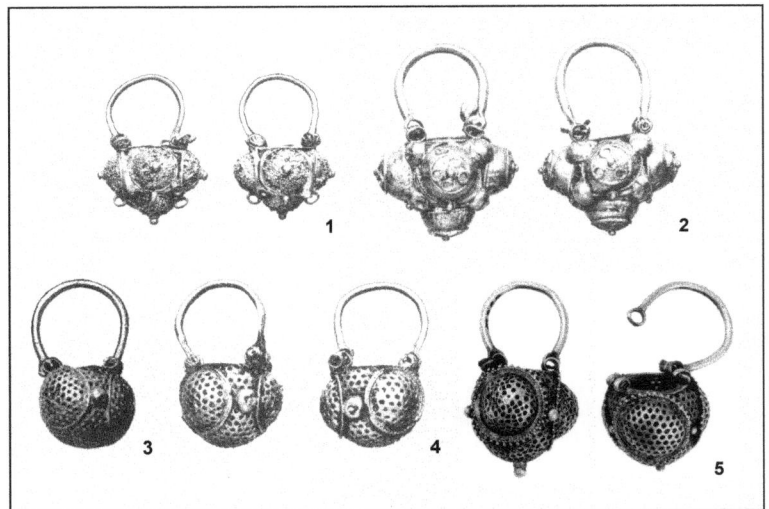

Fig. 10: Basket earrings from the eastern Mediterranean region. 1, 2 and 4: Benaki Museum Athens (Segall, *Katalog der Goldschmiede-Arbeiten*, pl. 50,234.235.237); 3: Egyptian Museum Cairo; 5: British Museum London (Yeroulanou, *Diatrita. Gold pierced-work jewellery from the 3rd to the 7th century*, p. 278 no. 463 and 464).

Earrings

Typically 'Byzantine' basket earrings, as well as four pairs of golden lunate-shaped earrings, have been found in burials of the region in question.[69] Parallels from the Mediterranean and the Balkan area as well as from museum collections, show that basket earrings with pierced-work baskets have a distribution confined to Italy, former-Yugoslavia and the Carpathian Basin.[70] By contrast, earrings with closed, bag-shaped baskets are also known from fifth-century contexts in Bulgaria and sixth-century contexts in Macedonia.[71] Very few basket earrings have been found in the core area of the Byzantine Empire. They cover the period from the third to the eleventh century.

In view of the fact that few examples have been published, further conclusions are difficult at this stage, but it is possible to distinguish between earrings composed of a central cube with four to six fastened hemispheric bowls and/or baskets[72] (presumably partly affected by Arab style) which can be dated to the middle Byzantine period and those earrings worked from three, usually pierced-work, hemispheric bowls/baskets (Fig. 10).[73] At the moment, because of a lack of stratified contexts, a precise date between the third and seventh century cannot be identified. Golden lunate earrings are well-known from the eastern Mediterranean area, but the fact that parallels cannot be made for all pieces from the region north of the Alps, suggests that not all of the earrings have a Byzantine provenance.[74]

[69] Basket earrings: G. Fingerlin, 'Imitationsformen byzantinischer Körbchen-Ohrringe nördlich der Alpen. Fundberichte aus Baden-Württemberg', 1 (1974): 597-627; E. Riemer, 'Byzantinische Körbchen- und Halbmondohrringe im Römisch-Germanischen Museum Köln (Sammlung Diergardt)', *Kölner Jahrbuch für Vor- und Frühgeschichte* 25 (1992): 121-136; Drauschke, *Zwischen Handel und Geschenk*, pp. 170 ff. Lunate-shaped earrings: Feldkirchen (Bavaria, Germany) grave 79: Knöchlein, *Studien zur Archäologie der Merowingerzeit im Rupertiwinkel*, p. 176 pl. 38F, 3-4. Linz-Zizlau (Austria) grave 83: H. Ladenbauer-Orel, *Linz-Zizlau – Das baierische Gräberfeld an der Traunmündung*, pp. 46-47, pl. 7.9; 22, 44. Petting (Bavaria, Germany) grave 99, pair with one Mediterranean original and one copy: D. Reimann, 'Byzantinisches aus dem Rupertiwinkel – zum Ohrringpaar von Petting', *Das Archäologische Jahr in Bayern* (1991): 143-145, fig. 113. Steinhöring (Bavaria, Germany) grave 11: S. Arnold, *Das bajuwarische Reihengräberfeld von Steinhöring, Landkreis Ebersberg* (Charybdis 5; Hamburg, 1992), pp. 154 f. fig. 1; pl. 4.2-3.

[70] Italy: E. Possenti, *Gli orecchini a cestello Altomedievali in Italia* (Ricerche Archeologia Altomedievale e Medievale 21; Florence, 1994); E. Riemer, *Romanische Grabfunde des 5. - 8. Jahrhunderts in Italien* (Internationale Archäologie 57; Rahden/Westf., 2000), pp. 45 ff. For former-Yugoslavia: J. Kastelič, 'Les boucles d'oreilles à corbeille en Slovenie', *Archaeologia Iugoslavica* 2 (1956): 119-129; Z. Vinski, 'Körbchenohrringe aus Kroatien', in *Die Wiener Schule der Völkerkunde. Festschrift des Instituts für Völkerkunde Wien 1929-1954*, eds. J. Haekel et al. (Vienna, 1956), pp. 564-568; U. Ibler, *Studien zum Kontinuitätsproblem am Übergang von der Antike zum Mittelalter in Nord- und Westjugoslawien* (Dissertation, University of Bonn, 1990), pp. 44 ff. For the Carpathian Basin: Garam, pp. 15-18, pl. 1-2.

[71] Riemer, *Romanische Grabfunde des 5. - 8. Jahrhunderts in Italien*, p. 61, fig. 9c. I. Mikulčić, *Spätantike und frühbyzantinische Befestigungen in Nordmakedonien: Städte, Vici, Refugien, Kastelle* (Veröffentlichungen der Kommission zur vergleichenden Archäologie römischer Alpen- und Donauländer / Münchner Beiträge zur Vor- und Frühgeschichte 54; Munich, 2002), fig. 193; 280, 1–3.

[72] Examples are known from Saraçhane, Istanbul: R.M. Harrison, *Excavations at Saraçhane in Istanbul I* (Princeton, 1986), p. 267 no. 597; and possibly Ephesus: *Collection H. Stathatos III: Objets antiques et byzantins* (Strasbourg, 1963), p. 287 no. 220, as well as from the collections of the Archäologische Staatssammlung München: L. Wamser and G. Zahlhaas (eds.), *Rom und Byzanz. Archäologische Kostbarkeiten aus Bayern. Ausstellungskatalog München 1998-99* (Munich, 1998), 192 f. no. 268; and the Benaki Museum, Athens: B. Segall, *Katalog der Goldschmiede-Arbeiten. Benaki Museum Athens* (Athens, 1938), pp. 152 f. no. 234 f., pl. 50.

[73] Possible examples are known from Asia Minor: E. Hoogendijk, 'Byzantine earrings from the Collection of the Rijksmuseum van Oudheiden in Leiden', *Oudheidkunde Mededelingen* (1994): pp. 139-151, 141 f. fig. 3. Also from the collections of the Benaki Museum, Athens: Segall, *Katalog der Goldschmiede-Arbeiten*, p. 153, no. 237; 160 no. 252, pl. 50. Also from the British Museum: A. Yeroulanou, *Diatrita. Gold pierced-work jewellery from the 3rd to the 7th century* (Athens, 1999), p. 278 no. 464.

[74] I. Baldini, 'Gli orecchini a corpo semilunato: classificazione tipologica', *Corso di Cultura sull'Arte Ravennate e Bizantina* 18 (1991): 67-101; I. Baldini Lippolis, *L'oreficeria nell'Impero di Constantinopoli tra IV e VII secolo* (Bibliotheca Archaeologica 7; Bari 1999), pp. 103 ff. no. 2.II.7 ff.; Yeroulanou, *Diatrita. Gold pierced-work jewellery from the 3rd to the 7th century*, pp. 279 ff. no. 475 ff.; Riemer, *Romanische Grabfunde des 5. - 8. Jahrhunderts in Italien*, p. 67, list 1.

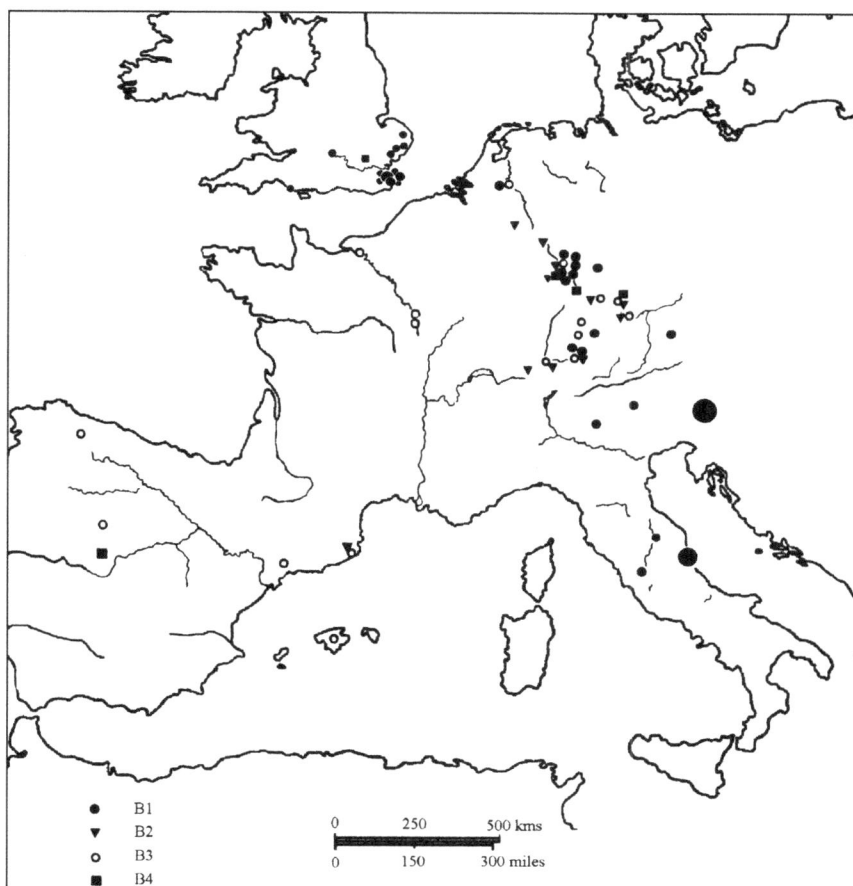

Fig. 11: Find spots of Mediterranean cast bronze vessels, type B (after Harris, p. 67 fig. 14).

Brooches

Byzantine brooches, imitation or otherwise, are nearly unknown in north-west Europe during this period. Among the few pieces, which mainly originate from the Mediterranean area, are two disk brooches found in burial 38 at Güttingen (Baden-Württemberg, Germany) and a square jewel brooch from grave 403 at Mengen (Baden-Württemberg, Germany).[75] They were reworked (perhaps north of the Alps) and were only secondary used as brooches.

Pectoral cross

A silver pectoral cross from grave 15 in Friedberg (Bavaria, Germany) is equally rare in having 'Byzantine' parallels. This is dated to the third quarter of the seventh century. It possesses numerous parallels from the

Mediterranean area, where such crosses are usually dated from the sixth to early-seventh centuries.[76]

Bronze vessels

So-called 'Coptic' cast bronze vessels represent the largest group of Mediterranean vessels in north-west Europe. It has become generally accepted that they originate in the eastern Mediterranean, even if a production centre in the western Mediterranean area cannot be excluded for some types.[77] Since P. Périn

---

[75] G. Fingerlin, *Grab einer adligen Frau aus Güttingen (Ldkrs. Konstanz)* (Badische Fundberichte, Sonderheft 4; Freiburg, 1964), pl. 2,1-2; 10,1.3; G. Fingerlin, *Die alamannischen Gräberfelder von Güttingen und Merdingen in Südbaden* (Germanische Denkmäler der Völkerwanderungszeit A 12; Berlin, 1971), pl. 18, 3-4. H. Zeiß, 'Die frühbyzantinische Fibel von Mengen, Ldkr. Freiburg i. Br.', *Germania* 23 (1939): 269-273; M. Egger, 'Das alamannische Gräberfeld von Mengen ('Hohle-Merzengraben')', in *FundMengen. Mengen im frühen Mittelalter* (Archäologische Informationen aus Baden-Württemberg 25; Stuttgart, 1994), pp. 55-69, fig. 41 and cover.

[76] H. Roth, 'Almandinhandel und -verarbeitung im Bereich des Mittelmeeres', *Beiträge zur Allgemeinen und Vergleichenden Archäologie* 2 (1980): 309-334, esp. 332 fig. 8; M. Trier, *Die frühmittelalterliche Besiedlung des unteren und mittleren Lechtals nach archäologischen Quellen* (Materialhefte zur Bayerischen Vorgeschichte A 84; Kallmünz/Opf., 2002), pp. 325 f. pl. 25.

[77] See: J. Werner, 'Italisches und koptisches Bronzegeschirr des 6. und 7. Jahrhunderts nordwärts der Alpen', in *Mnemosynon Theodor Wiegand*, eds. J. F. Crome et al. (Munich, 1938), pp. 74-86; J. Werner, 'Zwei gegossene koptische Bronzeflaschen aus Salona', *Zbornik Radova Posvećenik Michael Abramićiu I. Vjesnik za Arheologiju i Historiju Dalmatinsku* 56/59 (1954/57): 115-128. For discussion about places of production, see: H. Dannheimer, 'Zur Herkunft der "koptischen" Bronzegefäße der Merowingerzeit', *Bayerische Vorgeschichtsblätter* 44 (1979): 123-147; H. Roth, 'Urcei alexandrini: Zur Herkunft gegossenen "koptischen" Buntmetallgeräts aufgrund von Schriftquellen', *Germania* 58 (1980): 156-161; K. Werz, '"Sogenanntes" koptisches Buntmetallgeschirr' (Konstanz, 2005), pp. 65 f.. M.C. Carretta, 'Il catalogo del vasellame bronzeo Italiano Altomedievale'

---

mapped the distribution of the vessels in the West, afew more have been found – for example vessels from Avar-controlled areas (Hungary) – but the general principles of the distribution have not changed (Fig. 11).[78]

Glass vessels

By contrast, 'Byzantine' glass vessels are scarce. Examples tend to comprise stemmed goblets with feet, which are found mainly in southern Germany and the Rhine country with only few find-spots further west.[79] They are likely to have been manufactured in Italy, probably at either Invillino (*Ibligo*), Torcello or Rome, where there were early medieval glass workshops.[80]

Pilgrim flasks

Pilgrim flasks (*ampullae*) were often used 'souvenirs' of pilgrimage, and are, therefore, unusual here insofar as they might reflect the presence of Westerners who had travelled to the eastern Mediterranean area and, even where this is not possible to establish, permit insights into contacts and relations between East and West. Three types of fourth- to seventh-century flask have been identified: flasks from the Menas sanctuary near Alexandria, flasks from the Holy Land and those from smaller sanctuaries in western Asia. In north-west Europe, *ampullae* are well-known, but nearly all of them come from museum collections and only few derive from secure archaeological contexts. As a result, using them as evidence for Byzantine contacts with the Merovingian kingdom is still problematical.[81]

Plant remains and textiles

One must not forget the evidence for exotic plants, such as clove or incense, although these occur in very small quantities in the archaeological record.[82] The same applies to textiles. Silk has been identified in a few archaeological contexts: for example, there is a silk cross from grave 62 at Oberflacht (Baden-Württemberg, Germany). There is also a silk garment from Chelles (France).[83] Cotton and gold braid, other textiles of possible eastern Mediterranean origin, are also very rarely found in archaeological contexts.[84] Nevertheless, as a result of progress in textile archaeology, some gold braid textiles combined with silk has been identified in recent years, and it is interesting that their number increases strongly in the second half of the seventh century, especially from high-status burials in the Austrasian part of the Frankish kingdom.[85] At present, it is still unclear whether those textiles arrived as 'finished products' from the eastern Mediterranean or whether silk materials were processed further west in Italy or even in the Merovingian Empire itself. However, future analyses may well be able to show which gold braid textiles can be reliably identified as eastern Mediterranean products.

(Ricerche di Archeologia altomedievale e medievale 4; Florence, 1982), pp. 11 f.; P. Périn, 'La vaisselle de bronze dite "copte" dans les royaumes romano-germaniques d'Occident. État des la question', *Antiquité Tardive* 13 (2005): 85-97.

[78] P. Périn, 'A propos des vases de bronze "coptes" du VIIᵉ siècle en Europe de l'ouest: le pichet de Bardouville (Seine-Maritime),' *Cahiers Archéologiques* 40 (1992): 35-50; E. Bárdos, '"Kopt" bronzedény a Zamárdi avar temetöböl', *Somogyi Múzeumok Közleményei* 9 (1992): 3-40; Drauschke, *Zwischen Handel und Geschenk*, pp. 440 ff., list 8.

[79] F. Damminger, *Die Merowingerzeit im südlichen Kraichgau und in den angrenzenden Landschaften* (Materialhefte zur Archäologie in Baden-Württemberg 61; Stuttgart, 2002), pp. 114-118, fig. 36, list 5.

[80] V. Bierbrauer, 'Invillino-Ibligo in Friaul I. Die römische Siedlung und das spätantik-frühmittelalterliche Castrum' (Münchner Beiträge zur Vor- und Frühgeschichte 33; Munich, 1987), pp. 285 f.; L. Leciejewicz et al., *Torcello. Scavi 1961-62* (Istituto Nazionale d'Archeologia e Storia dell'Arte Monografie 3; Rome, 1977), pp. 114 ff., fig. 108-111; M.S. Arena et al. (eds.), *Roma dall'Antichità al Medioevo. Archeologia e Storia* (Nel Museo Nazionale Romano Crypta Balbi; Rome and Milan, 2001), pp. 308-310, no. II.3.303-342.

[81] See Bangert, this volume. Also: Ch. Lambert and P. Pedemonte Demeglio, 'Ampolle devozionali ed itinerari di pellegrinaggio tra IV e VII secolo', *Antiquité Tardive* 2 (1994): 205-231; P. Linscheid, 'Untersuchungen zur Verbreitung von Menasampullen nördlich der Alpen', in *Akten des XII. Internationalen Kongresses für Christliche Archäologie, Bonn 1991*, eds. E. Dassmann and J. Engemann (Jahrbuch für Antike und Christentum, Ergänzungsband 20; Münster, 1995), pp. 982-986.

[82] For cloves and incense: Horbourg, Dép. Haut-Rhin (France), grave 4/1884: *Korrespondenzblatt der Westdeutschen Zeitschrift für Geschichte und Kunst* 4, 1 (1885): Nr. 2, Sp. 1-3. Köln St. Severin (Nordrhein-Westfalen, Germany) grave 217: O. Doppelfeld, 'Das fränkische Frauengrab unter dem Chor des Kölner Domes', *Germania* 38 (1960): 89-113, 111. Schleitheim, Kt. Schaffhausen (Switzerland) grave 637: Burzler et al., *Das frühmittelalterliche Schleitheim*. On the provenance of cloves and incense, see: J. Werner, *Das alamannische Fürstengrab von Wittislingen* (Münchner Beiträge zur Vor- und Frühgeschichte 2; Munich, 1950), p. 45; J.I. Miller, *The spice trade of the Roman Empire 29 B.C. to A.D. 641* (Oxford, 1969), pp. 48; 102-104; W.W. Müller, 's. v. Weihrauch', in *RE Supplbd.* 15 (Munich, 1978), Sp. 700-777; Schoch, in Burzler et al. *Das frühmittelalterliche Schleitheim*, pp. 285-288.

[83] A. Streiter and E. Weiland, 'Das seidene Aufnähkreuz aus Oberflacht. Gewebeanalyse und Musterrekonstruktion', in *Textilien aus Archäologie und Geschichte. Festschrift K. Tidow* eds. L. Bender Jørgensen et al. (Neumünster, 2003), pp. 142-147; J.-P. Laporte and R. Boyer (eds.), *Trésors de Chelles: Sépultures et Reliques de la Reine Bathilde et de l'Abesse Bertille* (Ausstellungskatalog Chelles 1991; Chelles 1991).

[84] Cotton was identified in a female grave at Bülach St. Laurentius, Kt. Zürich (Schweiz): H. Amrein et al., 'Neue Untersuchungen zum Frauengrab des 7. Jahrhunderts in der reformierten Kirche von Bülach (Kanton Zürich)', *Zeitschrift für Schweizerische Archäologie und Kunstgeschichte* 56 (1999): pp. 73-114, esp. 95 f. fig. 32-33. Gold braid textiles are known from Lauchheim "Wasserfurche", Ostalbkreis (Germany) grave 795: Stork; Ch. Raub and H. Weiss, 'Untersuchung von Resten der Goldfäden eines Brokatgewebes aus Lauchheim, Ostalbkreis, Gräberfeld "Wasserfurche", Grab 795', *Archäologische Ausgrabungen in Baden-Württemberg* (1994): pp. 217-220; A. Stauffer and F. Weisse, 'Ein frühmittelalterliches Goldgewebe aus Lauchheim', *Fundberichte aus Baden-Württemberg* 22, 1 (1998): 729-736.

[85] A. Bartel et al., 'Der Prachtmantel des Fürsten von Höbing. Textilarchäologische Untersuchungen zum Fürstengrab 143 von Großhöbing', *Bericht der Bayerischen Bodendenkmalpflege* 43/44 (2002/03): 229-249; A. Bartel, 'Die Goldbänder des Herrn aus Straubing-Alburg, Untersuchungen einer Beinbekleidung aus dem frühen Mittelalter', *Bericht der Bayerischen Bodendenkmalpflege* 43/44 (2002/03): 261-272.

Balances and weights

Balances and weights are important typical 'Byzantine' small finds, although they are not very frequently found in north-west Europe.[86] Precision balances of Mediterranean origin are known in Belgium and in England.[87] In Germany, however, apart from the weights from grave 75 at Singen (Baden-Württemberg, Germany) and tomb 6 at Klepsau (Baden-Württemberg, Germany), which are dated to the sixth century, most finds belong to the Migration Period or represent local imitations.[88]

'Oriental' finds of the sixth and seventh centuries

From the above discussion it would appear that Byzantine finds do not increase substantially in numbers as we move from the early Merovingian period into the sixth and seventh centuries. In fact, the western Mediterranean area, including the north-west Balkans, played a crucial role in the production of several categories of object sometimes referred to as 'Byzantine'. One might be tempted to suggest that there were only very sporadic or coincidental contacts with the eastern Mediterranean region.

However, this is not the case, as we see when we look at the relatively large group of artefacts that are not typically 'Byzantine', but which must have arrived in the West through the eastern Mediterranean area and/or the Byzantine Empire. These suggest very intensive relations between Western Europe and these areas until around 700. The provenance of these objects is to be located in all probability between north-east Africa and south Asia, on the basis of raw material deposits and scientific analyses.

The garnet ranks high among these objects. It was used in large quantities as a gemstone fitting for brooches and other jewellery, and derived from fifth- and sixth-century south-east India and Sri Lanka.[89] The distribution of garnet disk brooches alone shows how widespread the use of this gemstone was in Central and Western Europe.[90]

Cowrie shells also fall into this category. *Cypraea pantherina,* thought to have been carried as amulets, come from the Red Sea, while the *Cypraea tigris* type come from the Indian Ocean. Their distribution in Western Europe (Fig. 12) is similar to the red garnet.[91]

Ivory, another 'oriental' import, occurs in north-west Europe mainly as rings, which served on the continent as the 'enclosure rings' of ornamented bronze discs (Fig. 13). Yet, in Britain the bronze discs are missing and ivory rings are interpreted as components of bags.[92] Analyses of the material confirm that they are made of African elephant ivory, probably the tusks of savannah elephants.[93] That means that the elephant ivory found in Western Europe was probably imported from north-east Africa. A survey of ivory rings in southern Germany and adjacent regions showed a very dense distribution, which can only be explained by a heavy inflow of the material.[94]

Some beads found in Western Europe also have an 'oriental' provenance. Shells from the coasts of East Africa, the Red Sea or the eastern Mediterranean were the raw material for 'discoid beads', usually called 'mother-of-pearl-beads' because of their shining surface. They occur in Merovingian tombs of the seventh through to the

[86] H. Steuer, 'Gewichtsgeldwirtschaften im frühgeschichtlichen Europa', in *Untersuchungen zu Handel und Verkehr der vor- und frühgeschichtlichen Zeit in Mittel- und Nordeuropa IV. Der Handel der Karolinger- und Wikingerzeit. Kolloquien Göttingen 1980-83,* eds. K. Düwel et al. (Abhandlungen der Akademie der Wissenschaften Göttingen, Philologisch-Historische Klasse, 3. F. 156; Göttingen, 1987), pp. 405-527, esp. 432 note 105; 433 f. note 106; completion, see: H. Steuer, 'Spätrömische und byzantinische Gewichte in Südwestdeutschland', *Archäologische Nachrichten aus Baden* 43 (1990): 43-59.
[87] J. Breuer and J. Alenus-Lecerf, 'La boite a poids monetaires de Lutlommel', *Archaeologia Belgica,* 86 (1965): 103-116; see also the collection in: Steuer, 'Gewichtsgeldwirtschaften im frühgeschichtlichen Europa', p. 440, note 129.
[88] Steuer, 'Spätrömische und byzantinische Gewichte in Südwestdeutschland'.
[89] S. Van Roy and L. Vanhaeke, 'L'origine des grenats à l'époque mérovingienne', *Vie Archéologique* 48 (1997): 124-137; S. Greiff, 'Naturwissenschaftliche Untersuchungen zur Frage der Rohsteinquellen für frühmittelalterlichen Almandingranatschmuck rheinfränkischer Provenienz', *Jahrbuch des Römisch-Germanischen Zentralmuseum* 45, 2 (1998): 599-646; D. Quast and U. Schüssler, 'Mineralogische Untersuchungen zur Herkunft der Granate merowingerzeitlicher

Cloisonnéarbeiten', *Germania,* 78, 1 (2000): 75-96; P. Périn, 'Die Herkunft der im merowingischen Gallien gefundenen Granate. Neue chemische und mineralogische Analysen', in *Post-roman towns and trade in Europe, Byzantium and the Near-East, Konferenz Bad Homburg 2004. Abstracts,* ed. J. Henning (Frankfurt, 2004), pp. 76-78; for divergent results, see: F. Farges, 'Mineralogy of the Louvres merovingian garnet cloisonné jewellery: origins of the gems of the first kings of France', *The American Mineralogist* 83 (1998): 323-330.
[90] K. Vielitz, *Die Granatscheibenfibeln der Merowingerzeit* (Europe médiévale 3; Montagnac, 2003).
[91] A. v. d. Driesch, 'Tierärtliche Bestimmung von Fundstücken', in H. Geisler, *Das frühbairische Gräberfeld Straubing-Bajuwarenstraße I: Katalog der archäologischen Befunde und Funde* (Internationale Archäologie 30; Rahden/Westf., 1998), pp. 372-374; K. Banghard, 's. v. Kaurischnecke', in *Reallexikon der Germanischen Altertumskunde XVI* (Berlin and New York, 2000), pp. 344-347; K. Banghard, 'Kauris im merowingerzeitlichen Europa. Ein Beitrag zur frühmittelalterlichen Fernhandelsgeschichte', *Münstersche Beiträge zur antiken Handelsgeschichte* 20, 1 (2001): 15-21.
[92] D. Renner, *Die durchbrochenen Zierscheiben der Merowingerzeit,* (Kataloge vor- und frühgeschichtlicher Altertümer 18; Mainz 1970); J.W. Huggett, 'Imported grave goods and the early Anglo-Saxon economy', *Medieval Archaeology* 32 (1988): 63-96, esp. 69, fig. 3; Harris, p. 174, fig. 61; C. Hills, 'From Isidore to isotopes: ivory rings in Early Medieval graves', in *Image and power in the archaeology of Early Medieval Britain. Festschrift R. Cramp,* eds. H. Hamerow and A. MacGregor (Oxford, 2001), pp. 131-146.
[93] J. Drauschke and A. Banerjee, 'Zur Identifikation, Herkunft und Verarbeitung von Elfenbein in der Merowingerzeit' *Archäologisches Korrespondenzblatt* 37, 1 (2007): 109-128.
[94] Drauschke, *Zwischen Handel und Geschenk,* 76 ff.

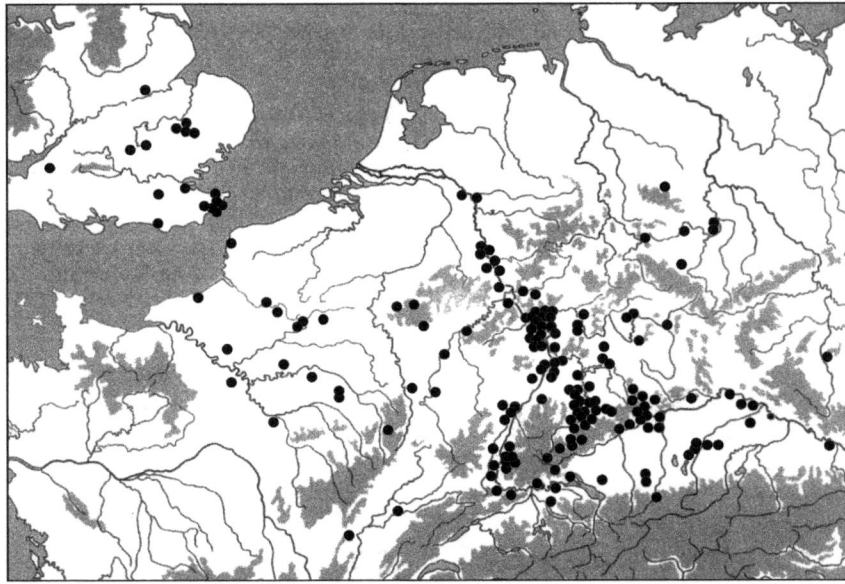

**Fig. 12: Distribution of Merovingian-period cowries
(after Banghard, 'Kauris im merowingerzeitlichen Europa', p. 346 fig. 32).**

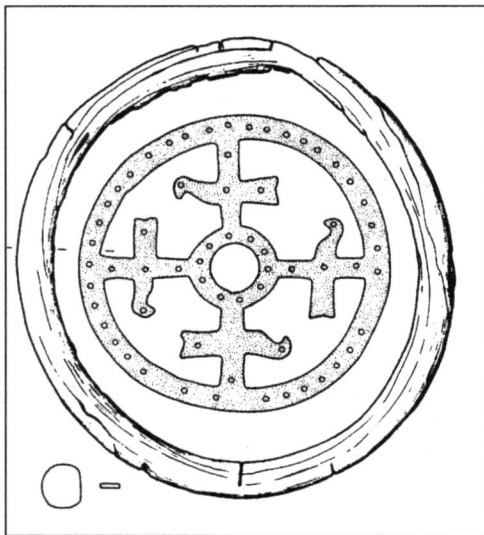

**Fig. 13: Bronze amulet disc with surrounding ring of
elephant ivory from Alburg, city of Straubing (Germany)
grave 500 (after Geisler, pl. 182, 13.14).**

beginning of the eighth century.[95] Numerous amethyst beads of the sixth and seventh century are also known from north-west Europe, although the source of the

amethyst deposits is not yet clear. South Asia or north-east Africa and/or regions around the eastern Mediterranean are all possibilities.[96] Given that there are numerous, almost identical finds of almond-shaped amethyst beads in the eastern Mediterranean area, which are found primarily on Byzantine necklaces, an 'oriental' provenance seems more convincing than an exploitation of Alpine deposits.[97]

The same applies to cylindrical beads made from sea foam, known from female graves of the second half of the fifth century to around 600.[98] The material has already been mentioned in association with early Merovingian belt buckles of Mediterranean origin (see above) and was also used – likewise in cylindrical form – for 'sword

---

[95] F. Siegmund and M. Weiß, 'Perlen aus Muschelscheibchen im merowingerzeitlichen Mitteleuropa', *Archäologisches Korrespondenzblatt* 19 (1989): 297-307; A. Lennartz, 'Muschelperlen – Perlmuttperlen – Schneckenperlen. Drei Namen für ein Phänomen?', in *Certamina Archaeologica. Festschrift H. Schnitzler*, eds. Ch. Keller et al. (Bonner Beiträge zur vor- und frühgeschichtlichen Archäologie 1; Bonn, 2000), pp. 191-202; for parallels from East Africa: M. Horton, *Shanga. The archaeology of a Muslim trading community on the coast of East Africa* (Memoirs of the British Institute in Eastern Africa 14; London 1996), p. 323, fig. 246, a-b.

[96] Drauschke, *Zwischen Handel und Geschenk*, 54 ff.

[97] For a Mediterranean (namely Italian) origin for these objects, see: J. Werner, *Münzdatierte austrasische Grabfunde*, (Germanische Denkmäler der Völkerwanderungszeit 3; Berlin and Leipzig, 1935), p. 75; R. Christlein, *Das alamannische Reihengräberfeld von Marktoberdorf im Allgäu* (Materialhefte zur Bayerischen Vorgeschichte 21; Kallmünz/Opf., 1966), p. 74 note 206; U. Koch, *Das Reihengräberfeld bei Schretzheim* (Germanische Denkmäler der Völkerwanderungszeit A 13; Berlin 1977), pp. 73 f.; U. Koch, *Das fränkische Gräberfeld von Klepsau im Hohenlohekreis* (Forschungen und Berichte zur Vor- und Frühgeschichte in Baden-Württemberg 38; Stuttgart, 1990), p. 124 note 44. For Byzantine parallels see, for example: Baldini Lippolis, pp. 134 ff. Nr. 1.c.

[98] For lists without differentiation of the raw material, see: A. Heege, *Grabfunde der Merowingerzeit aus Heidenheim-Großkuchen* (Materialhefte zur Vor- und Frühgeschichte in Baden-Württemberg 9; Stuttgart 1987), pp. 138 f. note 460; Ch. Grünewald, *Das alamannische Gräberfeld von Unterthürheim, Bayerisch-Schwaben* (Materialhefte zur Bayerischen Vorgeschichte A 59; Kallmünz/Opf., 1988), p. 118, note 90; R. Reiß, *Der merowingerzeitliche Reihengräberfriedhof von Westheim (Kreis Weißenburg-Gunzenhausen)* (Wissenschaftliche Beibände zum Anzeiger des Germanischen Nationalmuseums 10; Nürnberg, 1994), p. 105, note 170.

beads' of that date.[99] Their origin, or at least the origin of the raw material (sea foam/sepiolith), is probably to be looked for in the eastern Mediterranean area.[100]

Mention could also be made of further groups of objects, whose Mediterranean and/or 'Byzantine' origin is debated.[101] But the material presented here already suggests that the quantity and variety of goods transported from or through the eastern Mediterranean area to north-west Europe in the sixth and seventh century was very considerable and substantially greater than that of the fifth century. Therefore, we must assume continuing close relations between the Merovingian kingdom and the Mediterranean area. It is possible that the connection took place via southern France and Italy, for the evidence for direct connections with Constantinople is not compelling. Interestingly, the Central and Western European material discussed above points to a continuing inflow of material until at least about 700, which, it must be emphasised, is in contrast to the Mediterranean, where long-distance exchange is hardly recognisable in the archaeological record after the second half of the seventh century. Admittedly, the overall number of imports to Central and Western Europe strongly decreases in the second half of the seventh century, but it is hardly likely that these objects are all residual finds.

The 'Byzantine' nature of the Mediterranean finds

On the one hand, this evidence demonstrates a close relationship between the Byzantine-controlled eastern Mediterranean area and north-west Europe in the sixth and seventh centuries.[102] On the other hand, it has been demonstrated that some, apparently typical, 'Byzantine' artefacts are very likely to have been manufactured in the western Mediterranean and/or Italy or in the north-west Balkans, rather than in the 'core' area of the Byzantine world.

In order to reconcile these two findings it is clear that some differentiation needs to be applied to the term 'Byzantine'. To describe many of these finds simply as 'Byzantine' is unhelpful. Too often this term is primarily associated with the core area of the Byzantine Empire and the capital, Constantinople. As an indication of origin, this is not applicable for much of the material discussed here; moreover, it obstructs the view of the real reference systems, even if thereby the stylistic and typological relations of the individual artefacts are determined correctly.

It is, therefore, necessary to separate the stylistic and typological classification from the localisation of the probable workshops. This is because the definition of 'Byzantine' as a typological tool has developed very differently depending upon the material being discussed.[103] Besides, the now substantial progress made in research on early medieval Mediterranean products, means that reliable statements on a more or less representative material basis (depending upon the kinds of objects concerned) seem to be possible. Thus, the relationship between the distribution of Mediterranean objects and the localisation of workshops becomes more and more important. The criterion canon should be supplemented by technical-scientific investigations, which give, on the one hand, information about the raw materials used (including their provenance) and which could, on the other hand, illuminate procedures relating to manufacture, from which one can draw conclusions about the environment of origin. For example, F. Daim was recently able to identify belt types of 'Byzantine' production amongst eighth-century belts in the Avar Khanate, on the basis of a sharply defined catalogue of criteria, in which technical analyses took a central place.[104]

The stylistic development of a type, which is always a mirror of contemporary ideas about the 'correct' appearance of an object, permits an opportunity to make statements about cultural traditions standing behind that development. The distribution of the type enables us to supplement these statements, although they need not always be congruent. So, for example, typologically 'Byzantine' finds are often more frequently found outside the Byzantine Empire's borders than within them. This is sometimes a function of different cultural practices – for

---

[99] For lists without differentiation of the raw material, see: J. Werner, *Beiträge zur Archäologie des Attila-Reiches* (Abhandlungen der Bayerischen Akademie der Wissenschaften, Philosophisch-Historische Klasse, N. F. 38 A; Munich, 1956), pp. 120-128 list IV, pl. 75, map 11; Menghin, pp. 356-357, list C1.d, map 19; J. Cseh et al., *Gepidische Gräberfelder im Theissgebiet II* (Monumenta Germanorum Archaeologica Hungariae 2: Monumenta Gepidica; Budapest, 2005), p. 174, fig. 33.

[100] For a description of the sea foam-material, see: M. Herdick, ,Meerschaum – ein fast vergessener Rohstoff in der Archäologie', *Anschnitt* 48, 1 (1996): 35-36; Herdick, 'Vom Mineral zum Prestigeobjekt'.

[101] For example, millefiori-beads: U. Koch, ,Mediterrane und fränkische Glasperlen des 6. und 7. Jahrhunderts aus Finnland', in *Studien zur vor- und frühgeschichtlichen Archäologie. Festschrift J. Werner*, eds. G. Kossack and G. Ulbert, (Münchner Beiträge zur Vor- und Frühgeschichte, Ergänzungsband I, 2; Munich, 1974), pp. 495-520; A. Volkmann and C. Theune, 'Merowingerzeitliche Millefioriperlen in Mitteleuropa', *Ethnographisch-Archäologische Zeitschrift* 42 (2001): 521-553; or weapons such as lances and arrowheads, as well as armaments: U. v. Freeden, 'Awarische Funde in Süddeutschland?', *Jahrbuch des Römisch-Germanischen Zentralmuseum*, 38, 2 (1991): 593-627; U. Koch, 'Der Ritt in die Ferne. Erfolgreiche Kriegszüge im Langobardenreich', in *Die Alamannen*, ed. Archäologisches Landesmuseum Baden-Württemberg (Stuttgart, 1997), pp. 403-415; R. Kory, 's. v. Schuppen- und Lamellenpanzer', in *Reallexikon der Germanischen Altertumskunde XXVI* (Berlin and New York, 2004), pp. 375-403.

[102] Roth, 'Handel und Gewerbe vom 6. bis 8. Jh.', p. 350; Drauschke, *Zwischen Handel und Geschenk*.

[103] For this discussion in relation to definitions of 'Byzantine' art see, for example: R. Warland, 's. v. Byzantinische Kunst', in *Lexikon für Theologie und Kirche 2* (Freiburg, 1994), Sp. 863-867; C. Mango, 'Introduction', in *The Oxford history of Byzantium*, ed. C. Mango (Oxford, 2002).

[104] Daim, 86 ff.

example, within the barbarian realms the furnishing of graves was practised extensively. Sometimes, as we have seen, it is because typically 'Byzantine' objects were also produced beyond the borders of the Byzantine Empire.

In view of possible inaccuracies in the identification of production sites in the overall Mediterranean area, it is advisable to use first the term 'Mediterranean' for the objects in question, and then to supplement this with 'eastern' (or 'western'), if possible.[105] If still more detailed information on provenance is available (for example, if an object derives from Italy, North Africa or the Balkan provinces), a further differentiation of the term 'Byzantine' could take place.[106] In the eastern Mediterranean, the 'core' area around Constantinople must be distinguished from the northern Black Sea area and from the Near Eastern provinces and Egypt. As shown above, the study of the fifth- to seventh-century material culture of the Mediterranean area has progressed to a point where such designations are already possible for some groups of artefacts.

The problem of how objects arrived in north-west Europe

Trade dominates most explanations of archaeological distributions, including those examined here. Yet, the structure and conditions of this trade are almost never described in detail, and neither is the possible migration of persons bringing the 'strange' goods to north-west Europe. The contemporary written sources must, of course, be analysed as a first approach to the problem of artefact distribution mechanisms in Merovingian times. Merchants are well-documented, meeting the cost of living by the purchase and sales of goods.[107] The written sources hint at other possible interpretations, but it must be kept in mind that they are – like archaeological sources – incomplete and contain little or no information about areas not actually mentioned within them, for example the regions to the east of the Rhine.[108]

Despite these limitations, there are a variety of possibilities by which the distribution could have been achieved according to written sources. D. Claude has summarised some of these, including robbery and war booty, mutual exchange between high-status clerics, aristocrats and other 'free' people, and donations by the Byzantine emperor to the Merovingian kings. Re-

distribution took place as well, sometimes in ecclesiastical contexts, sometimes as gifts made by kings and other nobles to subordinate social groups or individuals. An intensified circulation of goods within the seigneurial systems must also be understood as a form of re-distribution. The taxation and collection of tariffs may have led to a forced exchange, too.[109]

The shown mechanisms can be assigned without difficulty to the categories of redistribution, reciprocity and market exchange (including trade), which belong to a model widely accepted and applied within anthropological studies.[110] This classification (Fig. 14) can help in the examination of, for example, the mechanism of 'trade'. That is, 'trade' can be organised as barter or based on a monetary economy. Goods or services resulting from over-production, and considered to be of equal worth, are exchanged between partners or institutions either by paying a visit to the trade partner or by visiting the market place. Each person participating in the exchange acts according their own perceived advantage. This is much more important than the social meaning of exchange: the mere existence of professional or long-distance merchants is not a compelling condition for the existence of trade.[111]

This model explains the distribution of goods using the concept of exchange. However, objects could have been transported over long distances by individuals, not necessarily with any intention to distribute or to exchange them. This, of course, applies particularly to migrations or exogamous procedures, as well as by itinerant craftsmen (Fig. 14).

It is clear that trade cannot be used as the sole explanation for the importation of goods into the Merovingian kingdom. There are other mechanisms involved in the late antique and early medieval transportation of goods in the Mediterranean area. It is possible, too, that the state was responsible for some forms of long-distance exchange, and that distribution was the result of a so-called 'de-commercialized' economy, at least in its most

---

[105] This has already been implemented by Fingerlin, 'Eine Schnalle mediterraner Form'; Kazanski; Quast, 'Garnitures des ceintures méditerranéennes'.

[106] Garam, pp. 12-13.

[107] See the sources collected by Verhulst.

[108] H. Roth, 'Zum Handel der Merowingerzeit auf Grund ausgewählter archäologischer Quellen', in *Untersuchungen zu Handel und Verkehr der vor- und frühgeschichtlichen Zeit in Mittel- und Nordeuropa III. Der Handel des frühen Mittelalters. Kolloquien Göttingen 1980-1983*, eds. K. Düwel et al. (Abhandlungen der Akademie der Wissenschaften Göttingen, Philologisch-Historische Klasse, 3. F. 150; Göttingen 1985), pp. 161-192, 164-171 table 1.

[109] Claude, 'Aspekte des Binnenhandels im Merowingerreich auf Grund der Schriftquellen', pp. 10-14.

[110] U. Köhler, 'Formen des Handels aus ethnologischer Sicht', in *Untersuchungen zu Handel und Verkehr der vor- und frühgeschichtlichen Zeit in Mittel- und Nordeuropa I. Methodische Grundlagen und Darstellungen zum Handel in vorgeschichtlicher Zeit und in der Antike. Kolloquien Göttingen 1980-1983*, eds. K. Düwel et al. (Abhandlungen der Akademie der Wissenschaften Göttingen, Philologisch-Historische Klasse, 3. F. 143; Göttingen, 1985), pp. 13-55, esp. 16-22; J. Jensen, 'Wirtschaftsethnologie', in *Ethnologie. Einführung und Überblick*, eds. H. Fischer (3. Auflage Berlin and Hamburg 1992), pp. 119-147, 134-143; see also: C. Renfrew and P. Bahn, *Archaeology: theories, methods and practice* (London, 1991), p. 310.

[111] Köhler, 21 f.; Jensen, p. 141.

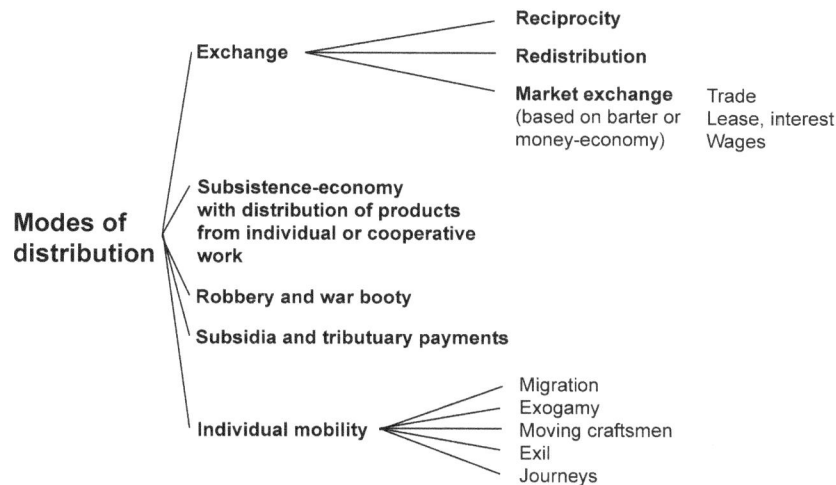

Fig. 14: Possible forms of distribution in accordance with anthropological models (with additions).

extreme form.[112] According to this model, the exchange of goods was mainly directed by the state, in the form of supplies (*annona*), and connections were principally between the estates of the church and the needs of the ruling elites. In this scenario, merchants would have acted merely as agents for the state.

However, it is important to remember that in complex, organised societies several exchange mechanisms can co-exist. In addition, it is necessary to distinguish between long-distance cross-Mediterranean contacts and regional markets, because whereas the former may have been driven by state intervention, the latter may have comprised money-based trade, which was dependent, to some extent, on supply and demand dynamics. It is not only conditions in the Mediterranean area which must be considered when seeking to explain the transfer of Mediterranean goods to north-west Europe, but economic circumstances within the Merovingian kingdom itself, particularly given that economic life was quite differently structured either side of the Rhine.[113]

It would seem that the two phases differentiated above were influenced by different transfer mechanisms, notwithstanding the groups of objects, their archaeological contexts and their chronological classification. The imports (whether from the eastern or western Mediterranean area) of earliest Merovingian times are dominated by very prestigious objects of high value and made of precious materials, which are particularly associated with high-status burials. It is not

surprisingly, therefore, that Mediterranean buckles, for example, led to many imitations. In view of this situation (and further evidence from grave-goods), it would appear that the individual mobility of people and personal contacts with the Mediterranean area were crucial for the transfer of goods from the south and east. Mercenaries could have acquired a buckle, a long and narrow *sax* or helmets when they served in the Byzantine army, for they are sometimes found together in one burial assemblage. Exceptional pieces, like the gilt-handled *spathae*, the Syrian glass flask from Bräunlingen, the numerous silver spoons or silk fabrics, give the impression of high-quality honours or gifts, although it remains questionable whether 'junior' leaders of the Germanic tribes were regarded as important enough to receive such allowances from the Byzantine Emperor. Perhaps not, and it must be noted here that objects deriving from Italy after the Ostrogothic conquest must probably be interpreted as gifts of the Ostrogothic rulers, rather than of the Byzantine court. Indeed, in view of the numerous Italian treasuries containing Byzantine silver spoons, it would be wrong not to include robbery and war booty as a 'transport factor'. Yet, within the Alamannic settlement range of south-western Germany, strong relationships with the middle Danube area can be seen, and these can be partly interpreted as indications of an influx of persons.[114]

A change in the variety of Mediterranean finds is clearly recognisable around 510-530. It is influenced by general developments in dress style of that time. Thus, the frequency of ivory rings occurring correlates to the custom of carrying ornamented bronze discs as amulets on a long ribbon as part of the female costume. Nevertheless, changes can be recognized, in my opinion, which are not related to changes in dress style. For

[112] See: C.R. Whittaker, 'Late Roman trade and traders', in *Trade in the ancient economy*, eds. P. Garnsey et al. (London, 1983), pp. 163-180. Similarly: P. Arthur, 'Eastern Mediterranean amphorae between 500 and 700: a view from Italy', in *Ceramica in Italia: VI-VII secolo. Kongress Rom 1995*, ed. L. Saguì (Florence, 1998), pp. 157-183.
[113] Roth, 'Zum Handel der Merowingerzeit auf Grund ausgewählter archäologischer Quellen', pp. 161 f.; H. Roth, 'Produktion und Erwerb von Edelmetallerzeugnissen', in *Festschrift für Otto-Herman Frey zum 65. Geburtstag*, ed. C. Dobiat (Marburger Studien zur Vor- und Frühgeschichte 16; Marburg 1994), pp. 517-522.

[114] D. Quast, 'Vom Einzelgrab zum Friedhof. Beginn der Reihengräbersitte im 5. Jahrhundert', in *Die Alamannen*, ed. Archäologisches Landesmuseum Baden-Württemberg (Stuttgart 1997), pp. 171-190; Quast, 'Auf der Suche nach fremden Männern'.

example, necklaces and/or beads, as well as ribbons, with amulets had been carried in early Merovingian times, too, but cowries and ivory rings, mother-of-pearl- and amethyst-beads are part of the archaeological record only after 510-530. Likewise, in some regions, bronze vessels are part of grave-good assemblages throughout the entire Merovingian period – however the cast bronze vessels of Mediterranean origin start to make frequent appearances in burials only around 600 and again in the middle of the seventh century. These changes might reflect new connections in the Mediterranean area opening up possibilities for the transport of new types of goods.

In contrast to the other categories of object examined in this paper, 'oriental' precious and prestigious objects actually increase during the later phase. Goods such as cowries, ivory rings, amethyst- or mother-of-pearl-beads are now found in larger quantities and are no longer components only of high-status graves, at least between about 570-580 and 670-680. Their vast geographical distribution is noteworthy. Given this, and given that we are concerned here with material which was not available in north-west Europe, it is likely that we are seeing a demand for these 'oriental' goods, which led to trade relations in the sense defined above. Moreover, in the western parts of the Frankish kingdom the effects of so-called 'privileged goods traffic' must be considered.[115] In other words, goods may have been transported over long distances without commercial activities (in a strict sense) being responsible.

It is not plausible that the 'oriental' goods are all a reflection of the activities of itinerant craftsmen, but they may comprise gifts and/or subsidies from the Byzantine Empire.[116] Booty taken in warfare is probably a preferable interpretation, particularly given that Frankish and Alamannic troops entered Italy several times during the course of the sixth century.[117] Yet, warfare cannot explain the chronologically, as well as geographically, constant distribution of Mediterranean and 'oriental' goods within the borders of the Merovingian kingdom as a whole. For this reason, it is necessary to differentiate the find material. The numerous items of Byzantine coins, Mediterranean jewellery and components of dress (earrings, brooches, pectoral cross, belt-buckles and exotic textiles) might have not been commodities in the sense of being traded items; for them the already mentioned alternatives are rather more satisfying explanations.

A further possibility is to understand the distribution of Mediterranean material as a consequence of the migration of distinct groups into the Frankish kingdom, especially during the sixth century.[118] However, this hypothesis cannot be proved at present. It is likely that some of the Mediterranean objects arrived into the eastern Merovingian kingdom in this way, but the proportion which might have done so is difficult to determine since the identification of different ethnic groups and 'strangers' in the archaeological record remains difficult.[119]

The Merovingian Empire – part of a globalized world?

In conclusion, we have seen that exchange mechanisms between the Mediterranean regions and the Merovingian kingdom can be seen in operation from the second half of the fifth century until the beginning of the eighth century. The archaeological sources suggest that the most important factors initially were inter-personal contacts, migration, gift-exchange and booty-taking, with trade becoming important later in the period. This relates well with the evidence from the Anglo-Saxon areas of Britain, where indirect trading relations appear to be responsible for the distribution of Mediterannean material (which

---

[115] The background for the so-called 'privileged' transport of goods were the attempts of Merovingian monasteries and churches to achieve a low-priced supply for their own requires, why they obtained privileges from the Merovingian kings such as those for St. Denis or Corbie. So-called *missi* accomplished the business and organized the transport from the Mediterranean ports in southern France to the north. D. Claude, 'Aspekte des Binnenhandels im Merowingerreich auf Grund der Schriftquellen', in *Untersuchungen zu Handel und Verkehr der vor- und frühgeschichtlichen Zeit in Mittel- und Nordeuropa III. Der Handel des frühen Mittelalters. Kolloquien Göttingen 1980-83*, eds. K. Düwel et al. (Abhandlungen der Akademie der Wissenschaften Göttingen, Philologisch-Historische Klasse, 3. F. 150; Göttingen, 1985), pp. 9-99, esp. 78 ff. A decrease of occupation merchants within the exchange of goods in the Merovingian Empire from the sixth to the seventh century is clearly visible. S. Lebecq, 'Les echanges dans la Gaule du Nord au VIᵉ siècle: une histoire en miettes' in *The sixth century. Production, distribution and demand*, eds. R. Hodges and W. Bowden (The Transformation of the Roman World 3; Leiden, 1998), pp. 185-202, esp. 190.

[116] For tributes paid to the Merovingian kings in 535, 571 and 578, see: E. Ewig, *Die Merowinger und das Frankenreich* (3. Auflage, Stuttgart, 1997), pp. 37; 43-45, or as tribute payments of the Lombard Kingdom paid in kind (for tributes paid between 591 and 618/19 see: U. Koch, 'Der Ritt in die Ferne', pp. 410 f.

[117] U. Koch, 'Mediterranes und langobardisches Kulturgut in Gräbern der älteren Merowingerzeit zwischen Main, Neckar und Rhein', in *Atti del 6° Congresso Internazionale di Studi sull'Alto Medioevo I. Mailand 1978* (Spoleto, 1980), pp. 107-121.

[118] The recent attempt by Graenert to interpret the archaeological record of southern material found in the Austrasian part of the Frankish kingdom as an effect of the migration of Lombard women is not convincing in every case. See: G. Graenert, 'Langobardinnen in Alamannien. Zur Interpretation mediterranen Sachgutes in südwestdeutschen Frauengräbern des ausgehenden 6. Jahrhunderts', *Germania* 78, 2 (2000): 417-447.

[119] This is not the place to engage in the debate, particularly vigorous in German Archaeology, on the extent to which ethnic groups can actually be distinguished in the archaeology of the Early Middle Ages. The different opinions are stated by: V. Bierbrauer, 'Zur ethnischen Interpretation in der frühgeschichtlichen Archäologie', in *Die Suche nach den Ursprüngen. Von der Bedeutung des frühen Mittelalters. Forschungen zur Geschichte des Mittelalters 8* ed. W. Pohl, (Österreichische Akademie der Wissenschaften, Philosophisch-Historische Klasse, Denkschriften, 322; Vienna, 2004), pp. 45-84; S. Brather, *Ethnische Interpretationen in der frühgeschichtlichen Archäologie*, (Geschichte, Grundlagen, Alternativen. Reallexikon der Germanischen Altertumskunde, Ergänzungsband, 42; Berlin and New York, 2004).

consists mainly of identical 'oriental' objects) during the same period.[120] This is important because the presence of the material in Britain (which cannot necessarily be explained as an effect of migration) is a clear indication of the importance of trade as a mechanism of exchange for the finds from the continent.

However, the volume of this trade cannot have been very extensive, since the relative quantities of goods are low in relation to the total assemblage of objects from Merovingian graves. The cast bronze vessels are the exception, rather than the rule. It seems very improbable that merchants travelled constantly over the Alps or along the Rhône, selling their goods within the borders of the Merovingian kingdom. It is hard to envisage them roaming from village to village ('Tröpfelhandel'), in order to exchange gemstones, cowries and ivory for the surplus products of Frankish rural activities. A more plausible explanation would take into account longer periods of time between the visits of merchants and search for their destination in urban settlements, particularly the markets of the western Frankish kingdom,

which were on the rise from the beginning of the seventh century onwards. In these areas, one might expect to obtain a good price and high demand for Mediterranean goods. The subsequent re-distribution of the objects from these central locations is an issue that cannot be discussed here, but which needs further research.[121]

From the general outline of contacts between the Merovingian kingdom and the Mediterranean world one can conclude that during this period Central and Western Europe were still a part of a 'globalised' (Byzantine-centred) world in a broad sense. But while contacts of the late fifth and sixth centuries seemed to have been more goal-directed – remembering the efforts of the Byzantine emperors to win the Frankish kings over to their side during the armed conflicts with Ostrogoths and Lombards in Italy – relations became less and less directional from the seventh century onwards, perhaps because the Byzantine Empire was busy with its own existential problems and lost sight of the barbarian kingdoms in the West.

---

[120] Harris, pp. 175 ff..

[121] See: Drauschke, *Zwischen Handel und Geschenk*, p. 366.

Ethiopian Christian material culture: the international context. Aksum, the Mediterranean and the Syriac worlds in the fifth to seventh centuries

Niall Finneran

University of Winchester

Introduction

The primary agency for social and cultural change during the period between the fifth and seventh centuries AD was arguably the Christian Church. The Church of this period was, however, essentially a fragmented community, still very much focused upon the eastern Mediterranean world, and centred upon the great Christian cities of Rome, Constantinople, Jerusalem, Antioch, Alexandria and Carthage. Each city was home to its own ideas and theologians-- 'brands' of Christianity--informed often by politics, charismatic ecclesiastics, national self-interest as well as issues of basic Christology.[1] These issues came to a head in the extraordinary Councils of Ephesus in 431 and Chalcedon in 451. As a result, Christianity was more divided than ever, becoming even more cosmopolitan. Membership of the 'Christian club' conferred great benefits, and the brands of Christianity created across Asia and Africa reflected local socio-political concerns. This paper looks at how – in what is traditionally regarded as a 'peripheral' region – the Aksumite Empire of northern Ethiopia, already a major international trading player, created its Christian identity from a very cosmopolitan perspective. Using primarily an archaeological rather than an art-historical perspective, we will consider how Ethiopian Christianity became globalized, how it drew in influences from across the Late Antique and early medieval Christian world and how these influences are reflected in the organisation of early Ethiopian Christian material culture.

Aksum: the international dimension

The Aksumite polity dominated what is now the northern Ethiopian/southern Eritrean highland region and the African Red Sea littoral between (approximately) the first-eighth centuries. Scholars now recognise its strong African antecedents, a complex socio-cultural phenomenon which was rooted in the eastern Sudanic-Nilotic worlds, rather than a continuum of the earlier, late-first millennium BC developments (sometimes given the cumbersome umbrella term 'pre-Aksumite culture') which owed much to cultural input from across the Red Sea in Southern Arabia. It is important that the 'African' roots of the Aksumite polity are stressed; historically the Ethiopian past has been created and viewed very much from an Asian-centric perspective.[2] By stressing the

African roots of Aksum, however, we must be careful that we do not lose sight of the important socio-cultural and ideological relationship between the Ethiopian/Eritrean highlands and the eastern Mediterranean (Fig. 1). Although the Aksumite achievement must be 'Africanised', it is also equally important that it also be placed very squarely within an eastern Mediterranean, Byzantine context, yet one which does not stress the traditional dichotomy of centre and periphery.

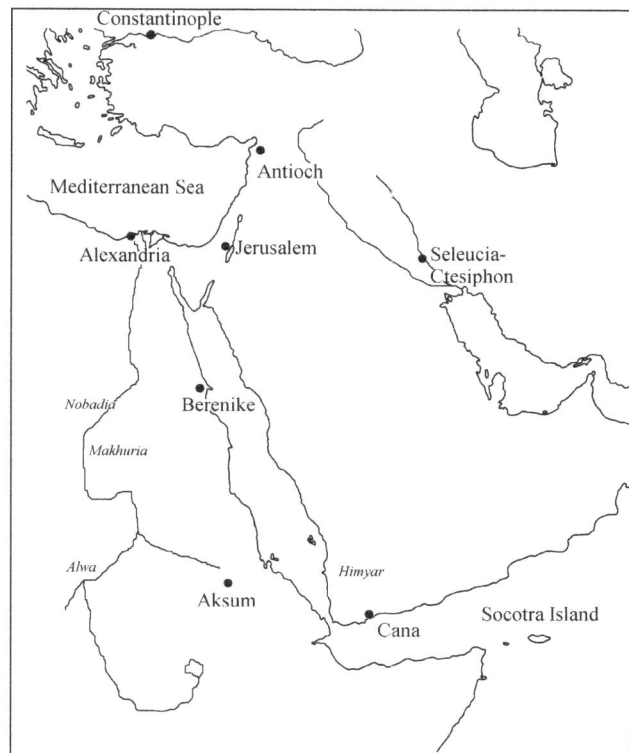

Fig. 1. Aksum and the Eastern Mediterranean

Because of its strategic position and as a source for luxury items much in demand in the Mediterranean world, the Horn of Africa was never an isolated geographical entity. Egyptian historical sources as far back as the Old Kingdom outline the trading relationship – utilising the Red Sea corridor – between Egypt and the Land of Punt.[3] This relationship continued into Ptolemaic

---

[1] For example, W. Frend, 'Nationalism as a factor in anti-Chalcedonian feeling in Egypt', *Studies in Church History* 18 (1982): 21-38.
[2] N. Finneran, 'The persistence of memory: national identity and

migrationism. A case study from African and Ethiopian archaeology', *Studies in Ethnicity and Nationalism* 3 (2003): 21-37.
[3] J. Phillips, 'Punt and Aksum: Egypt and the Horn of Africa', *Journal of African History* 38 (1997): 423-457. Historians now agree that this

times with the need to acquire war elephants for the wars against the Seleucids, and later, within the context of the primacy of the Alexandrian (Coptic) Episcopate over the Ethiopian Orthodox Church, an often fraught ecclesiastical relationship was forged.[4] The distinctive tri-metallic Aksumite coinage was minted from the end of the third to the seventh centuries; the weight of Aksumite gold coins was based upon the Roman standard in use prior to Diocletian's reforms in the 290s. The circulation of this coinage (gold coins have been found in Arabia and as far north as Israel) facilitated regional trade links, especially with the eastern Mediterranean world.[5] Ethiopia also looked eastwards; during Aksumite times (and before) there were extensive contacts with southern Arabia, the Sassanian Empire, India and possibly China. Recent archaeological work at the major Aksumite harbour at Adulis (Eritrea) as well as excavations at Aksum itself has cast new light upon the international material culture of the Aksumite world.

Marble used in church buildings from Adulis was shown to contain fragments of Proconessian marble from the Sea of Marmara region (Turkey), as well as a form of marble known as 'grand antique', sourced from the French Pyrenees.[6] Surface survey around the ancient anchorages of Diodorus Island yielded evidence of first-century BC eastern sigillata A wares, as well as pieces sourced from the region of Aqaba (Jordan), eastern Mediterranean Late Roman 1, 2 and 3 wares as well as north African cylindrical amphorae, implying a long time-scale of interaction with the Roman world.[7] It is also expected that a thorough maritime archaeological reconnaissance of a recently discovered shipwreck (the Black Assarca wreck) off Dahlak Kebir will also shed extensive light on the nuances of international Aksumite maritime trade.[8]

At Aksum itself, archaeological evidence for long-distance exchange relationships has come to light from many excavated sites.[9] Local Aksumite pottery, whilst

drawing upon pre- and proto-Aksumite vessel forms and decoration, soon accumulated influences from abroad. This may be discerned in the trend towards everted and ledge rims from the early Aksumite period onwards.[10] It is important to note that in many cases consumers – especially at D (domestic) Site, Kidane Mehret – recognised the inherent luxury value of the container as opposed to its contents.[11] In some cases the value of the container took on extra symbolism: children were buried in amphorae at Matara and Adulis. These amphorae are very distinctive markers for trade between Aksum and the Mediterranean worlds; Syrian-origin amphorae have been excavated from fourth- to fifth-century contexts from Ona Negast, Beta Giyorgis, and others suggest a Gaulish origin.[12] One Aksumite export above others was very highly prized. Concerted efforts by the Romans to source new markets for raw ivory were triggered by the fall off in north African ivory supply during the first century.[13] Soon Aksumite ivory was in great demand within the Mediterranean; it is even possible that the ivory chair or throne back excavated within the burial context of the Tomb of the Brick Arches may have indirectly influenced Byzantine craftsmen (the sixth-century Maximian's chair at Ravenna, Italy being such an example).[14]

Archaeological evidence for trading relations between Aksum and points further east is patchy. The discovery of a hoard of Indian coins from the Kushan kingdom at the monastery of Debra Damo is intriguing if opaque. The monastery itself was not founded until the sixth century and the coins themselves date from around the second century.[15] Aksumite pottery has also been identified at Kamrej, Gujarat, and beads discovered in funerary contexts at Aksum (for example, the Tomb of the Brick Arches) *may* betray an Indian origin.[16] Evidence for direct links with China is less clear cut. Sergew suggests that the region of 'Huang-Chi' noted by chroniclers of the Han dynasty (AD 220-589) as an important trading centre lying '12 months' journey, or 30,000 *li*' westwards could be identified with Aksum.[17] Chinese material at Aksum

place must have been located along the Red Sea coast; K. Kitchen, 'Punt and how to get there', *Orientalia* 40 (1971): 184-207.

[4] S. Munro-Hay, *Ethiopia and Alexandria: the Metropolitan Episcopacy of Ethiopia* (Warsaw, Za's Pan, 1997).

[5] S. Munro-Hay, *Aksum: An African Civilisation of Late Antiquity* (Edinburgh, Edinburgh University Press, 1991), pp. 180ff; W. Hahn, 'Aksumite numismatics: a critical survey of recent research', *Révue Numismatique* 6 (2000): 281-311.

[6] D. Habtemichael, Y. Gebreyesus, D. Peacock and L. Blue, *The Eritro-British Project at Adulis: Interim Report 2004* (Asmara and Southampton, University of Southampton, 2004); M. Heldman, 'Early Byzantine sculptural fragments from Adulis', *Études Éthiopiennes* 1 (1994): 239-252.

[7] Y. Geresus, R. Russom, D. Peacock, L. Blue, D. Glazier, J. Whitewright and J. Phillips 2005. *The Eritro-British Project at Adulis: Interim Report 2005* (Asmara and Southampton, University of Southampton, 2005).

[8] R. Pedersen, 'Under the Erythraean Sea: an ancient shipwreck in Eritrea', *International journal of Nautical Archaeology Quarterly* 27 (2000): 3-13.

[9] R. Tomber, 'Troglodites and Trogodites: exploring interaction on the Red Sea during the Roman Period', in *People of the Red Sea: Proceedings of Red Sea Project II*, ed. J. Starkey (Oxford, British Archaeological Reports International Series 1395 / Society for Arabian Studies Monograph 3, 2005), pp. 41-49.

[10] D. Phillipson, *Archaeology at Aksum 1993-1997* (2 vols.) (London and Nairobi, Society of Antiquaries of London/British Institute in Eastern Africa, 2000), p. 456.

[11] Phillipson, p. 484.

[12] R. Fattovich and K. Bard, 'Scavi archeologici nella zona di Aksum. Ona Enda Aboi Zegue e Ona Negast', *Rassegna di Studi Etiopici* 39 (1997): 49-70; K. Bard, R. Fattovich, A. Manzo and C. Perlingieri, Archaeological investigations at Beta Giorgis, Aksum, Ethiopia, *Journal of Field Archaeology* 24 (1997): 387-404.

[13] J. Phillips, 'Aksum and the ivory trade: new evidence', *Orbis Aethiopicus: Äthiopien und seine Nachbarn* (Gdansk, Gdansk Archaeological Museum, 1997), pp. 75-84.

[14] Phillipson, p. 119.

[15] A. Mordini, 'Gli aurei Kushana del convento Dabra Damo', in *Atti del Convegno Internazionale di Studi Etiopici (Roma 2-4 Aprile 1959)* (Rome, Accademia Nazionale dei Lincei, 1960), pp. 249-254.

[16] S. Gupta, P. Gupta, T. Garge, R. Pandey, A. Geetali and S. Gupta, 'On the fast track of the *Periplus*: excavations at Kamrej, 2003', *Journal of Indian Ocean Archaeology* 1 (2004): 9-33; Phillipson, p. 86.

[17] Sergew Hable Selassie, *Ancient and Medieval Ethiopian History to 1270* (Addis Ababa, Addis Ababa University Press, 1972), p. 71. A. Hermann, 'Ein alter Seeverkehr zwischen Abessinien und süd-China bis zum Beginn unserer Zeitrechnung', *Zeitschrift der Gesellschaft für*

may possibly be represented by a small forged iron and silver piece from Chamber D in the Tomb of the Brick Arches, but in truth there is little that constitutes hard archaeological evidence for a long-lasting trading relationship between Africa and China.[18]

The expansion of Islam through the Red Sea region in the seventh century effectively cut off Aksum from its co-religionists in the eastern Mediterranean, and also affected the regional trade dynamic. In time, the Red Sea ports lost their importance, and the focus of Indian Ocean trade fell, from the ninth century onwards, upon the coastal ports of the region termed *Zanj* by Arab geographers, or more popularly known as the Swahili Coast.[19] This, then, is a very broad and cursory overview of the key economic factors which lead us to define an internationalised economy for Ethiopia in Late Antiquity, an economic relationship based upon the import and export of materials aimed primarily at elite consumption. This contribution, however, seeks to take a different orientation, away from 'goods', be they exotic or mundane, and looks at the transmission of ideas, cosmology, perhaps even psychology. This is best understood in the shape of the 'export' of the Syrian (west-Syrian-rite) brand of Christianity from the eastern Mediterranean into the court of King Ezana of Aksum in the mid-fourth century, an export which was subsequently reinforced with the arrival of the Syrian Nine Saints in the fifth century, a phenomenon which witnessed the Christianisation of the countryside under the aegis of an eremitic monastic system based upon a Syrian, rather than Egyptian model.

In this paper, I seek to move away from the historical facts (which we shall briefly outline below) towards a more archaeological perspective. This route demands a consideration of the material culture traces of Syrian monasticism within an Ethiopian context; it demands a critique of how we may actually recognise (if it is possible) a Syrian brand of eremitic monasticism in the archaeological record, and how this organisation of space impacted upon the vernacular Ethiopian tradition. In short, is it possible to recognise, from an archaeological perspective, the 'global' flavour of the organisation of Ethiopian Christian material culture during this very important and formative period in the creation of a Christian Ethiopian identity? Before attempting to answer this question, a consideration of the wider historical framework is required.

Christianising Ethiopia: historical and archaeological perspectives

Rufinus' (c. 345-410) account of the introduction of Christianity to the Aksumite court is important given that

it is virtually contemporary with the events it describes, being written in around 410, some sixty years after the events it describes.[20] Rufinus states that two Syrian brothers from Tyre (Frumentius and Aedesius) were rescued from a shipwreck on the Red Sea coast and were taken to the court of the king of Aksum. Impressing the king with his faith, Frumentius had himself ordained bishop for Ethiopia by the Alexandrian Patriarch, Athanasius, and returned to undertake the conversion of the king and his court.[21] This is commonly suggested to have occurred in the 340s, although the nature of Ezana's 'conversion' is still open to question.[22] The Christianisation of the Aksumite court was thus accomplished through the agency of the twin powers of eastern Christendom: Syria and Alexandria, and subsequently the regions within which the great Christological controversy 'monophysitism' (itself an inaccurate label) and which would come to a head at the Council of Chalcedon in 451, found most support. There were other politico-ideological ramifications too; according to Athanasius' *Apologia ad Constantium Imperatorem,* Constantius II wrote a letter to the Aksumite co-rulers 'Ezana and Shaizana' demanding that they side with him in his support for the doctrine of Arianism. He urged that they promote his candidate for the Alexandrian Patriarchate, the Arian George of Capadoccia against Athanasius himself. This letter indicates that even within a short time, the Christian Ethiopian court was perceived as being a useful ally to the Eastern Roman emperors. Whilst there may have been obvious theological support for Arianism at the Imperial court, surely wider geopolitical concerns would play a part too.[23]

From an archaeological perspective the framework for conversion is what we might term a 'top down' model of conversion.[24] Historical parallels would include: the conversion of the medieval Nubian states in the sixth century; the conversion of the Caucasian kingdoms in Late Antiquity or the Anglo-Saxon kingdoms of England in the early seventh century.[25] This would contrast with the process of conversion visible in the Roman Empire

Erdkunde (1913): 553-561. G. Fiaccadori, 'Teofilo Indiano pt II', *Studi Classici e Orientali* 34 (1984): 271-308.
[18] Phillipson, p. 114.
[19] This was the *Azania* of antiquity; that is, the littoral of modern Kenya and Tanzania.

[20] J-P Migne (ed.) *Rufinus Historia Ecclesiastica* PL 21, 478-9, (Paris, 1849).
[21] This established the link between the Ethiopian and Coptic churches with lasted until autocephaly for the former in the 1950s. B. Dombrowski and F. Dombrowski, 'Frumentius/Abba Salama: Zu den Nachrichten über die Anfänge des Christertums in Äthiopien', *Oriens Christianus* 68 (1984): 114-169.
[22] S. Munro-Hay, 'The dating of Ezana and Frumentius', *Rassegna di Studi Etiopici* 32 (1990): 111-127; S. Kaplan, 'Ezana's Conversion Reconsidered', *Journal of Religion in Africa* 13 (1982): 101-109.
[23] In any event Arianism was essentially a spent force after the Council of Constantinople in 381. D. Rankin, 'Arianism', in *The Early Christian World*, ed. P. Esler (London, Routledge, 2000), pp. 975-1004.
[24] N. Finneran, *The Archaeology of Christianity in Africa* (Stroud, Tempus, 2002), p. 35.
[25] D. Edwards, 'The Christianisation of Nubia: some pointers', *Sudan and Nubia* 5 (2001): 89-96. For the Anglo-Saxon conversion, see P. Urbancczyk, 'The politics of conversion in north-central Europe', in *The Cross Goes North: Processes of Conversion in Northern Europe AD 300-1300* ed. M. Carver (York, York Medieval Press, 2003), pp. 15-27.

prior to 312. Here Christianity was a proscribed religion and the archaeological visibility of its earliest manifestations, such as in Egypt, would be complex and opaque.[26] The archaeological implications of 'top down' conversion would suggest a fairly immediate impact upon material culture and perception of space.[27]

Trilingual monumental inscriptions reveal a change in cosmological outlook: one refers to 'Lord of Heaven', a god in the singular and removes references to the Aksumite war god Mahrem. It is interesting too that while the Ethiopic version tends to tone down the Christian message, the Greek version is more overt in its Christian message.[28] The implication is clear: the message for the outside world is that Aksum is solidly Christian. The message for local consumption, however, is less equivocal, hedging more towards, perhaps, a period of ideological co-existence. Changes in coinage also reflect conversion; an issue of king *MHDYS* (successor of Ezana after c. 350) bears a direct Ge'ez (classical Ethiopic) translation of the vision of Constantine at the Battle of the Milvian Bridge: 'by this sign (the cross) you will conquer'. As the coinage was intended for use internationally, it made sense to stress very heavily a Christian identity. This was a message riddled with propaganda value.

Early Aksumite ecclesiastical architecture reflects a strong local architectural tradition as well as a potential Syrian inheritance rather than any northern African influence. As is often noted elsewhere in northern Africa (particularly in Egypt pharaonic and Ptolemaic temples), Asia and also Late Antique and early medieval Europe, the new Aksumite churches often took over pre-existing sacred sites. De Contenson notes that the church of Enda Cherqos near the pre-Aksumite cultic centre of Hawelti-Melazzo appears to incorporate architectural features (including Sabaean inscriptions) from an adjacent temple structure, and there are many other examples of strong spatial associations between Aksumite churches and pre-Christian sacred sites.[29] Aksumite church architecture appears to combine the standard basilican model prevalent in the Christian world during this with a strong local architectural flavour derived from secular building and graphically illustrated (albeit is a skeuomorphic manner) by the depiction of multi-storied buildings on the faces of the decorated stelae 1-3 at Aksum (Fig. 2). Particular interest attaches to the use of wooden bosses or through-ties ('monkey heads') in linear registers across the facades of the buildings. In plan the walls are indented. The only excavated Christian churches within

Fig. 2. Detail of the decoration on the base of stela 3 at Aksum showing distinctive Aksumite door frame and wooden bosses ('monkey heads'). This pre-Christian architectural style is reused in later church architecture (Photo: Niall Finneran)

the Aksum landscape are those from Beta Giyorgis and Wuchate Golo; the churches built on the southern flanks of Beta Giyorgis correspond to the areas identified by the Deutsche Aksum Expedition as 'Ruinen E and F'.[30] The basilica at Beta Giyorgis 'Superiore' possesses the sort of recessed architecture that one finds on the large palace buildings; special interest also attaches to the carved column bases as well as the ornate water spouts which recall the features on the wine presses nearby at Adi Tsehafi.

A somewhat later structure associated with an enclosure wall excavated at the area of Wuchate Golo north-west of Aksum would appear to be a rectangular basilican church with an associated cistern dating, on the basis of associated coinage, to the seventh or eighth centuries.[31] The three-aisled Aksumite basilica at Enda Cherqos also incorporates a baptistery installation, which incorporates a walk-in tank located in the southern flanking room of the apse, a configuration which is suggested by the excavator to follow Syrian practice (although it is, in fact a generic feature of eastern Mediterranean church architecture), and which is also reflected at the Aksumite churches of Adulis and Yeha.[32] The question of the baptistery is important. Large baptisteries with stairs suggest that

---

[26] E.g. E. Wipszycka, 'La Christianisation de l'Egypte aux IVe-VIe siècles. Aspects sociaux et ethiques', *Aegyptus* 68 (1988): 117-166.
[27] N. Finneran, 'Syncretism of space? The Christianisation of the Ethiopian landscape', in *Landscape Archaeology,* eds. H. Lewis and S. Semple (Oxford, British Archaeological Reports International Series, in press).
[28] S. Uhlig, 'Eine trilinguale Ezana-Inschrift', *Aethiopica* 4 (2001): 7-31.
[29] H. De Contenson, 'Les fouilles à Ouchatei Golo près d'Axoum en 1958', *Annales d'Ethiopie* 4 (1961): 3-16.

[30] L. Ricci and R. Fattovich, 'Scavi archeologici nella zona di Aksum B. Beta Giyorgis', *Rassegna di Studi Etiopici* 31 (1987): 123-99.
[31] De Contenson, 'Les fouilles à Ouchatei Golo'.
[32] H. De Contenson, 'Les fouilles à Haoulti-Melazo', *Annales d'Ethiopie* 4 (1961): 39-60.

adults were being regularly baptised, indicating that the structure dates from an initial period of conversion of the wider population. It is possible, however, that the associated cistern may not be a baptistery. At Wuchate Golo there are no steps to allow access to the tank, and its use may mirror the tradition of the use of the *laqqan* (Epiphany) and *mandantum* (Maundy) tanks of Coptic tradition. An analogue to this form of ceremony is found in the Ethiopian Timkat Epiphany ritual, a tradition which may betoken some deep-seated syncretic motif for the veneration of natural springs and water.[33]

Developments in elite Aksumite tomb architecture also reflect a Christian outlook. The Tomb of the False Door at Aksum is probably very early Christian in date, and although losing the stela as a grave marker, in terms of architecture it still pays homage to the tradition of Aksumite monumental architecture rather than any external Christian tradition. The tombs of Kaleb and Gebra Masqal clearly embody elements of a more Christianised style of tomb architecture. Aspects of their monumentality emphasise a break with pre-Christian Aksumite funerary tradition; firstly they are removed from the urban focus, located two kilometres up hill from the town – and it may be important that they are sited in close proximity to the monastery of Abba Liqanos.[34] Secondly their ground plan and structure clearly reflects the organisation of space of a Christian basilica. They are fundamentally spatially different from any tomb architecture hitherto seen at Aksum, and although the identity of the individuals who would have been interred here is still open to question, their scale and embellishment surely suggests a royal tomb.

Early Christian Aksumite architecture presents a melange, as far as we can tell, of local, probably secular, styles of architecture and the very standardised basilican plan, the closest analogues being those of the eastern Mediterranean, specifically Syria, as suggested by the use of rooms flanking the apse (the *prothesis* and *diakonikon*; Fig. 3). We cannot, at this stage, really trace any evidence of a strong Egyptianising influence. During the fourth and fifth centuries in Egypt, the basilican form predominated in the main urban centres, and later on within the monastery. The distinctive features of Coptic church architecture – the western return aisle, three altars and a pronounced spatial dichotomy between the *naos* and *heikal* (sanctuary), really only develop after the Islamic conquest in the mid-late seventh century.[35] Looking

elsewhere along the Nile, it is only possible to discern very vague similarities in church design.

The basic developmental Nubian church typology as defined by William Adams on the basis of the Nobatian material sees a gradual trend away from the standard basilican format (type 1, c. 550-750), towards an evolved and distinctly Nubian form of church building in the later centuries of the first millennium AD (Adams' type 3 and 4 churches) which witnesses a gradual decrease in size and naos area relative to the size of the sanctuary, and the development of a range of rooms within the narthex.[36] Makhurian churches (such as the Church of the Granite Columns and the Cruciform church at Old Dongola) being more centralised in character, may be suggestive of a stronger Byzantine influence, perhaps mirroring the form of the Palestinian *martyria*.[37] It is in any event virtually impossible in most cases to actually differentiate, on the basis of architectural plans alone, the difference between what constitutes on anti-Chalcedonian or Chalcedonian church.[38]

It is noticeable that the Nubian (and Coptic) trend towards a closing off of the sanctuary by means of an iconostasis or *Heikal* screen is reflected in Ethiopia but seemingly at a much later date. Although basically basilican in plan, the medieval Ethiopian church (as perhaps best exemplified by the rock-hewn churches of Tigray) exhibits a bewildering array of forms.[39] The churches develop a tripartite plan, a form of internal organisation which places the sanctuary, holy of holies (or *maqdas*) beyond the eyes of the congregation. Why do we find this trend in the eastern churches towards this closing off, this desire for secrecy? Suggestions that the basic Ethiopian church tripartite church division represents a copy of the Judaic temple may not be entirely wide of the mark. Perhaps there is a deep, ingrained Semitic trend in cultic architecture to delineating the sacred from the secular. Such an idea takes the church away from the idea of a meeting place, the *domus ecclesiae*, back to the notion of the temple as a house of the God.

[33] N. Finneran, 'Holy waters: Pre-Christian and Christian water association in Ethiopia. An archaeological landscape perspective', in *The Archaeology of Water: Social and Ritual dimensions,* ed. F. Stevens (London, University College London Monographs in Archaeology, in press).
[34] Although note that the presence of possibly earlier shaft tombs in the vicinity might suggest that this area was used as some form of cemetery (probably non-elite) in pre-Christian times; F. Anfray, 'L'Archéologie d'Axoum en 1972', *Paideuma* 18 (1972): 60-78.
[35] P. Grossman, *Christliche Architektur in Ägypten,* (Leiden, Brill, 2002).
[36] W. Adams, 'Architectural Evolution of the Nubian Church, 500-1400 AD', *Journal of the American Research Centre in Egypt* 4 (1965):87-139.
[37] S. Jakobielski, 'Nubian Christian Architecture', *Zeitschrift für Ägyptische Sprache und Altertumskunde,* 108 (1982): 33-48. The account suggests that an anti-Chalcedonian mission sponsored by Theodora, Justinian's consort, evangelised the kingdom of Nobatia in the north and Alwa in the south; Justinian's pro-Chalcedonian mission evangelised the middle kingdom, Makhuria. The picture of Christian conversion in the middle Nile is undoubtedly more complex. The *martyria* might reflect the picture of mission activity in the Middle Nile suggested by the (admittedly) partisan John of Ephesus. Edwards.
[38] cf. M. Mundell, 'Monophysite Church Decoration', in *Iconoclasm*, eds. A. Bryer and J. Herrin (Birmingham: University of Birmingham Centre for Byzantine Studies, 1977), pp. 62-63.
[39] D. Buxton, 'The rock-hewn and other medieval churches of Tigre province, Ethiopia', *Archaeologia* 103 (1971): 33-100.

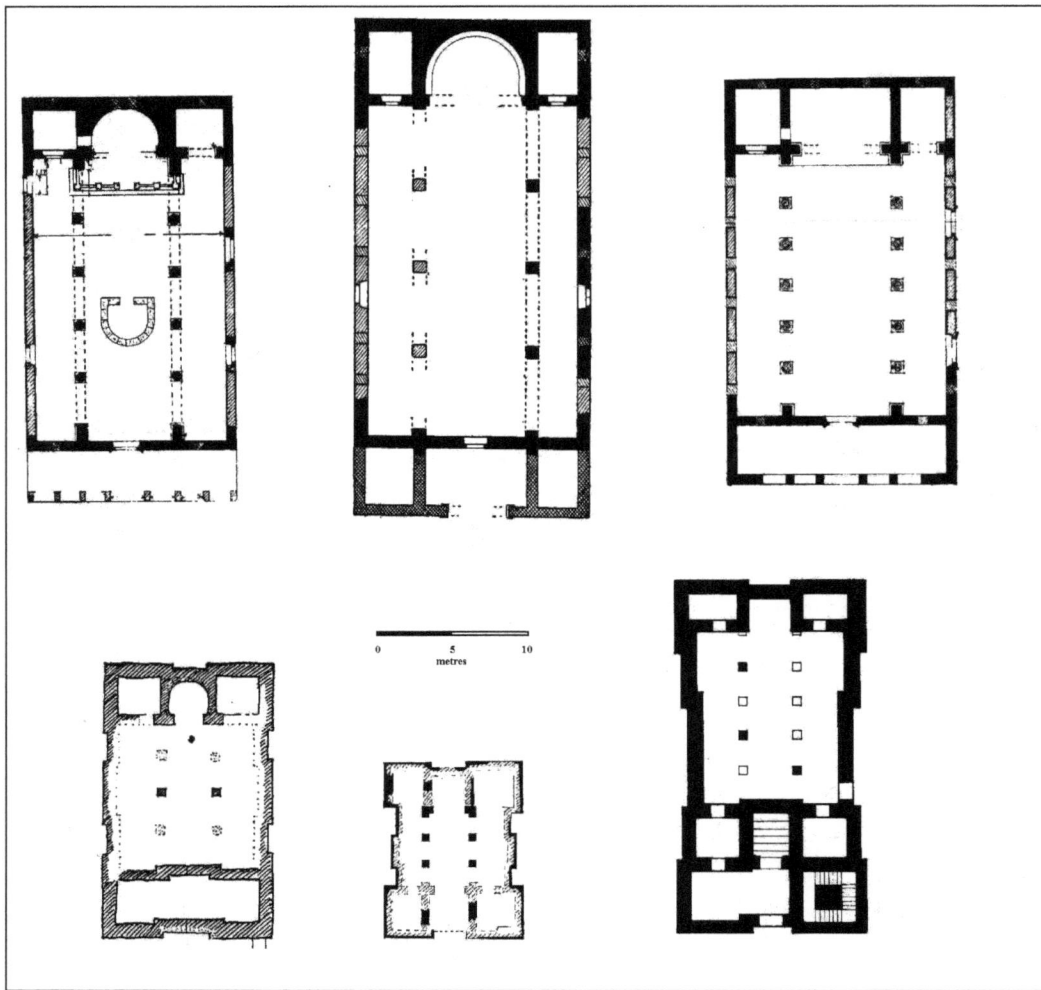

Fig. 3. Comparison between the Syrian basilica (top row) and the indented plan of the Aksumite basilica (below).
Top row left to right: Karab Shams; Jebel Hauran; Bakirha east church (all fourth-sixth centuries). Bottom row left to right:
Adulis; Qohaito; Aksum Tomb of Kaleb (Redrawn after Buxton 1971 fig. 36).

The twin strands of historical and archaeological evidence tell us much about the international factors present in the earliest phases of Christianity at the court of Aksum in the fourth-fifth centuries. In the first place, the available evidence suggests that Christianity was an urban phenomenon, churches are only found in major urban centres; the countryside was thus still predominantly 'pagan'. Secondly, the King essentially saw Christianity as a useful tool in his attempt at building international relations; it gained him 'membership' of an exclusive international cultural network focused upon the eastern Mediterranean (this much is clear from the maintenance of the international gold Aksumite coinage with its extensive iconographic stress upon 'being Christian' and its basis upon the Roman coinage standard). Thirdly, the cultural 'flavour' of Ethiopian Christianity was shaped by historical circumstance, that is, a strong Syrian connection, yet also embraced a great deal of local, syncretic variation. Let us now move on to the fifth and sixth centuries, and to a consideration of the

development of Ethiopian Christian material culture during a very eventful period.

Ethiopia and the world in the in the fifth-sixth centuries

During the fifth and sixth centuries we see Aksum take on a more overt international role in terms of foreign policy, often at the behest of the Byzantine authorities in Constantinople.[40] High-level political dialogue and diplomacy between the Roman and Aksumite courts showed just how well regarded the newly-Christian kingdom was; the sixth-century Byzantine ambassador, Nonnosus has left us an account (via the historian John

---

[40] We must assume that the notional adherence of the Ethiopian Church to the anti-Chalcedonian position was over-ridden by greater political concerns. This position contrasts with the political role of the Patriarchs of the Church of the East at Seleucia-Ctesiphon, whose allegiance to the Sassanian Empire often brought them into conflict with the Christians of the West.

Malalas) of the court at Aksum.[41] The historian Procopius tells us that the Byzantine Emperor Justinian wrote to king Kaleb of Aksum asking him to take military action against Dhu Nuwas, King of the Himyarites in southwestern Arabia, who was persecuting Christians there. Kaleb's inscription of victory is to be found at Marib, Yemen.[42] Stephanos of Byzantium included Ethiopians in his geographical encyclopedia *Ethnikon*, a testament to the fact that they were now regarded as more than human curiosities.[43]

The events of the council of Chalcedon in 451 must have clearly impacted upon Ethiopian Christian material culture, although it is questionable whether the Ethiopian church was actually represented there.[44] In any case, the Ethiopian church was ecclesiastically tied to the Coptic Patriarch at Alexandria, and it was this factor rather than any ingrained, local theological interpretation of the Christological controversy that kept the church here, theologically at least, beyond the fringes of Byzantium and in the anti-Chalcedonian 'camp'.[45] The period from the accession of Ezana to Kaleb also marks the zenith of Aksumite political and military power. Ezana, importantly, retained the identity as King of Arabia, organising extensive tribute-gathering expeditions (as would be suggested by his inscriptions at Aksum as well as those from Meroë). The author of the inscription at Adulis noted by Cosmas Indicopleustes in his *Christian Topography* is unknown, but was evidently a king of great military capability, for he claimed domains as far as the Nabataean port of Leuke Kome – which we may assume to be somewhere in the region of the Gulf of Aqaba in the northern Red Sea.[46] With the success of the expedition, southern Arabia was now brought under more direct political control of Aksum with the appointment of a 'viceroy', Sumyafa Ashwa.[47] Christianity was momentarily re-established in an Ethiopian model within southern Arabia; in 576 Abreha (Kaleb) built a cathedral at his new capital of Sana. This structure became known as al-Qalis, an Arabic corruption of the Greek word

ecclesia.[48] Sergew suggests that Greek architects were employed in its building and was most unlike any Ethiopian church, taking on more of a centralised form in the manner of Haghia Sophia at Constantinople.[49]

Another important historical source, the sixth-century Syriac Acts of Gregentius, seems to stress, however, that the Church of South Arabia was very much based upon Syriac (eastern 'Nestorian' and western 'Jacobite' (*sic*)) traditions rather than an implanted Ethiopian model.[50] It is even probable that four different 'churches' were at work in this area: the Byzantine, the Ethiopian, the West Syrian and the East Syrian; the competing motivations would have been political (even colonial) in the case of the former two churches, the case of the latter two very much an unstructured mission expansion. The island of Socotra was also annexed by Aksum, and a bishop was reported here by Cosmas Indicopleustes, but when Marco Polo arrived in the twelfth century he noted that the Christians there swore allegiance to the see of Seleucia Ctesiphon in Mesopotamia, thus implying membership of the eastern Syriac tradition, the Persian Church of the East.[51] If we take South Arabia as an example, the process of Christianisation could be used to support political and military colonialism, or, in the case of the Syriac churches, a much freer, more amorphous and less structured mission ethic. The distribution of east-Syrian monasteries through the Gulf, for instance (and incidentally also along the Silk Road) implies a mission process, free of political control and tied explicitly to the regional trade routes. It is during this period of extension of Aksumite political and military control into Arabia that we see, in essence, a re-Christianisation of the Ethiopian landscape via a generic Syriac pattern of monasticism. Hitherto, whilst the urban elite of Aksum had engaged with Christianity, a facet which gave them membership of an international 'club', and used this Christian identity as a justification for extension of political and military power, the Aksumite countryside was still largely a non-Christian preserve. This changed with the creation of a Christian monastic movement inspired, I believe, directly by the rural Syrian hermit.

'The Nine Saints'

Apart from the Frumentius connection – which in any case ultimately became the vehicle for Alexandrian, Egyptian, political control of the Ethiopian church – there is actually little direct evidence for relations between Aksum and Syria. Vague suggestions of Syrian influences in the art and architecture of the pre-Aksumite

[41] Munro-Hay, *Aksum*, 15ff.

[42] M. Kamil, 'An Ethiopic Inscription found at Marib', *Journal of Semitic Studies* 9 (1964): 56-7.

[43] D. Levine (ed.), *Greater Ethiopia: the Evolution of a Multi-Ethnic Society* (Chicago, Chicago University Press, 2000), p. 3. The Greeks had always seen Ethiopians as being primitive; cf. Sergew, *Ancient and Medieval Ethiopian History*, p. 51.

[44] M. Heldman, 'The Kibran Gospels: Ethiopia and Byzantium', in *Proceedings of the International Conference of Ethiopian Studies 5 (session A, December 19-22 1977, Nice, France; session B April 13-16 1978, Chicago, USA) Session B proceedings* ed. R. Hess (Chicago, Northwestern University, 1978), pp. 359-372; E. Honigmann, 'Un évêque d'Adulis au Concile du Chalcédonie?' *Byzantion* 20 (1950): 295-301.

[45] This rather falsely implies a monolithic bloc of national churches from Egypt, Syria, Ethiopia and Armenia.

[46] L. Cansdale, 'Cosmas Indicopleustes: merchant and traveller', in *Akten des XII Internationalen Kongress fur Christliche Archaeologie Studia di Anticha Cristiana LII* (Aschendorffsche, Munster, 1995), pp. 600-616; Munro-Hay, *Aksum*, p. 77; L. Kirwan, 'The *Christian Topography* and the Kingdom of Axum', *Geographical Journal* 138 (1972): 163-173.

[47] Munro-Hay, *Aksum*, p. 88.

[48] Its remains are still to be found within the Great Mosque at Sana'a, Jami al Kabir.

[49] Sergew, *Ancient and Medieval Ethiopian History*, p. 150.

[50] V. Christides, 'The Himyarite-Ethiopian war and the Ethiopian occupation of South Arabia in the Acts of Gregentius (circa 530 AD)', *Annales d'Ethiopie* 9 (1972): 115-146.

[51] I. Gillman and H-J. Klimkeit, *Christianity in Asia before AD1500* (Richmond, Surrey, Curzon Press, 1999), p. 81.

and Aksumite periods remain unproven.[52] Aurelian is said by the *Historia Augusta* to have captured Aksumite prisoners when he defeated the revolt of Zenobia of Palmyra (270-5) but this does not suggest a formal degree of Aksumite support for Palmyra.[53] The individuals concerned were probably mercenaries. The Syriac influence (by this I mean the Syrian Christian) is suggested to be most overt within the initial efforts at translating the Bible into Ethiopic from Syriac originals; and there is a rich tradition of Ethiopic church music – based upon St Yared's chant – within which there are a number of terms with roots in Syriac literary tradition.[54] The real nature of Syriac influence upon the literature of early Christian Ethiopia is far from as clear as traditional historical scholarship would actually imply.[55] It is difficult to unravel the connections between Syriac and Ge'ez terminology as both are Semitic languages and words have similar roots.[56] The arrival of the Nine Saints, however, introduces another possible conduit for Syriac influence.

In the fifth century, during the reign of Ella Amida, (Kaleb's grandfather) Ethiopian tradition tells of the arrival of nine pious holy men from Syria who introduced monasticism into Ethiopia and effectively evangelised the rural hinterlands of Aksum, finally cementing the domination of Christianity at all levels of Aksumite society. The places of origin of these saints are given in the Ethiopian synaxarion as well as their hagiographies (see below), and they clearly indicate an eastern Mediterranean origin, perhaps more precisely Anatolia and Antioch.[57] Also at this time another group of evangelisers known as the *Sadqan* ('righteous ones') were active in southern Eritrea (Shimazana) where a number suffered martyrdom at Matara; this might imply that the spread of Christianity through the polity was still very localised, and that the inhabitants of Matara may have enjoyed a degree of local autonomy.[58] The implication from most authors is that these are holy men fleeing persecution by the pro- Chalcedonian church authorities within the Byzantine Empire, but this appears unlikely. Who were they and what were their motives for coming so far south?

In truth, we know very little about these individuals whose names and places of origin are given below. Their hagiographies are presented in the traditional Ethiopic *gädl* (plural *gädlät*; the noun may be translated as the 'struggles'). In terms of literary tradition the *gädl* very much resembles the *Vitae* of western Christian tradition. A striking parallel, in fact, may found in the accounts of the missionary saints of early medieval Ireland, Wales and Cornwall, which mix the mundane with the miraculous.[59] Of particular importance for reconstructing the deeds of the Nine Saints are three translated hagiographies of saints Päntallewon, Arägawi and Afse: the *gädl Päntallewon*; *gädl Arägawi* and *gädl Afse*.[60] It is important to recognise that the *gädl* may not be a reliable or accurate account of the actions of the saint; they were written mainly in the post-Zagwe period (that is, the thirteenth century onwards) and are thus almost 800 years out of date. We should approach the historical accounts with a degree of caution, but it is clear that the impact of these individuals, however, was profound. Their images adorn a number of Ethiopian churches (Fig. 4) and they have become some of the most revered saints of the Ethiopian Church. We cannot be sure that this was in fact an organised, concerted missionary effort; there are no real indications apart from a few later historical sources that the nine saints came as one in some unified purpose. As far as we can see, there are no events that would imply a deeper political motivation on the part of the Byzantine court, or the ecclesiastical authorities at Antioch, to send the missionaries. Their purpose and goals remain opaque.

Table 1: The places of origin of the 'Nine Saints'

Arägawi:	*Rom/Romya (generic Ethiopic and Arabic term for Byzantine Empire)*
Päntallewon:	*Rom/Romya*
Gärima:	*Rom/Romya*
Liqanos:	*Qwestentenya* (Constantinople)
Guba:	*Qelqeya* (Cilicia)
Afse:	*Esya* (Asia)
Sehma:	Antioch
Alef:	Caesarea
Yemata:	*Qosyat* (unidentified)

It is also clear that there are problems identifying these individuals, in fact, as Syrians. The places of origin summarised above do not actually indicate a specific Syrian homeland for these individuals. Sergew points out that Liqanos and Päntallewon are actually Greek names;

[52] E.g. H. De Contenson, 'Les monuments d'art sudarabe découverts sur le site de Haoulti (Ethiopie) en 1959', *Syria* 39 (1962): 64-87.

[53] Sergew, *Ancient and Medieval Ethiopian History*, p. 86.

[54] C. Sumner, 'The Ethiopic Liturgy: an analysis', *Journal of Ethiopian Studies*, 1 (1963): 40-46.

[55] e.g. C. Conti-Rossini, *Storia d'Etiopia* (Milan, Officina d'Arte Grafica A. Lucini, 1928), pp. 155ff.; E. Ullendorff, *Ethiopia and the Bible* (London, British Academy, 1968).

[56] P. Marassini, 'Some considerations on the problem of 'Syriac influences' on Aksumite Ethiopia', *Journal of Ethiopian Studies* 23 (1990): 35-46.

[57] E.g. E. Budge, *The Book of the Saints of the Ethiopian Church: a translation of the Ethiopic Synaxarium* (Cambridge, Cambridge University Press, 1928), vol 1, pp. 116-118; Sergew, *Ancient and Medieval Ethiopian History*, p. 116; see below, table 1.

[58] Tadesse Tamrat, *Church and State in Ethiopia 1270-1527* (Oxford, Oxford University Press, 1972), p. 23; Sergew, *Ancient and Medieval Ethiopian History*, p. 128, note 20.

[59] N. Finneran, 'Extending the Christian Frontier in late antiquity: Monks, missions, monasteries and the Christianisation of space. Towards a wider chronological and geographical context for the archaeology of mission', *Ethnohistory*, in press.

[60] For the *gädl Päntallewon*: C. Conti-Rossini, *Vitae Sanctorum Antiquiorum 1, Acta Yared et Pantalewon; CSCO Scriptores Aethiopici volume 10* (Leeuven, 1955). For the *gädl Arägawi*: I. Guidi, 'Il Gadla Aregawi', *Rendiconti della Reale Accademia dei Lincei* (serie 5, vol. 2., 1896. For the *gädl Afse*: Sergew Hable Selassie, 'New historical elements in the Gedle Afse', *Journal of Semitic Studies* 9 (1964): 200-203.

NIALL FINNERAN ETHIOPIAN CHRISTIAN MATERIAL CULTURE

**Fig. 4. Depiction of the Nine Saints,
Abuna Yemata, Guh, Gheralta
(Photo: Niall Finneran).**

the others either Aramaic or Syriac (it is hard to differentiate) implying a place of origin within Palestine or Syria.[61] As Marassini points out, Romya is too general a geographical term, Constantinople and Cilicia are definitely not Syria, Asia again is a very generic term, Antioch and Caesarea are part of the wider Syriac-Aramaic world yet 'one cannot help wondering whether their citation in connection with the Nine Saints was not a matter of mere religious and literary fiction'.[62] This leaves the problematic 'Qosyat'; this has been variously identified as a corruption of Fustat (Cairo), a Persian toponym, or even a local, Ethiopian place.[63] Marassini is also dismissive of the Syrian nature of their names. In short, current scholarship suggests that the Syrian Nine Saints were only very tenuously connected with Syria. This ignores, however, their very profound impact upon the Aksumite landscape and society. They introduced a monastic system, and this is where perhaps a more imaginative archaeological approach might be able to shed light upon the problem of the origin of the Nine Saints.

The Nine Saints founded monasteries across the central swathe of the kingdom, close to and around the city of Aksum, at strategic centres (Fig. 5), at important nodes in the landscape. This is a pattern that we may also

recognise, perhaps, in the missions of Columbanus in western Europe at roughly this time.[64] In Ethiopian terms, the monastery was an innovation and one not clearly derived from the Egyptian model. During the fifth-sixth centuries, the Egyptian monastery developed towards a communal, cenobitic model based upon the rule of St Pachomius.[65] This model stressed communal prayer and living allied to a strong work ethic on the land. With some small modification this form of monasticism was translated into Nubia as well as the Levant.[66] Deriving from a hermitage of a single holy man – often via the semi-cenobitic *Laura* best seen in the Kellia group of the western Nile Delta – the Egyptian communal monastic complex; and if we can reduce it to an architectural generality, embodied a number of repeated elements: churches, cells, refectory, latterly a Qasr, or keep and an encircling wall which tended to be fortified by the end of the first millennium AD.[67] These are very distinctive architectural features within the landscape.[68]

---

[64] Finneran, 'Extending the Christian Frontier'.
[65] J. Goehring, 'Withdrawing from the desert: Pachomius and the development of village monasticism in upper Egypt', *Harvard Theological Review* 89 (1996): 267-285.
[66] J. Anderson, 'Monastic lifestyles of the Nubian desert: seeking the mysterious monks of Makuria', *Sudan and Nubia* 3 (1999): 71-83.
[67] E. Makowiecka, 'Monastic pilgrimage centre at Kellia, Egypt', in *Akten des XII Internationalen Kongress für Christliche Archaeologie* (Aschendorffsche, Munster, 1995), pp. 1002-1015 (=*Studia di Anticha Cristiana* LII).
[68] M. Rassert-Debergh, 'Monastères coptes anciens: organisation et décoration', *Le Monde Copte* 21-22 (1993): 71-93.

---

[61] Sergew, *Ancient and Medieval Ethiopian History*, p. 116.
[62] Marassini, p. 35ff.
[63] Marassini, p. 36.

Fig. 6. The pilgrim site of Qalat Siman, northern Syria (Photo: Niall Finneran)

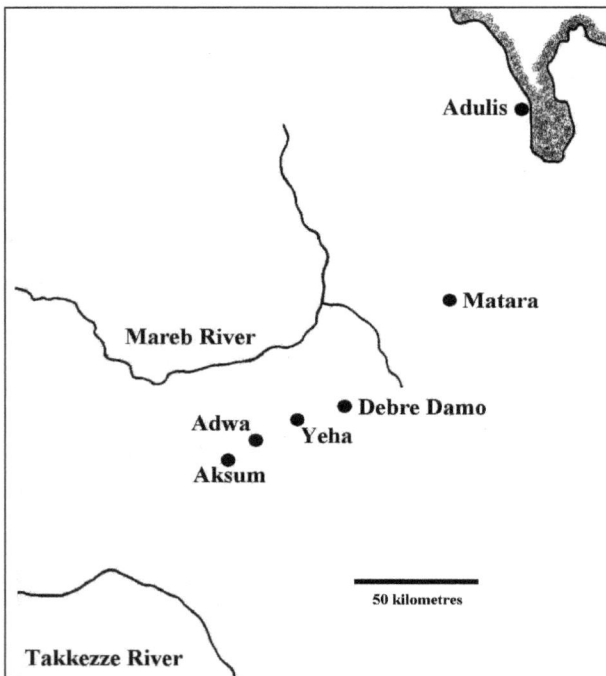

Fig. 5. Aksum and the key sites mentioned in the text.

In contrast, whilst cenobitic monasticism developed in Syria along a slightly different set of rules, the eremitic roots were more distinctive; more local – even perhaps reflecting a syncretic motif recalling pre-Christian veneration of mountains and high places.[69] Whereas the Egyptian hermit sought isolation in the desert, the Syrian holy man actually engaged with society taking on the role as a negotiator, a wise man, a judge.[70] This outlook contrasts strongly with the role of the Egyptian anchorite who tended to remain aloof.[71] The archaeology of Egyptian eremitic monasticism reflects this desire to remain apart, away from the secular world. Early Egyptian hermitages belong on the physical, social and psychological margins of society: caves or ancient pharaonic tombs.[72] In Syria a more 'visible' form of eremitic monasticism was developing pioneered by Simeon Stylites (c. 389-459).[73] The story of the most well-known of the pillar-sitting hermits of antiquity is to be found in a range of hagiographical accounts from Greek, Syriac, Coptic, Georgian, Armenian and Arabic literature.[74] Such was his fame that his pillar itself became a place of pilgrimage (Qalat Siman; Fig. 6) and his deeds influenced a number of other holy men to follow his actions. The tradition of the stylites in fact extended beyond Syria: St Alypius of Adrianople in Paphlagonia during the early seventh century, and a contemporary, St Theophilus the Confessor in Egypt. Intriguingly, the Ethiopic synaxarion mentions a certain St Agathon, probably an Egyptian stylite.[75] This has important implications for understanding the emergence of the Ethiopian brand of eremitic monasticism along the lines of the *Syrian* model, as we shall see. After their

---

[69] I. Pena, 'Aspectos peculiares del monacato sirio', in *Christian Archaeology in the Holy Land: Essays in Honour of V. C. Corbo,* eds. G. Bottini, L. Di Segni and E. Albiata (OFM, Jerusalem, 1990), pp. 561-569; S. Brock, 'Early Syrian asceticism', *Numen* 20 (1973): 1-19.

[70] P. Brown, 'The rise and function of the holy man in late antiquity', *Journal of Roman Studies* 61 (1971): 80-101.
[71] D. Frankfurter, 'Syncretism and the holy man in late antique Egypt', *Journal of Early Christian Studies* 11 (2003): 339-385.
[72] J. Goehring, 'Monastic diversity and Ideological Boundaries in Fourth-Century Christian Egypt', *Journal of Early Christian Studies* 5 (1997): 61-83; Finneran, *The Archaeology of Christianity in Africa*, pp. 76-77.
[73] D. Frankfurter, 'Stylites and phallobates: pillar religions in late antique Syria', *Vigiliae Christianae* 44 (1990): 168-198.
[74] A. Atiyah, *A History of Eastern Christianity* (London, Methuen, 1968), p. 186, note 1.
[75] H. Delahaye, 'Les Saints Stylites', *Subsidia Hagiographica* XIV (1923), pp. 135-136.

arrival at the court of Aksum, and their subsequent dispersal into the countryside, of all the Nine Saints only Päntallewon and Liqanos remained within the city, founding monastic cells upon high rock pinnacles which later became the churches, still visible, of the monastic communities of Abba Liqanos and Abba Päntallewon. The site of Abba Päntallewon especially may have been a site of pagan significance given the presence of an Epigraphic South Arabian inscription there noted by the Deutsche Aksum Expedition in the early twentieth century.[76] We may take the analysis of space a little further. Let us, for an instant, consider a phenomenological approach to the study of these monastic units. This approach, as articulated by Christopher Tilley demands an imaginative approach to understanding the archaeological landscape.[77] It demands empathy, it demands an appreciation, perhaps of the visual and symbolic qualities of created places in relation to natural spaces. Both pinnacles are distinctive landscape features in a region where flat-topped hills predominate. They made a very strong visual statement, dominating, yet symbolically and physically distanced from the city and secular life itself. The monastery of Päntallewon especially, even today, does have a profound impact upon the observer, accentuated by the height and narrowness of the natural feature upon which it is sited (Fig. 7).

Apart from a very obvious phenomenological approach to the impact of these two monasteries, the proximity of Liqanos and Päntallewon to the centre of political activity was, as Sergew points out important owing to their Greek origin and also their support for the accession of Tazena, the successor of Ella Amida.[78] They thus enjoyed a close relationship with the king, and must have been regarded as trusted advisers and sources of counsel. Their role, then, within the social life of Aksum, as well as the fact that they chose to distance themselves from society in terms of 'vertical' rather than 'horizontal' space would seem to imply that although possessing Greek names, Päntallewon and Liqanos were actually hermits in the Syriac tradition. We may, then, see the use of the rock pinnacle as an analogue to the pillar. There was no real attempt to use the pinnacles as a distancing factor; quite the opposite. Their visibility owes more to the Syriac tradition of eremitic monasticism than that followed in the Egyptian deserts, the idea that the hermit, the pious holy man, should actually engage with society. After all, the stylites on his pillar was often accessible via a ladder.[79] And what of the other Nine Saints? Their approach to reordering the landscape was similar: utilise a high site, a visible and striking feature, an analogue to the pillar, and maybe even one with strong pre-existing pagan significance.[80]

Abuna Arägawi's foundation at Debre Damo (Fig. 8) also occupies a high *amba*, a mountain which is suggested to have strong pre-Christian symbolic connections.[81] Unlike the other foundations, this eremitic establishment soon became a complex cenobitic community in its own right, one of the most important monasteries in Ethiopia. The basilican churches here are probably some of the oldest in Ethiopia, and yet again are witness to the meeting of the local style of Aksumite architecture (this is particularly clear on the facades) and the basic internal division of the church. Many of the carved motifs within the church itself embrace wider eastern artistic influences. Abuna Yemata chose to situate his cell within a virtually inaccessible rock pinnacle at Guh in the Gheralta region of eastern Tigray (Fig. 9). The modern monastic church here dates from the fifteenth century, as does the well-known depiction of the Nine Saints on the roof, yet one feels again the psychological needs behind the siting of this monastery. It was a reflection, surely, of the practice of the Stylites from Syria. These are hugely dramatic statements of power within the newly-Christianised rural hinterland of Aksum: the seizure and adaptation of sacred mountains, places physically closer to God.

Fig. 7. The monastery of Abba Päntallewon, Aksum (Photo: Niall Finneran).

[76] This may also be true of the summit of Abba Liqanos.
[77] C. Tilley, *A Phenomenology of Landscape* (London, Berg, 1994).

[78] Sergew, *Ancient and Medieval Ethiopian History*, pp. 116-117.
[79] Frankfurter, 'Stylites and phallobates'.
[80] Finneran, 'Syncretism of space?'
[81] D. Matthews, and A. Mordini, 'The monastery of Debra Damo, Ethiopia', *Archaeologia* 97 (1959): 1-58.

Fig. 8. Debre Damo
(Photo: Niall Finneran)

Fig. 9. Abuna Yemata, Guh, Gheralta (Photo: Niall Finneran)

The locations of the monasteries founded by the other Nine Saints are less clear cut, with one or two exceptions. Abba Afse went to the pre-Aksumite centre of Yeha and founded a monastery in proximity to the old pagan sanctuary there (another example of a Christianisation of a pre-Christian sacred space). Abba Garima (Isaac) settled at Medera, near Adwa; a monastic church dedication to the saint is to be found at Adi Kewih – but this is surely not the original establishment – and Abba Guba also settled in this region. The Abba Garima gospel book shows, in terms of structure of layout and decoration, the close links between Ethiopia and the Byzantine world, especially Syria, and has recently been radiocarbon dated to the sixth century, making this one of the earliest Christian codices anywhere in the world.[82] The modern town of Adwa is sited along the great eastern route towards the coast; the siting of two monastic units here had clear strategic considerations, and perhaps it would also be worth while taking into account – from a phenomenological perspective – the very distinctive mountain landscape of this region. Abuna Alef founded a monastery to the northeast of Aksum named Debre Halle Luya (location unknown), the location of Abba Sehma's mission is also unknown, but may be centred upon the region today known as Enda Abba Sehma to the southeast of Adwa. In all cases, these hermits sought to engage with society, they were active missionaries and as such their psychology and choice of location for their monastic establishment implies a strong Syrian connection. What though of Egypt, the other main political and cultural player in the creation of an Ethiopian Christian identity in Late Antiquity?

The monastery re-exported: Ethiopia, Egypt and beyond

The role of the Coptic Church in the development of Ethiopian monasticism is not pronounced, even though it maintained, through the Patriarchal linkage, a large degree of strong political influence. Quite simply, the Ethiopian monastery develops along very distinctive, local lines after an initial Syrian – or at least eastern Mediterranean – impetus. Although politically masters of the Ethiopian church, there is very little real Coptic influence upon the material culture of Ethiopian Christianity and this is something of a surprise given the links between the areas and the proximity of the Nile corridor. The evidence for connectivity – historical and archaeological – is surprisingly sparse. Even the Nubian connection is not too clear cut; in fact, it appears that Aksum was actually still looking towards the Red Sea and into Asia rather than up the Nile into Africa.[83] This

pattern of ecclesiastical influence, in terms of material culture and thought is mirrored by the archaeological evidence for trade at this time. Fragmentary Egyptian textiles found at the monastery of Debre Damo only date from the ninth century; their appearance suggests that they were ecclesiastical robes worn by monks.[84] Well-preserved skeletons at the rear of the cave church of the monastery of Yemrehane Krestos, Lalibela (an establishment dating from the early thirteenth century) are said to be those of Egyptian monks or pilgrims who had fled to Ethiopia to escape persecution and only a few decorative elements within medieval Ethiopian churches seem to suggest any Coptic influence. Even the Ethiopian icon tradition owes more to the Byzantine world than to Egypt. There are few other indicators at this stage, however, of an international Christian material-culture component; evidence for long-distance Christian pilgrimage with Egypt may be indicated by the discovery at Adulis of a holy water flask from the pilgrimage site of St Menas in the Mareotis desert to the southwest of Alexandria. These very distinctive ampoullae have been found across south-central Europe and particularly along the Danube corridor, as well as in the eastern Mediterranean regions.[85]

There a few contacts in the other direction; the thirteenth-century Ethiopian monk Tekla Haymanot is the only Ethiopian to have been canonised by the Coptic church.[86] The famed monk Moses the Black (c. 330-405) who lived in the Scetis desert (Wadi Natrun) south of Alexandria began life, in some accounts, as a brigand or a servant in an Egyptian household. After his martyrdom he became one of the most important figures in the history of early Coptic monasticism, yet his identification as an Ethiopian could be open to question and in any case his presence in late antique Egypt and the circumstances of his origins hardly suggests a formalised monastic link between Egypt and Ethiopia.[87] Moses the Black is most closely associated with the monastery of Baramûs (the Romans) in the Wadi Natrun where his relics now reside.[88] Until recently Ethiopian monks occupied the church of St John the Little in the Monastery of the Syrians (Deir es-Suriani, Wadi Natrun) having previously, according to the Arab historian al-Maqrizi, had their own monastery of St Elisha, but their presence has now died out and in terms of archaeology alone there is little that bears witness to the long-lived relationship between the Ethiopian and Coptic churches.[89] Ethiopian Christians turned away from Egypt, and perhaps, as a means of resistance to Alexandria actively sought to emphasise their Syrian roots. It is noticeable that the Ethiopian

---

[82] J. Leroy, 'L'évangelaire Éthiopien du couvent d'Abba Garima et ses attaches avec l'ancien art Chrétien de Syrie', *Cahiers Archéologiques* 11 (1960): 131-143; J. Mercier, 'La peinture Ethiopienne à l'époque axoumite et au XVIII siècles', *Comptes Rendus Academie Institutes des Belles Lettres* (2000): 35-71.

[83] B. Zurawski. 'Nubia and Ethiopia in the Christian period – some affinities', in *Aspects of Ethiopian Art from Ancient Axum to the Twentieth Century,* ed. P. Henze (London, Jed Press, 1993), pp. 33-41.

[84] Matthews and Mordini, 1959.

[85] Bangert, this volume.

[86] O. Meinardus, 'Ecclesia Aethiopica in Aegypto', *Journal of Ethiopian Studies* 3 (1965): 23-35.

[87] K. O'Brien Wicker, 'Ethiopian Moses', in *Ascetic Behaviour in Graeco-Roman Antiquity*, ed. V. Wimbush (Minneapolis, Fortress Press, 1990), pp. 329-348.

[88] O. Meinardus (ed.), *Monks and Monasteries of the Egyptian Deserts* (Cairo, American University in Cairo Press, 1999), p. 54.

[89] Meinardus, *Monks and Monasteries*, p. 131.

Fig. 10. Mar Musa al Habashi, Nabk, Syria (Photo: Niall Finneran)

monks in the Wadi Natrun sought sanctuary in the Monastery of the Syrians.

The presence of Ethiopian contacts with the Holy Land is also well-known.[90] In Jerusalem the Ethiopian convent situated above the Church of the Holy Sepulchre (along with the nineteenth-century compound in the New City), is all that remains of what was once a large Ethiopian community in the city. The relationship between Ethiopia and Jerusalem is mythically enshrined in the story of Solomon and Sheba and the foundation of the Ethiopian Solomonic dynasty. Ethiopian Christian pilgrims have

long visited the city and there are other threads of evidence which suggest an Ethiopian presence further to the north; the dedication of the Syrian Catholic monastery of Deir Mar Musa al Habashi, Nabk (north of Damascus; Fig. 10) must refer to the Egyptian Moses, although according to tradition the Moses in question here was the son of an Ethiopian king who became a monk firstly in Egypt and then in Syria. The monastery itself was founded in the sixth century, although the current church building dates from 1048.[91] In the Lebanon, Ethiopian

---

[90] E. Cerulli, *Etiopi in Palestina* (2 vols.) (Rome, Liveria della Stato, 1943).

[91] P. Dall'Oglio, 'Storia del Monastero di San Mose l'Abissino descrizione degli affreschi della sua chiesa', in *Il Restauro del Monastero di San Mose l'Abissino, Nebek, Siria* (Rome/Damascus/Nebek, Istituto Centrale per il Restauro Roma

monks occupied a number of hermitages in the Wadi Qadisha alongside Maronite, west Syrian and Armenian monks. An Ethiopic inscription (fifteenth century) and fresco has recently been discovered in the small church of Mar Assia (who was, interestingly enough, the Ethiopian Pǟntallewon); a Christian Aksumite coin of Ousanas has also been reported here.[92] We have, therefore, some tantalising archaeological clues to the presence of Ethiopian monastic communities in Syria during the medieval period, but the question remains: how long have they been there and how did they come to be there? Undoubtedly the mechanisms of the Jerusalem pilgrimage played a part in the movement, but perhaps there is a more long-lived link, one perhaps playing upon the ancient relations between Aksum and Syria in antiquity, a counter-balance to the fractious relationship with Alexandria. This is clearly an area which requires much more archaeological attention.

Conclusion

This paper has examined the archaeological evidence for the international factor in Ethiopian Christianity from the fourth century onwards. Although the Egyptian (Alexandrian) linkage is clear in terms of political control, the material culture evidence (even though it is allied with doubtful historical material) strongly suggests a strong Syriac impact. Ethiopian Christian material culture derives from the eastern Mediterranean, and was recast using indigenous architectural styles and spatial approaches. The adoption of Christianity was more than a spiritual decision on the part of the Aksumite court; it had clear economic and political ramifications, building as it did upon a long-lived history of trade and exchange between the northern Ethiopian highlands and the eastern Mediterranean world. What is perhaps surprising is that the Christian communities to the east, along the Nile, had so little impact upon the formation of Ethiopian Christian identity. When considering notions of globalization and internationalisation in Late Antiquity, it is useful to step beyond the usual constraints of examining trade and exchange, and consider another framework, a spiritual framework (Christianity, in its many guises) which provides a medium through which contacts were initiated, developed and maintained over long distances and over long periods of time. One could take this approach further, and consider the framework of Silk Road trade in the light of the expansion of East Syrian Christianity through central Asia, India and into China, focusing on how the mission process went hand in hand with social and political demands. Here at least we have shown that Ethiopia, hitherto regarded perhaps as a marginal zone, played, through the medium of Christianity, a very strong role in the Christian world of the fifth to seventh centuries.

Ministero della Cultura; Directorate of Antiquities and Museums, Damascus; Mar Musa monastic community, 1998).

[92] H. Abdel-Nour and B. Jabbour-Gedeon, 'L'ermitage rupestre et la grotte de Mar Assia', *Spéléorient* 1 (1996): 27-38.

Britain and China at opposite ends of the world? Archaeological methodology and long-distance contacts in the sixth century

Anthea Harris

University of Birmingham

Introduction

'Access to the courts of heaven is as easy from Britain as it is from Jerusalem, for the kingdom of God is within you'.[1] So wrote Jerome from his monastery at Bethlehem, in the closing decades of the fourth century.

Jerusalem being the centre of the Christian world, the implication was that Britain was at the extremity of that world, although still part of it. Jerome himself was living and writing in a Byzantine physical and conceptual context: he had been a monk in rural Syria, had spent time in Rome, Antioch and Alexandria, and was now writing to a flock scattered around the Near East. His perception of Britain as being 'at the end of the world', as he wrote in another of his letters, was shared, one can infer, by the people to whom he was writing; Britain was the geographical landmass at the western extremity of Byzantine thought. The British cleric, Gildas, writing more than a century later, and in western Britain, shared his impression: 'The island of Britain lies virtually at the end of the world,' he wrote, 'towards the west and north-west' (taking Jerusalem as his locus).[2]

This paper considers an aspect of the relationship between Byzantium and Britain in the sixth century, before turning to East Asia and those lands that might have been considered to lie at the eastern extremity of the Byzantine thought world, albeit probably not, in this case, a part of the Christian *oikoumene*. Comparison of the material transmitted and the method of its transmission enables us to interpret Byzantium's relationship with its two peripheries in new ways.

Coinage is the main category of material examined here. How was Byzantine coinage transmitted to the farthest point of the known West and East Asia, and why? What meanings, if any, can we attach to the transmission of such coins to both of these peripheries? How were the coins used in each of the recipient societies, and what points of comparison can be made which might

illuminate the study of long-distance contacts in this period?

Part One: Byzantine coinage in Britain

The question of Byzantine coin-finds in Britain remains a controversial one. Until relatively recently, most archaeologists dismissed these as modern losses, not without reason, as these coins were not discovered in secure archaeological contexts.[3]

However, in recent years the question of post-fifth century 'Eastern Roman' links with the West has come to the fore in a new way, as Britain has increasingly been considered in a late antique context, and as different categories of material have been considered together.[4] Consequently, some new light has been shed on the numismatic evidence, although there is still room for considerable debate.[5]

Detailed studies of the ceramic evidence, in particular those by Ewan Campbell, have sketched out a context in which coin evidence might be studied anew.[6] Yet in one sense the story of Byzantine ceramics in Britain has been one of disappointment and unfulfilled promise. It was initially supposed, after the publication (and publicising) of Ralegh Radford's work on the imported pottery at Tintagel in the 1930s, that Byzantine pottery would be found widely in Britain and that it would come to form key dating evidence for the fifth to sixth centuries, and

---

[3] G. C. Boon, 'Byzantine and other Exotic Ancient Bronze Coins from Exeter', in *Roman Finds from Exeter*, eds. N. Holbrook and P. T. Bidwell (Exeter, Exeter County Council and The University of Exeter, 1991), pp. 38-45.
[4] R. Collins and J. Gerrard (eds.), *Debating Late Antiquity in Britain, AD300-700* (Oxford, British Archaeological Reports British Series 365, 2004)
[5] The debate was reignited by K. R. Dark's discussion of the West Country coins in *Britain and the End of the Roman Empire* (Stroud, Tempus, 2000), p. 162.
[6] E. Campbell, 'The Post-Roman Pottery', in *Early Medieval Settlements in Wales AD 400-1100: a critical reassessment and gazetteer of the archaeological evidence for secular settlements in Wales*, eds. N. Edwards and A. Lane (Cardiff, University College Wales, Department of Archaeology, 1988), pp. 124-36; E. Campbell, 'New finds of Post-Roman imported pottery and glass from South Wales', *Archaeologia Cambrensis* 138 (1989): 59-66; E. Campbell, 'The archaeological evidence for contacts: imports, trade and economy in Celtic Britain AD 400-800,' in *External contacts and the economy of Late Roman and Post-Roman Britain*, ed. K. R. Dark (Woodbridge, Boydell, 1996), pp. 83-96.

---

[1] F. A. Wright (ed. and trans.), *Select letters of St. Jerome* (London, William Heineman, 1933), Letter 58:3. The idea that Britain lay at the extremity of the known world recurs several times in Jerome's writings: Letter 60:4; 77:10; 133:9; 146:1; *Dialogue against the Luciferians*, 15, in *Jerome: The Principal works of St Jerome*, ed. and trans. P. Schaff (New York, Christian Literature Publishing, 1892).
[2] Gildas, *The Ruin of Britain and other documents*, ed. and trans. M. Winterbottom (Chichester, Phillimore, 2002), p. 16. Gildas was, of course, well acquainted with the works of Jerome (e.g. p. 156).

91

perhaps even the seventh century.[7] The lack of dating indicators for the fifth and sixth centuries (with the exception of 'Anglo-Saxon' burials) has long been a source of frustration for archaeologists of this period. Hopes for a widespread new diagnostic tool were largely dashed, although several new sites with Byzantine pottery have been identified, almost all in western Britain. By the 1990s it had become clear that Byzantine pottery imports are found primarily within the south-western peninsula and south coast of Wales, with the largest assemblages known from Tintagel, Cadbury Congresbury, South Cadbury and Bantham, a sand-dune site on the coast of south Devon.[8] Occasionally, Byzantine pottery has been found at sites further east, such as London and Verulamium; yet these are usually argued to represent 'British enclaves' and there is no evidence that Eastern Mediterranean amphorae reached the 'Anglo-Saxon' areas of the country.[9]

A welcome by-product of the perceived lack of quantity in terms of the ceramic evidence has been invaluable advances in methodology, which have been crucial in drawing out the relevance of this material to our understanding of Britain's place in the sixth-century world. Charles Thomas and others led the way, refining method in the identification of Eastern Mediterranean and other imported pottery types in the 1950s to 1980s, while since the 1980s new steps have been taken in interpretation.[10] Campbell's work on the chronological and typological spread of the pottery indicated a period of importation lasting from about 475 to 550, permitting an early idea that these could represent one shipload to be deemed almost certainly incorrect.[11] Michael Fulford argued that the Tintagel material had a distinctly 'Constantinopolitan' signature, even if the ships were collecting additional material from the Byzantine colony in southern Spain before turning west and north up the Atlantic coast.[12] More recent work on Spanish ceramic assemblages, while confirming the presence of Eastern Mediterranean fine wares and amphorae in late-fifth and

sixth-century Hispania, has tended to support Fulford's thesis insofar as it has highlighted key differences in the Iberian and British assemblages.[13] In brief, these are three-fold: 1) the majority of fine ware sherds at British sites are Phocaean Red Slip Ware (PRSW/Late Roman C), whereas African Red Slip Ware (ARSW) dominates the imports at sites on the Iberian peninsula; 2) North African amphorae are rare in Britain, but form up to 75.6% of the ceramic assemblage on key Iberian sites (e.g. Tarragona); 3) Eastern Mediterranean amphora type Late Roman 2 (LR2/British Bi) is the dominant amphora type in Britain, but is rare on most Western Mediterranean sites and is completely absent from Braga, the Visigothic capital on the Atlantic coast, which might have been expected to benefit from the long-distance exchange involving Britain. By contrast, amphora type Late Roman 1 (LR1/British Bii) is the most common Eastern Mediterranean amphora type on Iberian sites.

The extent to which these voyages were controlled by the state is uncertain. An entrepreneurial project by Eastern Mediterranean merchants has been suggested, but Anne Bowman has shown that strictly commercially-motivated contacts were unlikely, given the investment and time required to reach Britain. Research on late antique shipping technologies has also started to illuminate this question, starting with Jonathan Wooding's suggestion on comparative maritime grounds that deep sea-voyages provided a likely model for Byzantine contacts with Byzantium.[14] Previously, it had been thought that short-haul merchant ships, perhaps trading via Gaul and Spain, might be responsible for the imports.[15] Deep-sea voyages direct from Gibraltar explain the very 'Byzantine' assemblage at Tintagel, as well as the Frankish and Spanish material.

Whatever the motivation, there was, in all likelihood, a period of ceramic importation beginning at or before the reign of Justinian I and continuing well past the mid-century point, perhaps associated with diplomatic motives.[16] It involved an assemblage deriving from the Eastern Mediterranean and Constantinopolitan in character, although the ships may have harboured in North Africa, possibly Alexandria or Carthage, before sailing west. The cargoes contained red-slipped table-wares and the standard range of amphorae along, possibly, with other Byzantine products. As we have seen, amphora type LR2 predominated, just as it did at

[7] For example, C. A. R. Radford, 'Tintagel: the castle and Celtic monastery. Interim Report', *Antiquaries Journal*, 15 (1935): pp. 401-19.
[8] For a summary, see A. Harris, *Byzantium, Britain and the West: the archaeology of cultural identity, AD 400-650* (Stroud, Tempus, 2003), pp. 144-52.
[9] Verulamium: D. F. Williams, 'The Amphorae from the Lower Slope', in *The Excavation of a Ceremonial Site at Folly Lane, Verulamium*, R. Niblett, London, 1999, pp. 286-7. London: D. Williams and C. Carreras, 'North African Amphorae in Roman Britain: a reappraisal', *Britannia*, 26 (1995): 231-52.
[10] A. C. Thomas, 'Imported pottery in dark-age western Britain', *Medieval Archaeology*, 3 (1959): 89-111; A. C. Thomas, *A provisional list of imported pottery in post-Roman Britain and Ireland* (Redruth, Institute of Cornish Studies, Special Report 7, 1981).
[11] J. Wooding, 'Cargoes in Trade along the Western Seaboard', in *External contacts and the economy of Late Roman and Post-Roman Britain*, ed. K. R. Dark (Woodbridge, Boydell, 1996), pp. 67-82; J. Wooding, *Communication and commerce along the Western sealanes, AD 400-800* (Oxford, British Archaeological Reports, International Series 654, 1996).
[12] M. Fulford, 'Byzantine and Britain: a Mediterranean perspective on Post-Roman Mediterranean Imports in Western Britain and Ireland', *Medieval Archaeology*, 33 (1989): 1-6.

[13] P. Reynolds, 'Hispania in the Late Roman Mediterranean: Ceramics and Trade', in *Hispania in Late Antiquity: Current Perspectives*, eds. K. Bowes and M. Kulikowski (Leiden, Brill, 2005), pp. 369-486, esp. 423ff. and Tables 14-16. I am grateful to Simon Esmonde Cleary for drawing my attention to this article.
[14] A. Bowman, 'Post-Roman imports in Britain and Ireland: a maritime perspective', in *External contacts and the economy of Late Roman and Post-Roman Britain*, ed. K. R. Dark (Woodbridge, Boydell, 1996), pp. 97-107; Wooding, 'Cargoes in Trade', pp. 67-82.
[15] C. Thomas, '*Gallici Nautae de Galliarum Provinciis.* A Sixth/Seventh Century Trade with Gaul, Reconsidered', *Medieval Archaeology* 34 (1990): 1-26.
[16] Harris, pp. 144-52.

sites receiving state supplies from the imperial government.[17] Outside the south-west peninsula, this material is found only at high-status secular and religious sites; within the south-west peninsula, it is present at a wider-range of sites, including farming settlements. Byzantine glass is also found in this area. To my knowledge, no Byzantine metal objects have been excavated at 'British' sites.[18]

It would have been surprising if sailors arriving from coin-using societies in the Eastern Mediterranean did not carry some coin on them, if only for their own private purchases in the course of their journey. This might account for some of the sixth-century and earlier low-denomination Byzantine coins found in Britain, although it is notable that few Byzantine coins have been found at sites which have also yielded Eastern Mediterranean pottery. The discovery of a decanummium of Justinian I with a Nicomedia mint-mark, dated c. 560-561, at Padstow (Cornwall) in 2006 is an exciting, although isolated find.[19] Wroxeter (Shropshire) is another rare exception: here, we have a bronze nummus of 430-5 at a site which also yielded imported (Palestinian) fifth- to sixth-century pottery.[20] In the light of recent research at Silchester (Hampshire), an old (and sometimes dismissed) find of a sixth-century follis of Justinian I might now be re-considered.[21] Clwyd, Merseyside and Cheshire should also be mentioned here, for these adjacent counties have also yielded several low-value sixth-century Byzantine coins, although not, as yet, imported pottery from stratigraphically-excavated contexts.[22] In fact, there might now be enough bronze

Byzantine coins from north-west England to suggest, tentatively, that they represent actual losses of the fifth-seventh century period.[23]

Gold coinage appears very seldom in the west of Britain. A solidus of Justinian I, with the Constantinople mint mark, from Tenby (Pembrokeshire), is exceptional, as is a tremissis of the late-sixth century, also with the Constantinople mint mark, from the Lancashire/Cheshire border.[24] Silver coinage is equally rare, and is in any case likely to be associated with the ninth-century Norse expansion: as suggested by the seventh-century silver hexagram of Heraclius Constantine in the famous Cuerdale hoard and the recent find of an early seventh-century Sasanian silver drachm of Chosroes II (628) from Anglesey.[25]

By contrast, in the east of Britain, gold Byzantine coinage is much more plentiful – even if we exclude those pieces that have been subject to alteration, probably for use as jewellery or amulets. To date, over 15 Byzantine gold coins of the fifth and sixth century have been identified and recorded from eastern Britain, in contrast to the three or four from the west and north.[26] Numbers have increased significantly since the establishment of the Portable Antiquities Scheme (PAS) in late 1997 and are likely to continue to do so (the coverage of the PAS expanded to cover all of England and Wales only in 2003).[27] This raises the (rhetorical) question of how many coins were recovered but not recorded before the turn of the 21st century.

There are analogous numbers of seventh-century coins, whose importation (by definition) took place well after the Justinianic period of contact. These are often found in analogous places and contexts to the fifth- and sixth-century solidi; that is, principally in the southern and eastern areas of England.[28] This estimate excludes the so-

[17] Ibid.

[18] In addition to the coin-finds, to be discussed below, there are some chance finds, which include the Byzantine liturgical censer from Glastonbury and lead weights, also from Somerset. C. Entwistle, 'A coin weight from Somerset', in Byzantium: Treasures of Byzantine Art and Culture, ed. David Buckton (London, The British Museum, 1994), p. 86.

[19] PAS Find ID CORN-72D1D7. www.finds.org.uk

[20] Nummus: R. Abdy and G. Williams, 'A Catalogue of Hoards and Single Finds from the British Isles, c. AD 410-675', in Coinage and History in the North Sea World: c. 500-1250. Essays in honour of Marion Archibald, eds. B. Cooke and G. Williams (Leiden, Brill, 2006), pp. 31. Pottery: P. Barker, R. White et al, The Baths Basilica Wroxeter. Excavations 1966-90 (London, English Heritage, 1997), pp. 120, 168, 231, 318.

[21] Abdy and Williams, p. 35; M. Fulford et al, Life and labour in late Roman Silchester: excavations in Insula IX since 1997 (London, The British Academy, 2006), pp. 280-85: 'Occupation of our three properties [in Insula IX] continues through the fourth and, we suggest, the fifth/sixth centuries' (p. 282).

[22] For the coin-finds, see: R. Philpott, 'Three Byzantine Coins found near the North Wirral Coast in Merseyside', Transactions of the Historic Society of Lancashire and Cheshire 1998, 148 (1999): 197-202. More recently, a follis of Justinian I with an Antioch mint-mark was found near the Mersey Tunnel at Seacombe, Merseyside. (PAS Find number LVPL-874C64). Another follis of Justinian I was found at Preston Brook (Cheshire), just south-east of Runcorn (PAS Find ID LVPL-1440), although the find of a follis of c. 1042-c.1050 (reigns of Zoe and Theodora, and of Constantine IX Monomachus) less than ten miles away at Norley (Cheshire) does put a question-mark over this find (PAS Find ID LVPL-1883). Images at www.finds.org.uk and http://www.fitzmuseum.cam.ac.uk/coins/emc. Although no pottery from stratigraphical excavations has yet been

found, there is a small number of chance finds, most notably a Saint Menas flask from nearby Meols. See also Bangert, this volume.

[23] However, not necessarily losses of the sixth century: witness the sixth-century decanummium of Justinian I from a rubbish pit at Hamwic, where there was apparently no activity during the sixth century itself. Abdy and Williams, 2006, p. 35. The discovery of a follis of Leo V (886-912) in a back garden at Wedmore, Somerset in 2005 also urges caution. PAS Find ID GLO-D4B576: www.finds.org.uk

[24] There is also a solidus of Tiberius III (698-705) from Tenby. Abdy and Williams, pp. 33-4.

[25] J. Graham-Campbell (ed.), Viking Treasure from the North West: The Cuerdale Hoard in its Context (Liverpool, Liverpool Museum, 1992). Anglesey: PAS Find ID LVPL-2174. www.finds.org.uk

[26] For an overview, see Harris, 2003, pp. 152-5, 163-4. More recent finds are reported in Treasure Annual Reports of 2003, 2004 and 2005 (London, Department for Culture, Media and Sport). Most notably, Byzantine gold solidi have been found in mid-Norfolk (Treasure case 2005 T474), Coddenham, Suffolk (tremissis of Anastasius (491-518) Early Medieval Coin corpus number 2001.0014) and Faversham, Kent (solidus of Maurice Tiberius (582-602), modified into a pendant by the addition of a gold suspension loop, EF-4810). Images at www.finds.org.uk and http://www.fitzmuseum.cam.ac.uk/coins/emc.

[27] For up-to-date numbers, see www.finds.org.uk.

[28] Abdy and Williams, pp. 23-58. Finds since 2000 include: an incomplete struck/ hammered copper alloy Byzantine follis of Heraclius, minted in Nicomedia in 610-11 from the parish of Middleton,

called 'pseudo-imperial' gold coins, although if these were to be factored into the analysis the picture would be even more pronounced.[29]

However, and conversely, there are very few low-value sixth-century Byzantine coins in the eastern areas of Britain. Exceptions include coins (usually representing 40 nummi) of Anastasius (491-518) from Burwell (Cambridgeshire), of Justinian I to Justin II (i.e. 527-578) from Amersham (Buckinghamshire), of Maurice Tiberius (582-602) from Norfolk.[30] Another sixth-century follis (12 nummi) was found at Core's End (Buckinghamshire).[31] There are also nummi from Richborough (Kent), Dunstable (Bedfordshire) and Thelnetham (Suffolk), all with a *terminus post quem* deposition date of c. 435. Yet another nummus with a *terminus post quem* deposition date of c. 435 was found at Verulamium, but this site must be considered an anomaly in eastern Britain, since it is often argued to have been a 'British' centre in the fifth to seventh centuries, and, indeed, has yielded Byzantine imported pottery.[32]

Why might this distinct patterning, with west and east as two discrete distributions, have emerged? It is possible that the bronze nummi represent direct imports into Britain, brought in alongside the ceramic and other materials in the century leading up to c. 550. It is salient that almost all of them are issues of or before the reign of Justinian, which would enable them to be linked to this period of ceramic importation. There seem few other circumstances in which such low-value coins would make their way to western Britain during this period. Whether or not this point is accepted, it must be borne in mind that small bronze denominations of this kind often do not survive well in the archaeological record; this being the case, we are probably seeing a very small sample indeed of a larger quantity of such coins.

It is possible that Byzantine gold coins were also imported directly from the Eastern Mediterranean, but this is a much more problematical point and, in any case, the function of gold coinage (in monetary terms and otherwise) may have been very different from that of bronze coinage. The frequent association of genuine Byzantine gold coins with pseudo-imperial barbarian issues, often with Frankish mint marks but sometimes even Visigothic or Burgundian ones, militates against direct importation. It is likely, given the evidence for a Continental, overland, long-distance network of exchange, that the coins were brought into Britain via this second route, rather than via the Atlantic and the Mediterranean.[33]

This second network of exchange involved overland and riverine passage along the Danube, over the Alps and down the Rhine to the North Sea, before passing up through the Thames estuary or further north to the Deben estuary. It is widely accepted as having brought into Britain a wide variety of objects from the barbarian world, not least Frankish glass, weaponry and dress items. Byzantine objects such as the bronze ('Coptic') bowls sometimes found in late sixth- and early seventh-century Anglo-Saxon graves, as well as the so-called 'exotic' items also found in early Anglo-Saxon graves, such as cowrie shells, ivory rings and objects incorporating semi-precious stones, are also confined to the east of Britain, are likely to have been imported via this second route.[34]

Yet, the possibility of direct importation of Byzantine gold coins cannot be ruled out at this stage. If the Byzantine interest in western Britain had a diplomatic or political aspect, as well as an economic one, it is likely that gifts in the form of precious metals were also imported, in addition to the ceramic material.[35] Both textual and archaeological evidence suggests that the imperial government resorted to this practice elsewhere, including with the Franks, the closest neighbours of the British.

If this was the case, the otherwise puzzling absence of Eastern Mediterranean precious metal coinage in the Western British archaeological record may be explained by the secondary distribution of the material – from the British kingdoms to the emerging kingdoms of the Anglo-Saxons, perhaps again in the form of diplomatic gifts or tribute. This might go some way towards explaining why East Anglia and Kent often yield the most high-status artefacts: as the most complex of the early Anglo-Saxon polities, these might have been expected to engage in diplomacy more readily. On this basis, the presence of Byzantine gold coins in Anglo-Saxon burial contexts might represent, in some cases, a tertiary distribution of material – perhaps from a regional

in Warwickshire (Find ID WMID-8FC217); a possible Byzantine follis from Gravenhurst, in Bedfordshire (Find ID BH-D28B76). A solidus of Phocas minted 607-709 was found at Bossall, in North Yorkshire (Find ID NCL-6A6EF5). Another solidus of Phocas, said to have been found in Sussex in 2005, was sold on Ebay in December 2005, without having been reported to the PAS. www.ebay.co.uk ID 8342462441.

[29] Abdy and Williams, pp. 23-58, where perhaps the most notable find listed (p. 14) (although now lost) is a hoard comprising ten tremisses, said to be of Justin I, found on the bed of the Thames in 1848, and likely to have been pseudo-imperial. More recently, examples reported to the PAS include: a fragment a late-sixth or early-seventh century silver-gilt Merovingian pseudo-imperial solidus, pierced for suspension, from Southease, in East Sussex (Find ID SUR-5B13A4). See also R. Abdy, 'After Patching: Imported and Recycled Coinage in Fifth- and Sixth-century Britain', in *Coinage and History in the North Sea World: c. 500-1250. Essays in honour of Marion Archibald*, eds. B. Cooke and G. Williams (Leiden, Brill, 2006), pp. 75-109.

[30] Burwell: PAS Find ID CAM-C730D3; Amersham: PAS Find ID BUC-6129B2. The Norfolk coin (PAS Find ID BH-781624) was minted in Maurice Tiberius's second regnal year 583/584. There is a possible sixth-century coin from North Yorkshire (PAS Find ID YORYM-0BEEF7), and a 5 nummi coin of Justinian I, possibly from Fressingfield (PAS Find ID SF-69E582). www.finds.org.uk

[31] PAS Find ID BUC-4840C3. www.finds.org.uk

[32] See above, note 8.

[33] Harris, ch. 5.

[34] Harris, pp. 139-94.

[35] *Ibid.*

ruler to a loyal local family. While necessarily speculative, this suggestion is consistent with theoretical models widely employed elsewhere in archaeology.

The frequent alteration of high-value coins (imperial and pseudo-imperial) and their subsequent deposition in burial contexts suggests a society with little concept of a monetary system. It should present no surprise, therefore, that this is where we see the clearest archaeological footprint of the imported coins. By contrast, societies with active concepts of monetary exchange tend to pass on coins fairly rapidly in exchange or, at a later point, melt them down for renewal. This is by no means to argue that imported coin was used in western Britain as part of a coherent monetary system; merely that it may have been exchanged with Anglo-Saxon elites, perhaps in extremis.[36]

That several of the well-known high-status burial deposits (Sutton Hoo, Mound 1; Mound 17) included coins contained within a purse – or in the case of Mound 17 at Sutton Hoo, garnets within a 'purse' – might suggest a society aspiring to participation in a monetary system, or at least one whose elites had aspirations in this direction.[37] It might also lend tacit support to William Filmer-Sankey's argument that the burials at both Snape and Sutton Hoo Mound 1 were intended to evoke the Roman imperial office in some way.[38]

To what extent do these patterns compare with other areas? The second part of this paper turns from the western extremity of the Byzantine thought world, to its eastern extremity, and to China. If Britain provides a model for how interaction on the fringes of the Byzantine thought world took place, we might expect to see similar material and analogous patterns of activity occurring there, too.

Part Two: Byzantine coinage in China

Byzantine contacts with China have attracted rather less attention than Byzantine contacts with Britain, although this situation is slowly beginning to change. Friedrich Hirth's late-19th century translations of Chinese reports of diplomatic missions to 'the West' first brought the subject to Western scholarly attention, while the few references to Chinese silk in the Roman and Byzantine textual sources are well-known.[39] Procopius's story of silkworms being smuggled into the Empire is probably

the most cited of these.[40] Procopius also claims that in the mid-sixth century the Byzantine government tried, unsuccessfully, to persuade Ethiopian merchants to travel to India in order to buy Chinese silk on their behalf.[41]

However, it was not until the second half of the 20th century that archaeologists started seriously to explore the question of linkages between the Byzantine Empire and East Asia. Scholars studying the material culture of the post-Han to Tang period in China drew attention to the quantities of 'foreign' goods imported into China between the fifth and the eighth centuries, largely on the basis of the study of museum collections.[42] In the main, it was scholars working on the relationship between the Persian Empire and its eastern neighbours who first started to consider the possibility of a Byzantine component to this relationship, albeit one mediated through a Sasanian cultural world and facilitated by the fluctuating political dynamics of the Central Asian kingdoms.[43]

Renewed interest in the study of the so-called Silk Road has also resulted in an exploration of Byzantine-Chinese contacts.[44] It is important to recognise from the outset that the Silk Road had both a northern, land-locked branch (itself divided into 'sub-branches') and a southern, maritime branch, and was a series of intermittently operating trading stations. It was not, therefore, a single 'road', along which organised groups of merchants rode from start to end, but a series of roads of varying lengths and quality. Rarely did merchants travel the entire length

---

[36] K. Dark, *Civitas to Kingdom, British Political Continuity, 400-800* (Leicester, Leicester University Press).

[37] M. Carver, *Sutton Hoo: Burial Ground of Kings?* (London, The British Museum Press, 1998), p. 183.

[38] W. Filmer-Sankey, 'The "Roman Emperor" in the Sutton Hoo Ship Burial', *Journal of the British Archaeological Association*, CXLIX (1996): 1-9.

[39] F. Hirth (ed. and trans.), China and the Roman Orient: researches into their ancient and mediaeval relations as represented in old Chinese records (Chicago, Ares Publishers, 1975); Friedrich Hirth, 'The Mystery of Fu-lin', *Journal of the American Oriental Society*, 33 (1913): 193-208.

[40] Procopius of Caesarea, *History of the Wars*, (ed. and trans.) H. B. Dewing (London, William Heinemann, 1919), VIII.17.1-8.

[41] Procopius of Caesarea, *History of the Wars*, (ed. and trans.) H. B. Dewing (London, William Heinemann, 1979), I.20, 9, 11-12.

[42] For example: M. Pfrommer, *Metalwork from the Hellenised East. Catalogue of the Collections* (Malibu, John Paul Getty Museum, 1993); P. O. Harper, 'Iranian Luxury Vessels in China from the late first millennium BCE to the second half of the first millennium CE', in *Nomads, Traders and Holy Men along China's Silk Road: Papers presented at the Asia Society, New York, November 9-10, 2001*, eds. A. J. Juliano and J. A. Lerner (= *Silk Road Studies*, 7) (Turnhout, Brepols, 2002), pp. 97-100; B. Marshak, 'Central Asian Metalwork in China', in *China: Dawn of a Golden Age, 200-750 AD*, ed. J. C. Y. Watt (New York, 2004), pp. 47-55. See Chen, this volume, for glass.

[43] M. Tampoe, *Maritime trade between China and the West: an archaeological study of the ceramics from Siraf (Persian Gulf), 8th to 15th centuries A.D* (Oxford, British Archaeological Reports, International Series 555, 1989); S. Lieu, 'Byzantium, Persia and China: Interstate Relations on the Eve of the Islamic Conquest', *Silk Road Studies, IV: Realms of the Silk Roads: Ancient and Modern*, ed. D. Christian and C. Benjamin (Turnhout, Brepols, 2000), pp. 47-65; J. Howard-Johnston, *East Rome, Sasanian Persia and the End of Antiquity: Historiographical and Historical Studies* (Aldershot, Variorum, 2006); V. S. Curtis, R. Hillenbrand and J.M. Rogers (eds.), *The art and archaeology of ancient Persia: new light on the Parthian and Sasanian empires* (London, I.B. Tauris Publishers/The British Institute of Persian Studies, 1998); P. O. Harper, *In search of a cultural identity: monuments and artifacts of the Sasanian Near East, 3rd to 7th century A.D.* (New York, Bibliotheca Persica, 2006).

[44] Publications on the Silk Road are too numerous to list here. For a recent bibliography, see S. Whitfield (ed), *The Silk Road: Trade, Travel, War and Faith* (London, The British Library, 2004). For a sense of the variety of debates relating to the Silk Road, see the journal, *Silk Road Art and Archaeology* and Brepols' series, *Silk Road Studies*.

of the Silk Road; thus, objects traversing the entire route arrived at their destination (or at least their place of deposition in the archaeological record), in most cases, via down-the-line exchange.[45]

Perhaps partly as a result of 20th and 21st century globalising tendencies, Chinese historians have themselves recently started to develop greater interest in the Byzantine world. Zhang Xu-Shan at Tsinghua University is one of the pioneers in this, recently examining the way that the Early Byzantine-Chinese relationship is presented in Chinese literature.[46] His study of both Procopius's work (ironically one of the few Early Byzantine texts that mention Britain) and Cosmas Indicoplustes's *Christian Topography*, a sixth-century text written by an Egyptian traveller to the East, has led him to conclude that the Byzantines had a geographically accurate idea of where China was located and were likely to know this from first hand experience.[47] Chen Zhi-Qiang's eagerly awaited translations of Chinese texts relating to Byzantium will transform the study of Byzantine-Eastern relations.[48] Xu Jia-Ling at Northeast Normal University in Changchun has also worked extensively on these texts, pointing out that from the Han to the Ming Dynasty periods, the Chinese were intensely interested in a land they knew as 'Fu-lin', and arguing that, whereas in before the fifth century this appellation referred to the Roman Empire, by the fifth and sixth centuries it seems to relate to the Anatolian region of the Byzantine Empire, and that by the T'ang Dynasty (618-907) it seems to be used to describe a rather vague and undefined area to the west of the Chinese Empire, which sometimes included the Central Asian khanates.[49]

As far as archaeologists of Byzantium are concerned, it is numismatists who have started to explore the Byzantine-East Asian relationship most systematically – François Thierry and Cécile Morrisson in Europe and, more recently, Lin Ying in Guangzhou.[50] Outside of numismatics, however, the work of Marlia Mango has perhaps been most influential. She has explored, through studies on silverware, possible maritime links with China and elsewhere on the Asian Pacific coast, demonstrating that vessels with typically late antique motifs are to be found as far east as south-east China.[51] Part of the reason may lie in the fact that the end of the Han period coincided with an increased interest in silver and gold within Chinese society, and coincided, too, with the opening up of links with India, as Buddhism gained popularity in China. Buddhist statuary was increasingly adorned with gold or with precious stones, transported from India (for example, the Goddess of Mercy statue from Xi'an, c. 547), and the use of these materials in funerary display indicates that their usage was not confined to religious use. This openness arguably brought Chinese and Byzantine elite-level aspirations into closer alignment, forming a cultural context in which contacts might be more readily archaeologically identifiable. After c. 589, gold and silver objects were produced in China itself, so the sixth century provides a unique opportunity to study imported material.

This is the background against which we must consider the variety of possible Early Byzantine objects that have been found in China, including glass, silver and silver-gilt vessels and coins. With the exception of the coins, most of the objects have only hesitantly been identified as 'Byzantine', and some have recently been re-classified as Late Roman or Sasanian, or even as Chinese imitations.[52] The evidence (from texts) of at least eleven Sasanian diplomatic missions to China during the fifth to sixth century and at least two Chinese return missions to Persia has understandably led scholars to err on the side of

---

[45] C. Renfrew, *Approaches to Social Archaeology*, (Edinburgh, Edinburgh University Press, 1984).

[46] Zhang Xu-Shan, 'The Name of China and its Geography in Cosmas Indicopleustes', *Byzantion*, 74 (2004): 452–462. See also Zhang Xu-Shan, *He Kina kai to Vyzantio: scheseis - emporio – amoivaies gnoseis apo tis arches tou 6ou hos ta mesa tou 7ou ai* (= *Historicogeographica, Meletemata, 3*), (Athens, 1998). I am grateful to Zhang Xu-Shan for speaking to me on this topic and for alerting me to this publication.

[47] J. W. McCrindle, *The Christian Topography of Cosmas, an Egyptian Monk* (London, Hakluyt Society, 1987). For recent scholarship on Cosmas, see: M. Kominko, 'The Map of Cosmas, the Albi Map, and the Tradition of Ancient Geography', *Mediterranean Historical Review*, 20 (2005): 163–186.

[48] Chen Zhiqiang, 'The Byzantines in the Chinese Eyes: Translation and Commentary of Relevant Ancient and Medieval Chinese Texts', Dumbarton Oaks Fellowship Reports, 2005-06, http://www.doaks.org/do_byz_fellowship_reports.html#_13. See also Chen Zhiqiang, 'Record of Byzantine food in Chinese texts', in *Eat, drink, and be merry (Luke 12:19)—Food and Wine in Byzantium. Papers of the 37th Annual Spring Symposium of Byzantine Studies, in Honour of Professor A. A. M. Bryer*, eds. L. Brubaker and K. Linardou (Aldershot, Ashgate, forthcoming 2007).

[49] Xu Jia-Ling, 'Byzantium or Seljuk Sultanate? On a piece of narrative on 'Fulin' in Sung-shih (History of Sung Dynasty)', abstract in *Proceedings of the 21st International Congress of Byzantine Studies, London 21-26 August 2006*, eds. E. Jeffreys and F. Haarer (London, International Congress of Byzantine Studies, 2006), vol. 3, p. 19. I am grateful to Xu Jia-Ling for discussing her work and making the text of this paper available to me.

[50] For example: F. Thierry and C. Morrisson, 'Sur les monnaies byzantines trouvées en Chine', *Revue numismatique*, series 6, 36 (1994): 109-45; Lin Yin, 'Western Turks and Byzantine gold coins found in China', *Transoxiana*, 6 (2003) n.p. http://www.transoxiana.org/0106/lin-ying_turks_solidus.html [accessed 10 January 2007].

[51] M. M. Mango, 'The archaeological context of finds of silver in and beyond the Eastern Empire', in *Acta XIII Congressus Internationalis Archaeologiae Christianae*, eds. N. Cambi and E. Marin (Vatican and Split, 1998), pp. 207-52; M. M. Mango, 'Beyond the amphora: non-ceramic evidence for late antique industry and trade', in *Economy and Exchange in the East Mediterranean during Late Antiquity* eds. S. Kingsley and M. Decker (Oxford, Oxbow, 2001), 93-5. See also M. M. Mango, 'Action in the Trenches: A call for a more dynamic archaeology of Early Byzantium' (Lecture to Plenary Session II), *Proceedings of the 21st International Congress of Byzantine Studies, London 21-26 August 2006*, eds. E. Jeffreys and F. Haarer (London, International Congress of Byzantine Studies, 2006), vol 1, pp. 83-98. See also, for example, E. J. Laing, 'Recent finds of Western-related Glassware, Textiles and Metalwork in Central Asia and China', *Bulletin of the Asia Institute*, 9 (1995): 1-18.

[52] Shih Hsio-Yen, 'Gold and Silver Vessels excavated in North China: problems of origin', *New Asia Academic Bulletin*, 4 (1983): 63-82, figs. 1-64.

caution and ascribe a Persian provenance where there is any doubt. Yet, conversely, some objects once thought to be Late Roman or Sasanian are now thought more likely to have a Byzantine provenance.[53] In several cases, what can be stated with any certainty is only that the object was produced in a 'late antique' cultural setting or, at least, in imitation of a late antique style. Much research is still necessary on Chinese 'foreign' finds of the fifth to eighth centuries.

The most frequently-occurring and securely identifiable Byzantine finds in China are gold solidi.[54] Lin Yin has recently described 24 Chinese graves that have yielded genuine Byzantine solidi minted before 800 (with sometimes more than one solidus to a tomb), drawing attention to the northern provinces of Gansu and Hebei as the regions which have yielded the most Early Byzantine solidi through archaeological excavation.[55] Byzantine coins are also found in the region of the Turfan Oasis, in what was the Gaochang kingdom in the fifth to sixth centuries, most notably from the well-known cemetery site at Astana, where several contemporary tombs have yielded Byzantine solidi.[56] Approximately 40 Byzantine solidi and imitation coins are presently known.

Solidi are, in most cases, found in graves in association with other high-status objects and materials, such as jade, glass, metalwork and jewels. For example, the grave of Li Xizong (d. 540), which contained three Byzantine solidi, also contained a silver cup of Sasanian origin.[57] Fifth- to seventh-century Chinese mortuary evidence has not received anywhere near the attention of its Western counterparts in theoretical terms; however, preliminary work suggests that the coins deposited in such tombs were intended to display status, actual or aspirational, in a hierarchical society and were not regarded as components of a monetary exchange system.[58] Some of the coins were retrieved from the mouth of the inhumed body – a practice which is well-known in the Graeco-Roman

tradition, including Byzantium, as well as in Chinese and Central Asian history.[59] One such solidus, for example, was found in the tomb of an Eastern Wei dynasty princess who died in 550 (534-550), thus providing a mid sixth-century *terminus post quem* for its deposition.[60] Byzantine coins are not found in analogous contexts in Britain, although Philip Grierson suggested that the Merovingian coins deposited at Sutton Hoo Mound One could be seen as an Anglo-Saxon equivalent of 'Charon's obol', the inclusion of money in the mouth to pay for passage to the other world.[61] Of course, the practice was too widespread to tell us anything specific about sixth-century long-distance contacts, but it does perhaps permit an insight into the extent of the process of globalisation by this point in the first millennium AD.

By the time of their deposition, several Byzantine gold coins and their imitations had been pierced, almost always near the crown of the Emperor's head, suggesting that they were used as neck pendants or as head-dress accessories with the imperial image worn to the front. For example, four of the five Byzantine solidi from the tomb of Tian Hong (d. 575) in Ningxia Province, were pierced. The five solidi ranged in date from 457 to 542.[62] One of them, a solidus depicting Justin I and Justinian I as co-emperors, issued in 527, was both clipped and pierced in four places. One of the other pierced coins was found in the dead man's mouth. Likewise, the solidus of the reign of Theodosius II, discovered at Xiangride, in Dulun County, in western Qinghai, in 2002, is pierced – in this case – in two places.[63] This coin was found in a burial context, in what is thought to be an early Tibetan (Tuyuhun) cemetery; since it was lying adjacent to the skull of the dead person, it is likely that it formed part of a head-dress. Interestingly, the coin showed signs of having been much worn at the time of its deposition. The location of this latter coin, incidentally, may point to the shift south of the Silk Road in response to internecine

[53] M. Pirazzoli-t'Serstevens, 'Pour une archéologie des échanges. Apports étrangers en Chine-transmission, réception, assimilation', *Arts Asiatiques*, 49 (1994): 21-33. I am grateful to Craig Clunas for drawing my attention to this publication.

[54] Xu Pingfang, 'An Archaeological View of the Silk Road in China', in Xu Pingfang et al, *Land Routes of the Silk Roads and the Cultural Exchanges between the East and West before the 10th Century. (Desert Route Expedition International Seminar in Urumqi [Aug 19-21, 1990])*. (Beijing, New World Press, 1996), pp. 239-89. I am grateful to Wang Tao for drawing my attention to this publication and to Xu Jia-Ling for help with translation.

[55] Lin Yin, 'Western Turks and Byzantine gold coins'.

[56] Mu Shunying, Qi Xiaoshan, Zhang Ping, *The Ancient Art in Xinjiang, China* (Urumqi, Xinjiang Art and Photography Press, 1994), p. 61; H. Wang, 'How much for a camel? A new understanding of money on the Silk Road before AD 800', in *The Silk Road: Trade, Travel, War and Faith* ed. S. Whitfield (London, The British Library, 2004), pp. 24-33.

[57] Lin Yin, 'Western Turks'; J. C. Y. Watt (ed.), *China: Dawn of a Golden Age, 200-750 AD* (New York, Metropolitan Museum of Art, 2004), p. 254, fig. 153.

[58] F. Thierry and C. Morrisson, 'Sur les monnaies byzantines trouvées en Chine', *Revue numismatique*, series 6, 36 (1994): 109-45. See also Chen Zhiqiang, 'On the Mistakes in Research on Byzantine Coins Found in China', *Nankai Journal*, 5 (2004): 57-65.

[59] E. Ivison, 'Burials and urbanism in Late Antique and Byzantine Corinth', in *Towns in Transition: urban evolution in Late Antiquity and the Early Middle Ages*, eds. N. Christie and S. T. Loseby (Aldershot, Scolar Press, 1996), pp. 99-125; C. S. Lightfoot, E. A. Ivison, et al, 'The Amorium Project: The 1998 Excavation Season', *Dumbarton Oaks Papers*, 55 (1999): 371-99; E. Ivison, 'Charon's Obol or Apotropaic Talisman? Coins in medieval Byzantine Graves', *XXe Congres des Études Byzantines*, Paris, France, August, 2001; Table Ronde: *Rituel et Cérémonie* (Paris, *Congres des Études Byzantines*, 2001).

[60] Hong Mei Xu, 'A Gold Coin of the Eastern Roman Empire, Excavated in Dulun County, Qinghai Province', www.nara.accu.or.jp/hp/English/topics/participants/report2.html [accessed 10 January 2007].

[61] P. Grierson, The Purpose of the Sutton Hoo Coins, *Antiquity*, 44, (1970): 14-18.

[62] M. Alram, 'Coins and the Silk Road', in *Monks and Merchants: Silk Road Treasures from Northwest China, Gansu and Ningxia Provinces, 4th – 7th century*, eds. A. L. Juliano and J. A. Lerner (New York, Harry Abrams, 2001), pp. 271-91, nos. 96-99. See also: www.chnm.gmu.edu/whm/unpacking/objectanalysis2.html

[63] Hong Mei Xu, 'A Gold Coin of the Eastern Roman Empire, Excavated in Dulun County, Qinghai Province', www.nara.accu.or.jp/hp/English/topics/participants/report2.html [accessed 10 January 2007].

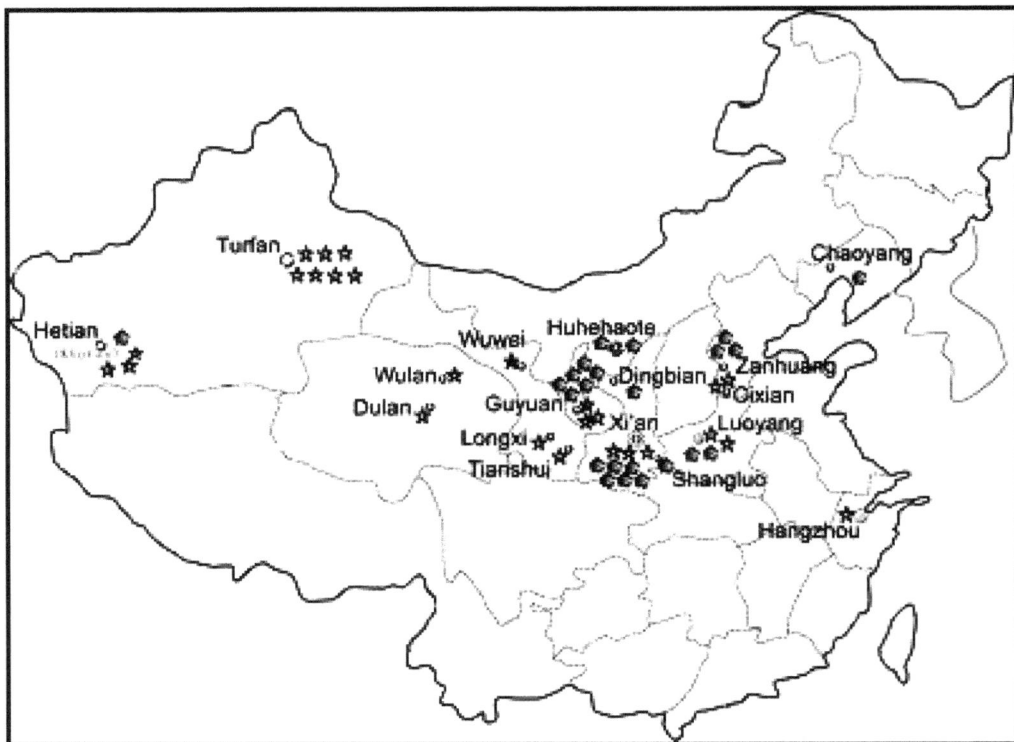

Fig. 1. Map showing geographical distribution of Byzantine gold coins across northern China. Lin Yin, 2005 (with permission)

warfare amongst the small polities in the Central Plains region. Several analogous fourth-sixth-century coins have been found in this area, including a solidus of Justinian II, found in 1999 in Wulan County.

The imitation Byzantine coins are sometimes merely hammered gold foil, impressed with the image of the obverse of the coin, and have no reverse to speak of. It is highly unlikely that these were ever used as money. It is possible that they were produced specifically as funerary items, either from sixth- and early seventh-century genuine Byzantine coins or from imitation coins probably produced in Central Asia and passed onto the Chinese in diplomatic exchange. Imitation Byzantine coins are found in Chinese high-status tombs well into the eighth century, although the prototypes on which they are based are no later than the reign of Heraclius (610-641), suggesting that the flow of coins may have come to an end in the early seventh century.

Eastern Central Asia was a (bronze) coin-producing society in the late-fourth to sixth centuries, in contrast to northern China itself, and so local people would have been familiar with the concept of the purchasing capabilities of money. Coins were minted in the Qiuci Kingdom (present-day Kucha) and are thought to have continued in circulation until the seventh or eighth century. Gold and silver coins were not represented in the local monetary system, although silver coins are plentiful in tombs. Over 1,000 are known from Gaochang, mainly from the Astana cemetery, and these are usually Sasanian

or Arab-Sasanian in origin.[64] Gold coins are very rare and, when they do occur, are Byzantine solidi or their imitations. The discovery of a large hoard of silver Sasanian and Arab-Sasanian coins and 13 gold bars at Wuqia, in present-day north-western Xinjiang Uighur Autonomous Region, might suggest that while silver coins were directly imported from the Sasanian Empire, imitation gold coins were locally produced, although some authentic gold coins must have existed, as master copies.[65]

Conveniently, many high-status tombs in sixth-century China can be dated by inscription, which has permitted Lin Yin to demonstrate that solidi were deposited within the borders of China itself between 575 and 612.[66] The tomb of Tian Hong in Ningxia province is particularly instructive in this respect.[67] The grave itself dates to 575, and five Byzantine solidi were included in the burial

---

[64] J. K. Skaff, 'Sasanian and Arab-Sasanian Silver Coins from Turfan: their relationship to International Trade and Local economy', *Asia Major*, 11 (1998): 67-115.
[65] Wang Binghua, 'Gold and Silver discovered in Boma, Xinjiang', in *The Glory of the Silk Road: Art from Ancient China*, ed. Lin Jian (Dayton, Dayton Art Institute, 2003).
[66] Lin Yin, 'Western Turks'; Lin Yin, 'Sogdians and Imitations of Byzantine Gold Coin Unearthed in the Heartland of China', *Ērān ud Anērān: Studies presented to Boris Ilich Marshak on the Occasion of His 70th Birthday* (= Transoxiana Webfestschrift Series I), 2003, http://www.transoxiana.org/Eran/Articles/lin_ying.html [accessed 10 January 2007].
[67] Lin Yin, 'Solidi in China and Monetary Culture along the Silk Road', *Silk Road Newsletter*, 3.2 (2005): n.p http://www.silkroadfoundation.org/newsletter/vol3num2/4_ying.php [accessed 10 January 2007].

assemblage, ranging in date from 457 to 542. So, at least one of these coins travelled from Byzantium to China between 542 and 575, a relatively short window of 33 years, spanning the mid-century point.

The Sasanians, as is often argued, dominated northern routes to China in the sixth century and it is likely that several of these coins did enter China as a result of Sasanian mercantile activity. However, given that the Sasanians were at war with the Byzantines for much of this period, it is perhaps unlikely that they would have had a ready source of solidi and certainly Sasanian diplomatic envoys to the Northern Dynasties' imperial court at Luoyang were unlikely to have brought Byzantine coin with them.[68]

If, during this narrow window of time, Byzantine coins were not distributed by the Sasanians, then how did they arrive in China? It is possible that some were brought via India, as Michael Alram has suggested.[69] However, for northern and north-western China we may find part of the answer in considering those Central Asian kingdoms which played an important role in promoting the fortunes of one Chinese dynasty over another during the middle decades of the sixth century. It is salient that several of the tombs Lin Yin lists as having Byzantine coins have been identified as the graves of persons of Sogdian origin, either high-status officials or merchants. One such tomb yielded three Byzantine imitation solidi, as well as an imitation Sogdian gold coin.[70] It is necessary, therefore, to understand the relationship between the Sogdians and the Chinese in more depth.

The Sogdians were an important group in fifth- to seventh-century north-west Chinese society, and long-distance contacts cannot be understood without taking their role into consideration.[71] They facilitated trade along the northern branches of the Silk Road, interacting with local Chinese, and by 439 Sogdian traders are recorded as being settled in several northern Chinese towns, their numbers continuing to expand throughout the fifth, sixth and seventh centuries.[72] By the mid- to late-sixth century, some Sogdians had achieved high office in the northern Chinese imperial court, serving the Emperor particularly in the north-west: northern Shanxi and the Ganu corridor, the area linking China to the Silk Road.[73]

The mid-sixth century document, 'Record of the Buddhist Monasteries in Luoyang', records that there were in excess of 10,000 families from 'west of the Pamirs to Daqin [Byzantium]'.[74] Many of these families would have been of Sogdian origin.

It is possible that some Sogdians were in contact with the Byzantines as well.[75] During the fifth century, Syriac Christian literature started to be translated into the local Sogdian language, suggesting that there was a sizable group of Christians in Sogdiana by this date.[76] This is not necessarily evidence for Byzantines, for these were likely to have been Nestorian congregations, anathematised by the Constantinopolitan Church at the Council of Ephesus in 431 and, in any case, strongly represented in the Persian, as well as the Byzantine, Empires.[77] Nevertheless, the 'Christianisation' of elements of Sogdian society brought them into closer cultural alignment with the Byzantine world, and may have created an implicit taste for late antique-style objects which facilitated relations with their western neighbours – both Persian and Byzantine.

Sogdiana was subject to demographic and political change, as well as religious change, which placed it in a vital position between east and west. By the end of the fifth century and the beginning of the sixth century, Turkic groups had populated much of the region. Like the Alans, who inhabited part of the steppe to the north-west, the Sogdians oscillated in their political loyalties.[78] Although initially allied with Persia, during the second half of the sixth century they were rebuffed by the Persians and, as a consequence, made deliberate contact with the Byzantine court instead. The late sixth-century Byzantine writer, Menander the Guardsman, describes this encounter of 568/9, writing, 'Maniakh, the leader of the Sogdians, took this opportunity and advised Sizabul

[68] The court was moved from Datong (Pingcheng) in 493.
[69] Alram, 'Coins and the Silk Road', p. 285, n. 3.
[70] Lin Yin, 'Sogdians and Imitations of Byzantine Gold Coin'.
[71] B. I. Marshak and N. N. Negmatov, 'Sogdiana', in *History of Civilisations of Central Asia, vol. 3, The Crossroads of Civilisations, AD 250 to 750*, ed. B. A. Litvinsky (Paris, Unesco Publishing, 1996), 233-80.
[72] *Nomads, Traders and Holy Men along China's Silk Road: Papers presented at the Asia Society, New York, November 9-10, 2001*, eds. A. J. Juliano and J. A. Lerner (= *Silk Road Studies*, 7) (Turnhout, Brepols, 2002). É. de la Vaissière, 'The Rise of Sogdian Merchants and the role of the Huns: the historical importance of the Sogdian Ancient Letters', in *The Silk Road: Trade, Travel, War and Faith*, ed. S. Whitfield (London, The British Library, 2004), pp. 19-23, 23.
[73] J. C. Y. Watt, 'Art and History in China from the Third to the Eighth Century', in *China: Dawn of a Golden Age, 200-750 AD* ed. J. C. Y.

Watt (New York, Metropolitan Museum of Art, 2004), pp. 13-45, 36. Zhang Qingjie, 'New Archaeological and Art Discoveries from the Han to the Tang period in Shanxi Province', *Orientations*, 34 (2002): 54-60.
[74] Watt, 'Art and History in China', p. 29.
[75] First explored by K. Hannestad, 'Les relations de Byzance entre la Transcaucasie au Ve et Vie siècles', *Byzantion*, 25-27 (1955-57): 421-56.
[76] N. Sims-Williams, 'The Sogdian Merchants in China and India', in *Cina e Iran: Da Alessandro Magno alla dinastia Tang*, ed. A. Cadonna and L. Lanciotti (Florence, Olschki, 1996), pp. 45-67.
[77] The famous stele, from Chang'an (Xi'an), describes the coming of (Nestorian) Christianity, claiming that Aluoben brought the 'True Scriptures' to Changan in 635. The stele itself dates to 781. S. H. Moffet, *A History of Christianity in Asia, Vol. 1, Beginnings to 1500* (New York, 1992); N. Standaert (ed.), *Handbook of Christianity in China, Vol. One: 635-1800* (Leiden, Brill, 2001), pp. 1-4, 12-15. For recent scholarship on Nestorian monuments in China, see I. Gardner, S. Lieu and K. Parry (eds.), *From Palmyra to Zayton, Epigraphy and Iconography* (= *Silk Road Studies* X) (Turnhout, Brepols, 2005), pp. 189-278.
[78] For the Alans, see Agustí Alemany, 'Sixth Century Alani: between Byzantium, Sasanian Iran and the Turkic World', *Ērān ud Anērān: Studies presented to Boris Ilich Marshak on the Occasion of His 70th Birthday* (= Transoxiana Webfestschrift Series I), 2003, http://www.transoxiana.org/Eran/Articles/alemany.pdf [accessed 10 January 2007]; Agustí Alemany, *Sources on the Alans* (Leiden, Brill, 2000), pp. 79-111.

[the leader of the Western Turkic khanate] that it would be better for the Turks to cultivate the friendship of the Romans and send their raw silk for sale to them because they made more use of it than other people. Maniakh said that he himself was very willing to go along with envoys from the Turks, and in this way the Romans and the Turks would become friends. Sizabul consented to this proposal and sent Maniakh and some others as envoys to the Roman Emperor carrying greetings, a valuable gift of raw silk and a letter'.[79]

While the Sogdians were concerned to sell silk and other commodities to the Byzantines, the Byzantine government's primary concern was to make a strategic alliance against the Persians. When Maniakh returned to Sogdiana in 569 the Byzantine diplomat, Zemarchus (Symmachus), travelled with him, meeting with the khan three times, before travelling back to Byzantium in 571/2.[80] He took with him diplomatic gifts from the emperor, Justin II, and it is likely that these included large quantities of Byzantine solidi, as was customary in Early Byzantine diplomacy. It is not known whether he took gold and silver vessels with him, although if he had he would have found that they were not the only silverware in the khan's collection. Apparently, the khan showed the envoy an impressive array of vessels, 'golden urns, water-sprinklers and also golden pitchers… many silver objects, dishes and bowls, and a large number of statues of animals, also of silver'.[81] The text gives no suggestion that Zemarchus's party recognised these as Byzantine in origin, so presumably they were Sasanian or Central Asian in origin.

As the Persian threat increased, the Byzantines again renewed their relations with the Sogdians. In 571, another embassy from the western Turkic kingdom travelled to Constantinople and, in 576, Byzantine diplomats, led by the envoy Valentinos, set out for Sogdiana. In an act that testifies to the regularity of contacts between the two polities, Valentinos was accompanied by 106 'Turks', then resident in Constantinople, probably as merchants. The Sogdian diplomatic service was kept busy: within a generation the Chinese also engaged in intensified diplomatic activity with the Sogdians, sending Pei Ju, a Sui Dynasty official there in 605.[82]

Diplomatic gifts from the Byzantines to the Sogdians may have increased in number in the early seventh century as the military situation worsened and as the Sogdians ('Western Turks') aided the Byzantines in Transcaucasia. As Lin Yin has pointed out, the

Byzantines perceived the Sogdians to be 'thirsty for gold' and, given that Heraclius gave 200,000 solidi to the Avars at this time, in return for their help against the Persians, it is likely that the Sogdians were given analogous gifts.[83]

No coin hoards have been found in Sogdiana itself, and so (while allowing for the possibility of them having been melted down) it is credible that the coins were subject to secondary distribution; they may have been offered as gifts to superiors, or as bribes to perceived inferiors. That Byzantine coins were brought into China by the Sogdians themselves is, of course, suggested by the finds of solidi in the graves of Sogdians (or people of Sogdian descent) living within China. Contact with, or at least knowledge of, Byzantium is suggested by the discovery, in 1999, of a carved stone sarcophagus in Taiyuan (Shanxi province), identified as the tomb of Yu Hong, an official of Sogdian origin, and his wife.[84] Yu Hong's interment in the sarcophagus took place in 592. The sarcophagus comprises nine main carved panels, four of which have been identified by Boris Marshak and James Watt as representing 'foreign' polities or peoples: India, Arabia, Iran (or Sogdiana) and the Byzantine Empire.[85] That the latter should be represented on such a tomb (incidentally, next to Iran) might indicate that it occupied a key position in the world-view of the dead man and his community.

Taiyuan and its vicinity have yielded at least two other archaeological finds of immense interest to scholars of sixth-century East-West relations, although neither of them are themselves western in production. An agate and amber necklace, together with a carved amber plaque, from the tomb of Kudi Huiluo and his wives, has an uncertain origin, but it has been suggested that the amber may derive from the Baltic region. If this is the case, it would have been imported in 'raw' form, since the motif on the plaque is distinctly Northern Qi.[86] Perhaps more important is a glazed earthenware flask from Taiyuan, dated to the Northern Qi dynasty (550-577), bears a depiction of a lion tamer flanked by two lions.[87] The motif is close enough to the popular early Christian image of Daniel in the Lions' Den, which also appeared on pottery flasks in this period, to warrant comment. In composition, it is also analogous to the depictions of St Menas flanked by two camels, which appear on fifth- to seventh-century Menas flasks.[88] It is possible that the flask is based on a Byzantine design which was either

[79] R. C. Blockley (ed. and trans.), *The History of Menander the Guardsman*, (Liverpool, Liverpool University Press, 1985), frag. 10.1, p. 115. However, compare Theophanes, who claims that Justin II was able to show silk to the Turkic envoys: Harry Turtledove (1982) (ed. and trans.), *The chronicle of Theophanes: an English translation of anni mundi 6095-6305 (A.D. 602-813)* (Philadelphia, University of Pennsylvania Press, 1982), frag. 3.
[80] *History of Menander the Guardsman*, frag. 10.3.
[81] *Ibid*.
[82] Xu Jia-ling.

[83] Lin Yin, 'Western Turks'.
[84] Shaanxi Archaeological Institute et al., 'Taiyuan Suidai Yu Hong mu qingli jianbao', *Wenwu* [*Cultural Relics*], 1 (2001): 27-52. See also A. L. Juliano, 'Chinese Pictorial Space at the Cultural Crossroads', *Ērān ud Anērān: Studies presented to Boris Ilich Marshak on the Occasion of His 70th Birthday* (= Transoxiana Webfestschrift Series I), 2003, http://www.transoxiana.org/Eran/Articles/juliano.html [accessed 10 January 2007.
[85] B. Marshak and J. C. Y. Watt, 'Sarcophagus', in *China: Dawn of a Golden Age, 200-750 AD*, ed. J. C. Y. Watt (New York, Metropolitan Museum of Art, 2004), pp. 276-81.
[86] Watt, *China: Dawn of a Golden Age*, pp. 249-50, fig. 147.
[87] Watt, *China: Dawn of a Golden Age*, p. 250, fig. 148.
[88] Bangert, this volume.

Fig. 2. Panel from Sui dynasty sarcophagus, said to depict the Byzantine Empire. Note vine-scroll and figures trampling grapes in a vineyard (After Shaanxi Archaeological Institute, 2001).

consciously adapted to specifically Chinese cultural norms or was misinterpreted as a circus motif.

It is possible, although perhaps unlikely, that the Sogdians were even given a Byzantine dog as part of their dealings with 'the west', for a curious note in a Tang dynasty biography (*cefu yuangui*) records that in 619 representatives of the Gaochang kingdom, possibly accompanied by Sogdians, presented two 'Fu-lin' (a term usually referring to Byzantine provenance) dogs to the Chinese emperor.[89] The dogs were said to be able to run as fast as a horse while holding a candle in their mouth. Even if the dogs were only *said* to be of Byzantine origin, it could suggest a desire on the part of the Sogdians and other Central Asian political authorities to appear to be in close contact with the Byzantine Empire, at least in the eyes of the Chinese Emperor. This might be expected to deter any potential mistreatment by the Chinese imperial government, which was expressing an interest in absorbing the eastern Central Asian kingdoms and in 630 was successful in doing so.[90]

It is more likely that coins, not dogs, were exchanged in the course of Chinese – Sogdian / Central Asian diplomacy and, given the prestige of gold, solidi were probably amongst these. These might explain the presence of solidi in Chinese royal graves, and permit those in the graves of high officials to be interpreted as secondary gift-giving.

Coin was not the only material expression of prestige and wealth, of course; neither was coin the only means of transacting an economic exchange. Recent research on the economy of eastern Central Asia has illuminated the extent to which coins were supplemented by other forms of exchange.[91] Contracts from the Turfan region concerning sales of large items such as houses, land and renting of property refer to prices in bolts of silk between the fourth and early sixth centuries, but in silver coin from the mid-sixth century onwards. By the early seventh century, for example, five silver Sasanian coins could apparently buy a house; two Byzantine gold coins a slave. Helen Wang describes this as a 'major change' in the use of currency in Central Asia and observes that there appears to have been a hierarchy of currency, with silver (and presumably gold) preferred for expensive transactions, especially those involving labour. Before the mid-sixth century the concept of coinage was much weaker, with gold and silver measured by weight, rather than by units (coins). Moreover, of the 40-plus tomb inventories from the Turfan region, those dated between 567 and 592 do not mention gold and silver at all. Thereafter, gold is mentioned in the tomb inventories, although it remains absent from the contracts themselves. As Wang suggests, 'the knowledge of, and desire for, gold and silver coins preceded and remained far greater than their general availability'.[92] In such an environment, Byzantine coins or their imitations would have been sought-after objects, serving an important role in emerging Central Asian socio-economic complexity.

Wang has also observed that while Sasanian coins in *eastern Central Asia* are predominantly fourth century and late-sixth and early-seventh century in date, Sasanian coins in *central China* are mainly fifth and sixth century in date. She suggests that this reflects the use of different routes from the Sasanian Empire to the East. The eastern Central Asian coins may have been brought via the northern Silk Route to Qiuchi and Gaochang, whilst the central Chinese coins may have been brought by a more southerly route, via Bactria-Wakhan across the Pamirs-Tashkurgan-Yarkand-Khotan-Kroraina, then eastwards either via Dunhuang, or through the Tsaidam Basin to the Koko Nor lake, then via Lanzhou to central China.[93]

---

[89] Lin Yin. 'Western Turks'.
[90] The eastern Turkic kingdom was revived in the 680s, before being defeated in 744 by the Uighurs, one of their subject peoples.

[91] Evgeniy Zeimal, 'The circulation of coins in Central Asia during the Early Medieval period (Fifth to Eighth centuries AD)', *Bulletin of the Asia Institute*, 8 (1994): 245-67; Wang, 'How much for a camel?', pp. 24-33; H. Wang, *Money on the Silk Road: the evidence from Eastern Central Asia to AD 800* (London, British Museum Press, 2004).
[92] Wang, 'How much for a camel?', p. 32; Wang, *Money on the Silk Road*.
[93] Wang, 'How much for a camel?', p. 29.

This is likely to reflect the political vicissitudes of the Central Plains in the fifth-sixth centuries and the need to move to a more southerly route. Caution must be exercised, however, and the mere date of a coin's minting does not indicate its date of deposition: witness the solidus of Theodosius II (408-450) from the tomb of Li Xizong (576), at Zanhuangxian (Hebei province).[94] Nevertheless, the lack of fifth and sixth-century Sasanian coins in eastern Central Asia might suggest a lack of Sasanian *activity* here during those years, and would be consistent with the suggestion earlier in this paper that a plentiful supply of Byzantine coins was unlikely to have been available to Sasanian merchants and envoys during the mid-sixth century. If so, this suggests that the Byzantine coins, along with the Sasanian silverware and other Western objects, were less likely to have been mediated through Sasanian activity, than through Sogdian or even Byzantine activity.

It is still unclear whether direct contacts were made between the Byzantines and the Chinese during the mid-sixth century, whether diplomatic or mercantile or even religious. The mode and pathway of transmission of 'Byzantine' objects is uncertain, while the lack of jade and porcelain on Byzantine (or other 'western') sites argues against direct contacts.[95] However, what does seem clear is that after the re-unification of China under the Sui dynasty in 589 and the increase of Chinese influence in Central Asia, the Chinese made diplomatic overtures to the Byzantines.[96] The negotiations probably involved gifts of coin on the part of the Byzantines and gifts of silk on the part of the Chinese. These diplomatic activities were to peak in the Tang dynasty, perhaps in response to the Arab incursions into former-Persian territory and Central Asia, before falling away again thereafter.

The presence of fifth- and sixth-century Byzantine coins at the Astana cemetery in Gaochang, and elsewhere in the western Hexi corridor and north-west China could, therefore, represent diplomatic gifts from subordinate Central Asian elites to the rulers of newly-emerging Chinese kingdoms which, while divergent, were sufficiently organised to demand 'tribute missions'.[97] It is possible, in addition, that some of the coins found on Chinese sites represent a small component of monies given as part of the Byzantine government's negotiations with the Sogdians between 568 and 576. Given that most of the Early Byzantine coins in China date from the reign of Justinian I and earlier, yet were not deposited until after 575, this might just be the case.

Comparing Britain and China in the sixth century

Simplistic comparisons between the Byzantine-British and the Byzantine-Chinese relationship on the basis of the Byzantine numismatic evidence are impossible. Not only is the archaeology of Britain very different from the archaeology of China, but archaeological agenda vary widely, and the organisation of field archaeology is very different; this has implications, of course, for the way that the evidence is treated.[98] For example, the energies channelled since the 1930s into identifying imported pottery in Britain have no parallel in the Chinese archaeological community. While the evidence for imports into fifth- to seventh-century Britain has been greeted with enthusiasm because of its potential diagnostic value, in China the evidence for imports has not received such a positive reception. For a long time, some areas of Chinese archaeology were resistant to the idea of 'foreign intervention', and the large-scale archaeological campaigns undertaken in the Cultural Revolution years tended to emphasise Chinese indigenous achievements instead.[99] It is perhaps salient, in respect of this point, that two of the key sites for 'foreign' influence, the Astana and Karakhoja cemeteries in the Turfan region, were initially dug between 1966 and 1969.[100] One wonders whether some of the evidence from those excavations would have been interpreted differently had the sites been dug at a later date.

In the last decade, perhaps the greatest challenge of Chinese archaeology has been trying to keep pace with urban development, which continues to take place on a

---

[94] M. Alram, 'Coins and the Silk Road', in *Monks and Merchants: Silk Road Treasures from Northwest China, Gansu and Ningxia Provinces, 4th – 7th century*, eds. A. L. Juliano and J. A. Lerner (New York, Harry Abrams, 2001), pp. 271-91, 284.

[95] After the end of the Han period, jade became more available to wealthy elites, and was no longer solely the preserve of the aristocracy. Given that it was imported from the Xinjiang region in western China, one might expect it to appear on 'Western' sites if direct and consistent exchange had taken place. White porcelain vessels were first produced in the period of the Northern Qi dynasty (550-577), and are found in a high-status tomb dated to 575 in Anyang, Henan Province. Li Li, *China's Cultural Relics* (Beijing, Foreign Languages Press, 2004), pp. 25-6, 124.

[96] D. A. Graff, 'Strategy and Contingency in the Tang defeat of the Eastern Turks, 629-630', in N. di Cosmo (ed.), Warfare in Inner Asian History (500-1800) (Leiden, Brill, 2002), pp. 33-71; S. Adshead, *T'ang China: The Rise of the East in World History* (Basingstoke, Palgrave, 2004); Hans Bielenstein, *Diplomacy and trade in the Chinese world, 589-1276*, (Leiden, Brill, 2005).

[97] Alram, 'Coins and the Silk Road'.

[98] K. C. Chang, 'Archaeology in China since 1949', *Journal of Asian Studies*, 36 (1977): 623-46 (esp. 624-5); J. Olsen, 'The Practice of Archaeology in China Today', *Antiquity*, 61 (1987): 282-90; Enzheng Tong, 'Thirty Years of Chinese archaeology (1949-1979)', in *Nationalism, Politics, and the Practice of Archaeology*, eds. P. L. Kohl and C. Fawcett (Cambridge, Cambridge University Press, 1995), pp. 177-97.

[99] Chang, p. 634: 'Chinese archaeologists tend to emphasize the indigenous nature of Chinese civilization and sometimes regard the external-origin advocates as cultural imperialists. Such indigenous views are in their turn dismissed by Western writers as Chinese ethnocentrism and chauvinism'. Cheng Te-K'un, 'Archaeology in Communist China', *The China Quarterly*, 23 (1965): 67-77; L. von Falkenhausen, 'On the historiographical orientation of Chinese archaeology', *Antiquity*, 67 (1993): 839-849; L. von Falkenhausen, 'The regionalist paradigm in Chinese archaeology', in *Nationalism, Politics, and the Practice of Archaeology*, eds. P. L. Kohl and C. Fawcett (Cambridge, Cambridge University Press, 1995), pp. 198-217.

[100] Anonymous, *New Archaeological Finds in China: Discoveries during the Cultural Revolution* (Beijing, Foreign Languages Press, 1974), p. 3.

vast scale. Comparisons with even the 'rescue' period of British archaeology are unsatisfactory, for the rate of the destruction of the Chinese archaeological resource is unprecedented.[101] One wonders what percentage of the overall assemblage of Byzantine coins is represented by the sample actually identified. Chinese archaeology is a growth discipline and there are vast quantities of archaeological work being undertaken in present-day China; yet the pressure under which excavators (and those involved in post-excavation) labour is phenomenal.[102] In such conditions, one would hardly expect a few sherds of unglazed pottery to be identified as 'Byzantine' by an excavator dealing with several thousand sherds of pottery, let alone other finds and features. We must, therefore, for methodological reasons, hesitate before declaring a definitive lack of Byzantine pottery on Chinese settlement sites.

Present-day archaeological practices aside, the respective sixth-century geopolitical situations in China and in Britain were also different. Britain covered an extremely small landmass by comparison with China, which then, as now, stretched from India in the south to Mongolia in the north, from the Pacific in the east to Afghanistan and the Central Asian kingdoms in the west. Britain, much of which had formally been part of the Roman Empire, was well-known to the imperial government in Constantinople and its adjuncts in Ravenna and Rome, although its precise relationship with the Empire after 410 is a matter of some debate. China, by contrast, had always existed beyond the periphery of the Roman Empire, and there has never been any suggestion that the Romans developed a 'foreign policy' towards it. China had been a highly developed state society for far longer than the Roman Empire, with complex bureaucracies, systems of warfare, literacy and monumentality.[103] In many ways, the contrast with Britain could not be stronger.

However, there are some points of similarity. The sixth century witnessed population movement and cultural change in both China and Britain. James Watt writes, 'The situation with regard to the ethnic groups in China in the third to early sixth century is not unlike that in Europe in the early Middle Ages, and many approaches employed in recent scholarship relating to ethnicity in early medieval Europe can also be applied to China'.[104]

At mid-century point both northern China and Britain were experiencing severe political disorder. In China, like Britain, the sixth century witnessed political unrest and war.[105] After the collapse of the Han dynasty in the early third century, a succession of dynasties and kingdoms vied for power. The country was eventually divided into two main political sectors, one each side of the Yangtze River (i.e. 'Northern-Southern dynasties' period). Successive 'Northern Dynasties' ruled between 386 and 589: the Northern Wei, Eastern Wei, Northern Qi, Western Wei and Northern Zhou. However, in 557, northern China was plunged into a form of intermittent civil war which lasted until 589 when the Sui dynasty came to power. The south, incidentally, was successively ruled by the 'Southern Dynasties' of the Song, Qi, Liang and Chen, all with Nanjing as capital, before partially being absorbed into the Sui kingdom. China was largely re-unified under the T'ang dynasty in 618.

For Britain, the mid-sixth century situation is described vividly by Gildas in his well-known *De Excidio Britanniae*.[106] Gildas's evocation of a Britain torn apart by warring factions, and by the encroachment of the Saxons, cannot be taken as historical 'fact', of course, but archaeologists have, nonetheless, not dismissed Gildas when interpreting the archaeology of this period, not least in the way that they have tended to focus on *either* the 'British' evidence *or* the 'Anglo-Saxon' evidence and studies have constructed sixth-century life in terms of a series of binary oppositions – British and Anglo-Saxon; Christian and pagan; inhumations and cremations; unfurnished graves and furnished graves.[107] Culturally, Britain and China were following different trajectories. While the 'Britons' shared a Christian religious identity and knowledge of the Latin language with the Byzantines, the Chinese entered into these exchanges with a very different set of religious beliefs, languages, and norms and expectations as their cultural framework.[108] Ironically, one might argue that the relationship between the Byzantines and the Anglo-Saxon areas of Britain was more analogous to the Byzantine-Chinese relationship than either the Byzantine-Western British relationship or the Western British-Anglo-Saxon relationship.

The same point could be made in relation to methodological differences. The archaeology of sixth-century China differs greatly, in many aspects, from the archaeology of sixth-century Western Britain. Most saliently, while cemetery evidence dominates the archaeology of China, Western British graves of this

---

[101] Chan Wai-Yin, Ma Shu-Yun, 'Heritage preservation and sustainability of China's development', *Sustainable Development*, 12 (2003): 15-31.
[102] The Institute of Archaeology at the Chinese Academy of Social Sciences is the best starting point for news about recent Chinese excavations: http://www.kaogu.cn/ and also provides links to the abstracts of Chinese archaeological journals, including *Kaogu* (Archaeology), *Kaoguxuebao* (Acta Archaeological Sinica), *Kaoguxuejikan*(Archaeology Periodicals) and *Wenwu* (Cultural Relics).
[103] D. Twitchett, M. Loewe and J. K. Fairbank (eds.), *The Cambridge History of China, Vol. 1., The Ch'in and Han Empires, 221 B.C.-A.D.220* (Cambridge, Cambridge University Press, 1986).
[104] Watt, 'Art and History in China', p. 8.

[105] Watt, 'Art and History in China', p. 8.
[106] Gildas, *The Ruin of Britain and other documents*.
[107] E.g. S. Lucy and A. Reynolds (eds.), *Burial in early medieval England and Wales* (London, Society for Medieval Archaeology, 2002).
[108] Paul Demiéville, 'Philosophy and Religion from Han to Sui', in *The Cambridge History of China, Vol. 1., The Ch'in and Han Empires, 221 B.C.-A.D.220*, eds. D. Twitchett, M. Loewe and J. K. Fairbank (Cambridge, Cambridge University Press, 1986), pp. 808-72.

period are devoid of grave-goods.[109] For many more years, therefore, than their Chinese counterparts, archaeologists here have been forced to focus on settlement excavation and analysis and have, as a by-product, refined techniques and methodologies to a high level.[110]

By contrast, archaeologists of the Anglo-Saxon areas of sixth-century Britain have a wealth of mortuary data available to them and have, until relatively recently, often been criticised for over-reliance on this body of evidence.[111] Yet whatever the shortcomings of Anglo-Saxon archaeology as a discipline, the archaeological record of sixth-century eastern Britain, like that of China in the same century, is well equipped to identify elite-level interaction, constructions of identity via high-status objects and the use of material culture in funerary display.[112] Methodologically, these are helpful similarities, which might permit a comparative archaeological study of these two regions experiencing rapid social and political consolidation during the sixth century.

Conclusion

During the course of the sixth century, links between the Byzantine Empire and these two regions at the fringes of what was, to it, the 'known world', were initiated and exploited. While political considerations may have been instrumental in both sets of linkages, these were very different relationships, despite the points of commonality in their archaeology. Byzantine interest in Britain, despite the enigmatic flourish at mid-century point that we see reflected in the ceramic evidence, appeared to have waned towards the end of the century. By contrast, contacts between the Byzantine Empire and China appear to have been strengthened towards 600, as the Chinese state achieved re-unification. The seventh-century evidence, outside the scope of this paper, suggests a more direct relationship between the two empires.[113]

For most of the sixth century, however, contacts between Byzantium and China were conducted indirectly, via intermediaries such as the Sogdians and other Central Asian peoples. Yet these relations, too, were principally political in content: the Byzantine government's initial motivation for approaching the Sogdians had been to acquire allies against the Sasanians. While down-the-line exchange, particularly that involving the Sasanians, may have played a part in taking Byzantine objects into China, the overall assemblage of Byzantine, or Byzantine-derived, objects found in China (glassware, and silver-gilt and gold vessels) is more consistent with high-level political contexts, for these are not the sort of goods exchanged as part of trading practices. It would seem that, for both Britain and China, inhabiting different part of the periphery of the Byzantine thought world, politically-driven relations may have been the catalyst for the creation of links with the Byzantine Empire.

---

[109] E. O'Brien, *Post-Roman Britain to Anglo-Saxon England: burial practices reviewed* (Oxford, British Archaeological Reports, British Series 289, 1999).

[110] Contrast this with the way that Chinese archaeological publications focus principally on material culture. E.g. Xiaoneng Yang (ed.), *The Golden Age of Chinese Archaeology: Celebrated Discoveries from The People's Republic of China*, (Washington DC, National Gallery Washington, 1999), although see also Xiaoneng Yang (ed.), *New Perspectives on China's Past: Twentieth-Century Chinese Archaeology* (Yale University Press, 2004).

[111] S. Lucy. *The Anglo-Saxon Way of Death: Burial Rites in Early England* (Stroud, Sutton, 2000), chapter 1; S. Lucy and A. Reynolds, 'Burial in Early Medieval England and Wales: Past, Present and Future', in *Burial in early medieval England and Wales*, eds. S. Lucy and A. Reynolds (London, Society for Medieval Archaeology, 2002), pp. 1-23.

[112] H. Williams, *Death and Memory in Early Britain* (Cambridge, Cambridge University Press, 2006.

[113] Zhang Xu-Shan.

www.ingramcontent.com/pod-product-compliance
Lightning Source LLC
Chambersburg PA
CBHW051303270326

41926CB00030B/4708